I strongly support this wonderful book!

— CORNEL WEST, Professor, Princeton University

In an age when religion is increasingly viewed through the lens of conflict, *Minefields & Miracles* is an important and timely reminder of the power and possibility of interfaith engagement and religious reconciliation. A must-read for interfaith advocates, scholars, and practitioners...

— VARUN SONI, Ph.D., Dean of Religious Life, University of Southern California

One of the greatest challenges of our contemporary society is the threat of disorientation and confusion in face of the amazing diversity that we are able to encounter as never before. To be able to truly embrace this diversity in the fullness of its enrichment, requires one to be well grounded in one's own identity, values and heritage. Ruth Broyde Sharone is blessed with this deep rootedness in her own Jewish tradition and draws on the universalism at its core to open up to and embrace the sense of the Divine presence in the other and especially in other religious traditions that give expression to it.

— RABBI DAVID ROSEN, Director,
American Jewish Committee's Department for Interreligious Affairs

An insightful, revealing autobiography of a journey that starts with discrimination and leads into a powerful involvement with the interfaith movement. Ruth's ability to become borderless involved her traveling the world to discover more and more how much we are each a child of God and, therefore, all the same in spite of our religious beliefs. Ruth inspires us to experience true freedom "when we celebrate as one enormous human family."

— JAYANTI KIRPALANI, European Director, Brahma Kumaris

Writing from a heart made wise by her years of rich experience in the interfaith movement, Ruth Sharone's book goes beyond polite formalities and has the potential to create a breakthrough in interfaith dialogue and action both on the global and personal level.

— REV. MICHAEL BERNARD BECKWITH, Founder and Spiritual Director,
AGAPE International Spiritual Center

Journey with Ruth. Whether it's a story of a minefield or miracle, be prepared to get caught up in the adventure. Ruth tells it like it is. She's a visionary of a better world made manifest through courage, tenacity, and heart. She sets the bar high for those who follow in her footsteps. This book is a must read for all on the path of interfaith work. You will be challenged to be your best self in your own minefields and miracles. You will see parts of yourself on every page and feel upheld. You will come to know that you are not alone in this great global adventure…interfaith endeavors. And you will feel blessed to be a part of it.

— THE REV. DR. GWYNNE GUIBORD, Founding President, The Guibord Center–*Religion Inside Out*

With the religious and culture conflicts now raging across the globe, there is nothing more important than initiatives like that of Ruth Broyde Sharone's book *Minefields & Miracles*. A strong supporter of her work, I pray that she succeeds in her interfaith mission and thereby creates harmony in our troubled world.
— AMBASSADOR AKBAR AHMED, Ibn Khaldun Chair of Islamic Studies, American University

Ruth Broyde Sharone, living as we all do in a sharply divided brutal world, has this wonderfully crazy idea to which she has dedicated the full force of her incredible will and imagination: that it is possible to achieve a common universal ground of humanity where people of many faiths, honoring themselves and their own religious traditions, can live together in trust and in compassion. Her new work, *Minefields & Miracles* shows how difficult and yet how rewarding this quest can be. It also reveals that here at work is a fine mind, a courageous spirit, and an empathic heart. Thus armed, she has gone forth to engage others in the liberation of their essential humaneness from the enmity, suspicion, fear, and ignorance that hold it in captivity. In so doing, she brings encouragement and hope to all who yearn to make real her soaring ambition.
— RABBI LEONARD BEERMAN, Rabbi Emeritus of Leo S. Beck Congregation, Los Angeles

Sharing 'faith journeys' with one another is a precious, powerful tool in the burgeoning interfaith movement. Ruth Broyde Sharone's faith story, *Minefields & Miracles*, turns out to be a page-turner, a compelling, fearless quest to reach across the toughest interreligious boundaries to develop peaceful friendships. Ruth is a master storyteller, traversing the world, making films, weaving webs of connection, and inspiring us to do the same. She epitomizes what people mean when they ask us to become the change we want to see in the world. Read her book.
— REV. PAUL CHAFFEE, Editor, *The Interfaith Observer*

With warmth and humor, Ruth Broyde Sharone takes us on a personal narrative through the educational pleasures and the often startling pitfalls that accompany the hard work of interfaith dialogue. Her experiences and enthusiasm should lend encouragement to people seriously interested in this spiritual discipline, pursued in the cause of peace.
— GUSTAV NIEBUHR, Religion writer and author, *Beyond Tolerance: Searching for Interfaith Understanding in America*

Ruth Broyde Sharone has written a most important book, witnessing how concrete, 'on the ground' interfaith encounters can transform the earth into an oasis of peace and justice. Her courage, her passion, caring and commitment, her friendships created through warm interaction and meaningful activity have already created immense progress in the contemporary world of interfaith activity and relations. An important read for all interested in the world of interfaith action.
— RABBI MEL GOTTLIEB, President, Academy for Jewish Religion, CA (AJRCA)

It is the responsibility of all people with an aspiration to spiritual perfection to help develop a deep recognition of the value of other faiths, and it is on that basis alone that we can cultivate genuine respect and cooperation.

— HIS HOLINESS THE DALAI LAMA

Readers will connect instantly with this open-hearted, often touching, occasionally hilarious, and always disarmingly personal account of inter-religious adventures and misadventures over a long and colorful lifetime. You may finish this book in an hour or two, but you'll be thinking about it days later.

— JACK MILES, Pulitzer Prize winning author of *God A Biography*

Our world is contracting, drawing ever closer. The old borders and boundaries that separated our communities also protected us from many challenges to our instinctive assumptions. But the boundaries are collapsing. In the modern world we can no longer retreat into sealed enclaves to secure our identities. We are forced to relate and interact with people who often seem radically different, even frightening. But most of us are not equipped for the task. Ruth Broyde Sharone is a border-crosser, a guide who takes us across the borders by way of her own personal odyssey. Through a personal narrative that is at once entertaining and inspiring, she gives us insight and wisdom and not a little healthy innocence, all of which are deeply needed today. Make sure you read this book.

— REUVEN FIRESTONE, Co-Director, Center for Muslim-Jewish Engagement
University of Southern California

It's time for Americans to stop talking about interfaith dialogue and get on with the business of interfaith activism! This is something Ruth Broyde Sharone obviously understands. We can all learn from her (mis)adventures.

— REZA ASLAN, Political commentator and author of
No god but God: The Origins, Evolution, and Future of Islam

Ruth Broyde Sharone's crucial and passionate work in the interfaith community reflects the same values that are cherished in the spiritual community. The vocabulary is not always the same, but the overlap is unmistakable. This book is a must read for individuals who seek to be "collaborators with the Holy" in the quest for peace.

— MARIANNE WILLIAMSON, spiritual teacher and best-selling author of *Return to Love*

The world needs more narratives of how faith can be a bridge of cooperation, rather than a barrier of division. I deeply thank Ruth Broyde Sharone for sharing her inspiring stories of bridge-building around the world. "

— EBOO PATEL, Founder & President, Interfaith Youth Core

I have been involved in interfaith work for more than 30 years. And I have seen and heard lots of interfaith stories from around the world. But I have never encountered an interfaith testimonial with the depth and breadth of this one. Ruth Broyde Sharone's Minefields and Miracles should be required reading for anyone who is serious about interfaith dialogue.
— PAUL MCKENNA, Scarboro Missions, Toronto, Creator of The Golden Rule Poster

Ruth Broyde Sharone takes you on a peacemaking journey and shows you what works and what does not work. To follow in her footsteps and see the world of peacemaking through her eyes gives you both hope and strips away illusions. Having worked with her and seen the subtle and delicate arch with which she gets people to see each other fully and to open the heart, I am delighted that she put it all in her wonderful book which besides its important content is also a page turner. I urge you to read the book, to learn from her, and to engage with your neighbors in the openhearted peacemaking work that can heal our planet."
— RABBI ZALMAN SCHACHTER-SHALOMI, co-founder of the Jewish Renewal Movement, co-author of *All Breathing Life Adores Your Name* and *A Hidden Light*

The many personal encounters that Ruth describes so vividly convey the excitement, the challenge and enrichment of sharing with people of different cultures and religions. Her book also gives an overview of the recent national and international development of interfaith co-operation. The history of the twenty first century may well depend on our answer to Ruth's question, "Will the new friendships survive if old conflicts re-ignite or will we once again be divided by the barbed-wire of the past?" The hope, as she says, is for us "to get involved and make a commitment to positive change, to become co-creators and reweave the fabric of our world."
— REV. DR. MARCUS BRAYBROOKE, President of the World Congress of Faiths, co-founder of the Three Faiths and author of more than 40 books including *Beacons of the Light*

Ruth lives and breathes the interfaith ideal. Principled, compassionate, curious, and, above all, deeply listening to those around her. She quotes Rumi, "Somewhere beyond the idea of right and wrong, there is a field: I'll meet you there." Ruth continues to strive to meet us in that field and her book is one guide to get there.
— VALARIE KAUR, Filmmaker, author, civil rights lawyer, Sikh activist and Interfaith leader

Ruth crosses borders, transgresses boundaries, and in her words is an "interfaith alchemist". It is through her interfaith work that the world is transformed into a better place. All those interested in participating in that transformation are urged to read this book and learn from her experience and her wisdom.
— AMIR HUSSAIN, Professor of Theological Studies, Loyola Marymount University, Los Angeles

Minefields and Miracles is one of the most honest and sincere undertakings in the 21st century on interfaith work and real dialogue. Broyde Sharone is passionate about the children of Abraham and her own faith as a Jewish woman. Intersecting multiple sacred worlds with secular politics she manages to offer the reader a place of solace as we are brought into her personal stories and hear the voice within her soul. She writes: *"Call me foolhardy. A dreamer. Naïve. I will not argue with you. I am all of those things and more. I come from a long line of dreamers. Perhaps that is why I am willing to enter the minefields of the interfaith world even though I have been forewarned and occasionally burned by the explosions."* Her honesty and idealism is what we need today as we are placated by so many misperceptions of one another, I recommend her book, and applaud her conviction as a human being in a complex yet hopeful world.
— DR. MEHNAZ M. AFRIDI, Assistant Professor of Islam & Director of Holocaust, Genocide, and Interfaith Center, Manhattan College, NY

This is such a compelling story! Told clearly, simply and passionately, it reflects Ruth Sharone's amazing capacity in film and now in the written word to convey the practice and the power of citizen diplomacy, how one individual and groups of friends and colleagues can create hope where there is despair, empowerment where there is fear and uncertainty, love where there is suspicion, and the power to change where there has been depression and helplessness. If learned helplessness is the essence of depression then Ruth's method is learned helpfulness, the empowerment that comes from the dogged determination to make connections beyond adversarial lines where no one else has—and to document it simply and clearly! Bravo to Ruth for showing the power to weave in new ways American society and global civilization.
— DR. MARC GOPIN, James H. Laue Professor, Director of the Center for World Religions, Diplomacy and Conflict Resolution, George Mason University

Minefields & Miracles is a work of critical and contemporary significance; it considers the process of interfaith and intra-faith matters. The author starts with the problems and possibilities in Abrahamic religious relations, but she does not stop there. Her vision is global. She recognizes the insights and values of Eastern traditions as well. She shows that each religious tradition is part of human religious heritage. To claim our common humanity and intrinsic spirituality through dialogue, she says we have got to be free, friendly and open-hearted. Her own example is to walk together, talk together and work together for the welfare of humanity. The book is an inspiring call to action.
— K.L. SESHAGIRI RAO, Professor Emeritus, University of Virginia; Chief Editor, *Encyclopedia of Hinduism*, Co-Editor, *Interreligious Insight*

An engaging interfaith biography…people new to the movement or seeking to understand it, will find this personal testimony informative, inspirational and inviting.
— REVEREND WILLIAM LESHER, President Emeritus, Board of Trustees, A Council for a Parliament of the World's Religions

Ruth Broyde Sharone seeks to find peace seeking hearts from people of any faith; her quest is noble and her book introduces the reader to this colorful, mine-filled and mindful world.
— RABBI DAVID WOLPE, Senior Rabbi, Sinai Temple, Los Angeles

If you yearn for a bridge from despair to hope, from division to community, I urge you to read Ruth Broyde Sharone's Minefields & Miracles. It will inspire you and challenge you to match the author's vision, courage, faith and commitment with your own. This is how light increases and the world changes.
— THE REV. CANON CHARLES GIBBS, Executive Director, United Religions Initiative

Ruth invites to reflect on our own biases as if we are sitting together sipping tea and having a great conversation. After reading the book, I felt reignited with hope and possibilities to imagine that yes, we can reach into our hearts and recognize that we are all members of the human family as we all share the same sky and are united in one cosmic heart.
— YOLAND TREVINO, United Religions Initiative, Global Council Chair

I am so glad Ruth Broyde Sharone is writing this splendid book. Interfaith momentum is the strongest, irresistible energy in the world today.
— SWAMI SWAHANANDA, Head Master, Vedanta Society of Southern California and elder of the Ramakrishna Order of India

Ruth Broyde Sharone's own interfaith journey is the foundation for this autobiographical thought piece on the increasing importance of interfaith activity for social interaction. This account will inspire the next generation to cross boundaries and take ideological risks for the sake of peace.
— REV. JERRY D. CAMPBELL, President, Claremont School of Theology and Claremont Lincoln University

Ruth Sharone has a special gift for each of us in this series of reflections as she encounters the interfaith world. With her own eyes and the eyes of the camera she captures the spirit of humankind. She travels around the world and brings home to each of us how the beautiful and sacred plays out in our lives. Everywhere she goes she experiences "Godliness" in each human being.
— RABBI STEVEN JACOBS, Founder, Progressive Faith Foundation

Minefields & Miracles
Why God and Allah Need to Talk

by
Ruth Broyde Sharone

Global Peace Publishing

Minefields and Miracles
Why God and Allah Need to Talk

Copyright © 2012 Ruth Broyde Sharone
Reprinted 2017

All rights reserved, including the right of reproduction in whole or in part in any form without the written permission of the publisher except in the case of brief quotations embodied in critical articles and reviews.

First published in 2012 by Mixed Media Memoirs LLC
Chestnut Hill, MA 02467
www.mixedmediamemoirs.com

Reprint Edition by Global Peace Publishing 2017
Culver City, CA 90232
www.globalpeacepublishing.com

Library of Congress Control Number: 2012900891

Editor, Leah Abrahams

Cover and book design by Laura Treichel

Mandala on cover created by Sebastian Schimpf
Bali-based Artist and Designer
www.endless-loving.com

ISBN-13 978-0-9992563-0-5
ISBN-10 0-9992563-0-0

Manufactured in the United States of America

10 9 8 7 6 5 4 3 2 1

Dedication

In blessed memory of my mother and father, Raya and Sam Broyde,
who taught me to love Judaism and humanity

and to Nana Verna, my adopted grandmother,
beloved "Queen of Hearts"

A Fourfold Song
by Rabbi Abraham Isaac Kook

There is one who sings the song of his own life, and in himself he finds everything, his full spiritual satisfaction.

There is another who sings the song of his people. He leaves the circle of his own individual self, because he finds it without sufficient breadth, without an idealistic basis. He aspires toward the heights, and he attaches himself with a gentle love to the whole community of Israel. Together with her he sings her songs. He feels grieved in her afflictions and delights in her hopes. He contemplates noble and pure thoughts about her past and her future, and probes with love and wisdom her inner spiritual essence.

There is another who reaches toward more distant realms, and he goes beyond the boundary of Israel to sing the song of man. His spirit extends to the wider vistas of the majesty of man generally, and his noble essence. He aspires toward man's general goal and looks forward toward his higher perfection. From this source of life he draws the subjects of his meditation and study, his aspirations and his visions.

Then there is one who rises toward wider horizons, until he links himself with all existence, with all God's creatures, with all worlds, and he sings his song with all of them. It is of one such as this that tradition has said that whoever sings a portion of song each day is assured of having a share in the world to come.

And then there is one who rises with all these songs in one ensemble, and they all join their voices. Together they sing their songs with beauty, each one lends vitality and life to the other. They are sounds of joy and gladness, sounds of jubilation and celebration, sounds of ecstasy and holiness.

The song of the self, the song of the people, the song of man, the song of the world all merge in him at all times, in every hour…

Lights of Holiness, Vol II, pp. 458-459

Preface

Margaret Mead, the great anthropologist, was slightly off-track when she opined that it took only a small group of thoughtful, committed citizens to change the world. It does not necessarily require a small group; one person charged by her dreams and fueled by her determination and energy is capable of galvanizing a movement and making a difference. It has been my great privilege and blessing to work alongside Ruth Broyde Sharone for the Parliament of the World's Religions and to found the Southern California Committee for a Parliament of the World's Religions (SCCPWR). It is a joy to see this book offered to the world, at last, detailing her dreams, her struggles and triumphs. I am convinced that it will inspire and empower those receptive souls who are willing to attend to its many lessons and insights.

Ruth in her own way is a miracle-worker. Nor is that just hyperbole. There are many examples in the book of Ruth's imagination and drive: the Freedom Seders, first in Israel and Egypt and then in other parts of the world, built around the Exodus narrative of the Israelites' liberation from bondage; her remarkable film *God and Allah Need to Talk* shown widely not only in the U.S. but also in Europe, the Middle East, and Latin America; her idea of citizen diplomacy involving diplomatic missions and their cultural-political outreach; and the hundreds of interfaith events and meetings that she has either helped to organize or has participated in. Anyone who has put together such events does not need to be told about the sweat and tears, and occasionally blood, that these initiatives involve. To be at it for more than 20 years and to grow in the process bespeaks firm, unshakeable commitment and resolve.

The deeper challenge of interfaith work, however, is the personal and intrafaith one. To be truly open and hospitable to the "other" involves the willingness to be seriously challenged and transformed as a religious practitioner and as a person. This existential demand is especially severe when it involves a Jewish woman, who loves both Judaism and Israel, and who is also solicitous and caring, as Ruth is, about the welfare of Muslims and of Arabs and Palestinians. Her deep-seated respect for Muslims and for Islamic faith and culture has won her a lot of friends in Muslim communities, but it has also brought her a fair share of vituperation and grief. Ruth has remained steadfast, and indeed has grown as a person, in the midst of such negativity—what she refers to in the book as "minefields."

Purity of heart, says Kierkegaard, is to will one thing only and to sacrifice everything, including one's personal well-being for that cause. In Ruth's case that "one thing" has been the quest for peace achieved through deeper interreligious understanding and respect. That purity and passion are palpable in her and have enabled her to win the trust of people, even those with sharply divergent orientations and viewpoints. For example, she documents in the book her hard-won friendship with a Bangladeshi Muslim man who strongly disagrees with her about Israeli-Palestinian politics. She also describes how easily misunderstandings and mistrust can grow in this area of interfaith communication when we are most exposed and vulnerable, and how we have to be willing to be scrupulously honest with ourselves and understanding and forgiving of others. Her reconciliation with friends and acquaintances involved in such misunderstandings is deeply moving.

There are multiple riches in this book. But what stands out for me, and I hope for others, is her boldness of vision and the personal qualities that Ruth brings to the task of translating this vision into reality. She touches on some of the deepest existential challenges facing us as a human species: "Are we doomed to eternal warfare or is there a common ground of humanity that unites us regardless of our (different) dearly-held beliefs?" "Can we expand our consciousness and our capacity to accept one another?" "Can we create bonds of trust and friendship that will not jeopardize or compromise our own beliefs, while we simultaneously show honor and respect to those on a different path?"

And, finally, the urgent question of our time that in a sense encapsulates the previous ones: "Are we finally ready to achieve world peace through our efforts and can interfaith dialogue actually hasten that process?"

Ruth is indeed a dreamer and a visionary but is also immensely practical and—like the best of dreamers—is willing to work hard to make such dreams a reality using all her formidable energy, wit, commitment, and boundless love for human beings in the process. In our local interfaith community we have witnessed with our own eyes the miracle that she is. It is my fervent hope that the miracles that she has created both in this beautifully written book and in her life are widely experienced. They are significant and inspiring steps along the arduous road to world peace.

Joseph Prabhu, Professor of Philosophy
California State University, Los Angeles
Co-Chair, Interfaith Ambassadors for a Parliament of the World's Religions

Table of Contents

Introduction 1

Chapter 1
    My Wake-Up Call 5

Chapter 2
    My Latin American Immersion 15

Chapter 3
    American Homecoming, Detour to Europe, and the Call to Israel 37

Chapter 4
    The Holy Land 47

Chapter 5
    My Palestinian Heritage and My First Palestinian Friend 53

Chapter 6
    German-Jewish Encounter: Another Time, Another Place 75

Chapter 7
    Multiple Narratives, Multiple Truths, and One Dream of Peace 81

Chapter 8
    Let There Be Peace on Earth, and Let It Begin With Me 95

Chapter 9
    I Have a Dream 103

Chapter 10
    Two Women One Journey 117

Chapter 11
    Festival of Freedom 125

Chapter 12
    Be Careful What You Wish For 147

Chapter 13
    From Terror to Reconciliation 169

Chapter 14
    God and Allah Need to Talk: A Billboard That Changes My Life 179

Chapter 15
　　Willing to Be the Stranger 193

Chapter 16
　　A Taste of Interfaith Paradise 203

Chapter 17
　　Think Globally, Act Locally 219

Chapter 18
　　Nineteen Persians and Me: The Call of Rumi 231

Chapter 19
　　The Summer of My Spider Bite 245

Chapter 20
　　Citizen Diplomacy 255

Chapter 21
　　Green Bay Revisited: The Packers, Cheese, and Interfaith 275

Chapter 22
　　Beyond Theories: Where the Rubber Meets the Road 283

Chapter 23
　　A New Era in Washington 289

Chapter 24
　　Lessons from the Rain Forest 299

Chapter 25
　　Is There Peace Among the Peacemakers? 307

Chapter 26
　　Weaving the Global Interfaith Web 319

Bibliography 347
Acknowledgements 353
Discussion Questions 357

Introduction

In April of 2000 I landed in an interfaith minefield, but I didn't know it at the time.

I was in Cairo, Egypt on the first lap of the fourth Middle East interfaith pilgrimage that I had helped to organize. Rabbi Marcia Prager and her husband, Cantor Jack Kessler, were our spiritual leaders. In what appeared to be a miraculous and auspicious turn of events, our group of thirty-six was offered a rare opportunity to meet with the head Imam of Cairo and with Egyptian government dignitaries in Al-Azhar, one of the most important mosques and Muslim learning centers in the world.

They held a press conference in the mosque to welcome us, and we were invited to introduce our peace mission publicly. After we spoke we unfurled and proudly displayed a thirteen-foot silk banner bearing messages for peace and freedom in more than twenty-five languages. We explained that these messages had been inscribed by people from all over the world. We emphasized to our Muslim hosts the importance of working closely with all the children of Abraham and, in turn, we were told by our hosts they were in perfect alignment with our mission. Shutters clicked. Lights flashed. Cameras rolled. And we were on an "interfaith high."

After the press conference, Mustapha, an eager and intelligent young reporter from a leading Egyptian newspaper, requested a private interview that same evening. We accepted. He arrived at our hotel at 8:00 PM to interview us: Rabbi Marcia, Joseph (our Muslim tour leader), and me.

We were all impressed by Mustapha's intelligence, and by his thoughtful questions about the nature of peace. How, he wanted to know, did we think peace could one day be achieved in the Middle East, which was home to one of the most intractable conflicts in the world?

"The answer lies in us," Rabbi Marcia told him, her hand touching her heart. "We will have to create the peace ourselves."

When he left us we were convinced that he, too, was a seeker of peace. It buoyed our spirits to meet a journalist sympathetic to our cause at the very beginning of our journey. We knew it was vital not only to convince people we might encounter about the benefits of interfaith dialogue and the importance of sharing our faith stories, but we also wanted to identify people in the media who would publicize our work and let others know that pursuers of peace are everywhere and willing to travel to spread the word.

A few months later, I was given a translation of the article written by our young, "sympathetic" journalist. In a front-page story strewn with lies and half-truths, our peace pilgrimage was vilified. The writer denounced the Imam for receiving us at the mosque, calling him naïve and susceptible to our "so-called peace mission." The writer also accused me personally of making films to harm Arab women and children.

We had been deceived.

You may be wondering as I did at the time: Why do I want to work in these minefields? Why should I continuously expose myself to relentless lies and accusations?

Call me foolhardy. A dreamer. Naïve. I will not argue with you. I am all of these and more. I come from a long line of dreamers. Perhaps that is why I am willing to enter the minefields of the interfaith world even though I have been forewarned and occasionally burned by the explosions.

But I must be honest. My existential dilemma goes even deeper than issues related solely to interfaith engagement. I struggle with the same nagging questions about the nature of humankind that have preoccupied men and women for millennia:

Are we doomed to eternal warfare, or is there a common ground of humanity that unites us regardless of our dearly held beliefs?

Is there an actual place—a unified field—where we can all intersect peacefully?

Can we expand our consciousness and our capacity to accept one another?

Can we create bonds of trust and friendship that will not jeopardize or compromise our own beliefs while we simultaneously show honor and respect to those who are on a different path?

And, adding my own twenty-first century personal question to the list:

Are we finally ready to achieve world peace through our own efforts and can interfaith dialogue actually hasten that process?

These thorny questions have insinuated themselves into my life, into the very marrow of my bones. To find answers for myself, I embarked on a journey of more than two decades, following the trail—and in some instances actually creating a trail—for interfaith engagement. I am living—not dying—to know if it is possible for us to get along with one another. No, not just get along. Get ahead. Ahead of our fears. Ahead of our blindness and beyond our

Introduction

differences or, as the Poet-of-Love Jallaladin Rumi says so eloquently, to meet in a field of ideas "beyond wrongdoing and rightdoing." The unified field.

I have come to believe that the most important and urgent work being done on the planet today is the work of interfaith engagement. Yet regardless of how crucial our mission may be, people always ask us the same question: What propels you to enter these minefields?

I believe I am responding for myself and for all my interfaith colleagues around the world when I say: We enter this territory because we must. We are compelled by visions of interfaith harmony no less mesmerizing than the ones that captivated the imaginations of our explorer ancestors: visions of a new world, of unlimited potential, of great opportunity and spiritual wealth.

We know with certainty that our interfaith world is curved, not flat. So do we also know that our faith is not linear. Our faith is particle and wave, as are we.

As voyagers, guided by our heavenly stars and constellations, we believe that just beyond the horizon is a fertile and welcoming world where people of many faiths can live in mutual respect and compassion, a land of unity within diversity, and diversity within unity. It is a world so rich in potential for inner and outer peace, that we are willing to risk all. We are willing to abandon the comfort of our familiar individual religious communities and well-worn scriptures, and to enter the unknown territory of "the other."

We are curious, adventurous, and our hearts are open. We are fascinated by the individual and personal spiritual paths of our sisters and brothers. We are also devoted to our own path, and happy to be pursuing it. And we do not feel a need to have everyone believe or worship as we do.

We enjoy comparing rituals and beliefs. We marvel at our similarities and we take note of our differences. We call out to the Creator and the Universe in our distinct voice, but we also hear the sincerity in the voices and melodies that are not our own.

We tell stories about ourselves and our experiences. Our stories merge, converge, and diverge. We marvel at the variations of themes. We play our individual instruments and we submit ourselves to the Grand Orchestra.

We look like everybody else and have no distinguishing body marks. We come in all skin colors, ages and genders, all sizes and shapes. You will recognize us because we are border crossers—not across national and political lines, but across spiritual and religious boundaries. We feel at home both in our own community, and in other people's communities. We move freely and easily between multiple worlds but we do not require passports or inked stamps to know when we left and when we returned. We may even inhabit those parallel worlds simultaneously.

We are border crossers because even as we recognize the philosophical and religious borders that separate us, we do not allow them to keep us from honoring our fellow travelers. And as we interfaith explorers discover one another, and as our networks of interfaith grow and expand across the globe like a giant golden web, we know with certainty we have not undertaken this bold adventure in vain.

At the end of the interview Mustapha, the Egyptian journalist, tried to prepare us for what might happen, but we were not savvy enough at the time to understand his parting words, as you will see in Chapter 12, entitled "Be Careful What You Wish For."

Our experience in Egypt was a minefield, one of many. But the miracles we can individually and collectively create through interfaith work are also many.

Won't you join us?

We don't set out to save the world; we set out to wonder how other people are doing and to reflect on how our actions affect other people's hearts.

~Pema Chodron

CHAPTER 1
My Wake-Up Call

I encountered my very first interfaith minefield when I was a freshman in college.

I was not allowed to live on campus during my first quarter because I lived only an hour's commuting distance from the university by bus. However, during winter quarter many students dropped out and the university was eager to fill their empty spots, so they offered me a room on campus. It was a godsend for me during the winter when navigating the icy, slippery streets of Chicago.

To my delight, I also received permission from the Student Housing Office to continue living at the dorms through the spring quarter. In retrospect I realize it was my first experience living on a daily basis in an environment that was predominantly Christian.

It was strange, at first, but as I made friends with students of various religious backgrounds, the differences seemed to pale. In fact, my first year I became very close friends with three wonderful Christian girls, and we made plans to room together the following fall quarter. Mary Ann and Rita were Catholic, and Joan was Presbyterian. I knew they attended church and prayed to Jesus, and they knew I went to a synagogue and was active in the Hillel Foundation for Jewish students. All four of us unanimously decided we would room together the following year and, in a stroke of amazing luck, I drew number two during the annual housing lottery. That meant I would be given priority in selecting a dorm room for the next year, and it simultaneously meant that all of my three roommates would be included in the early dorm selection. We rejoiced because we knew exactly which dorm we would choose: the one closest to the classrooms—so we could outwit the Chicago winter.

You can imagine my surprise when one day our dorm housemother asked to see me privately and told me I would not receive a dorm room assignment for my sophomore year. Moreover, my prospective roommates were all summoned and the housemother informed them I wasn't going to be allowed to continue living on campus. She instructed them to choose another roommate. They were shocked by that information, but they refused to select anyone else.

When I pressed our housemother for more information, she suggested I speak to one of the major campus administrators, because my case was "special."

"Why is it special?" I asked.

"He'll tell you," she said, her eyes shifting uncomfortably.

I made an appointment to see the Director of Admissions. My roommates waited nervously in our old dormitory, hopeful that I could arrange everything in short order, and that our housing problem would soon be resolved.

I entered a spacious office and noted the traditional mahogany furniture, forest green wallpaper, and a Tiffany desk lamp.

"You shouldn't be living on campus to begin with," the administrator told me immediately after I was seated. He wasted no time in coming to the point. "You live within commuting distance, and we need room for students who come from far away."

"But I have been living on campus for two quarters," I protested. "What about the students who live only ten minutes away and who are allowed to live on campus?"

"Well, that's different," he countered, "because their mothers are involved in sorority affairs, and because they are good students."

"But I have a straight 'A' average and I am very active on campus in extracurricular activities as well," I said in my defense.

"Nevertheless, it's just impossible," he insisted. "So, why don't you consult with your rabbi?" he suggested and then paused for effect.

My mouth opened and closed. I watched his face with disbelief. Why did he suddenly mention my rabbi? Why did the issue of my religion suddenly come up in a conversation that had nothing to do with religion? I couldn't believe what I had heard him say. My rabbi? Did he even know where I prayed or if I prayed? And how did he know I was Jewish? Slowly it dawned on me what was happening!

I remembered I had indicated my religious affiliation on my university application. At the time every student was required to submit a photo and indicate his/her religious affiliation.

I looked at him for a long time before I replied. His gaze never wavered.

"Why would I want to ask my rabbi?" I queried innocently.

"Well, perhaps he could help you find housing with a Jewish family near the university."

"And why would I need to look for housing with a Jewish family?"

"You know, for dietary reasons," he explained, his fleshy hand gesturing expansively to demonstrate his generosity and good will. And then he smiled. I will never forget that smile.

I had just encountered my first interfaith minefield, and I can still feel the shrapnel in my solar plexus, and hear the sound of the explosions in my head—my first wake-up call.

I don't remember the rest of our conversation. I do remember leaving his office in a state of shock, and returning to my three friends who were waiting to hear what they were convinced would be good news.

"He told me to talk to my rabbi, to find housing with a Jewish family. For dietary reasons," I related to them verbatim.

"For dietary reasons?" they repeated in unison. My friends were incredulous. I nodded.

"For dietary reasons?" Mary Ann echoed once again. The four of us looked back and forth at one another, in silence.

It's true. Observant Jews are very conscientious about their diet and will not eat in a place or in a home where they can't be sure the food is kosher. Very often they carry their own food with them in order to observe the strict dietary laws. My mother kept a kosher home, with separate plates and silverware for meat and dairy dishes. She would only eat fish in most restaurants, but never meat unless she knew it was a kosher establishment. My father, my sister, and I were more liberal and did not observe those laws strictly outside our home.

When I entered the world beyond my immediate environment, I discovered that the range of dietary practice among Jews was wide and diverse, even within the same family. But in our dorm, my dietary habits had never been a subject of discussion with the housemother. I didn't advertise the fact that I didn't eat shellfish or pork or mix milk and meat. I simply abstained from eating those foods when they were offered, and I never drank milk or ate any dairy products at any of the meals when meat was served. My close friends knew about my dietary restrictions, but it was never discussed in public.

Recently when we were reminiscing about our college days, Mary Ann reminded me that our housemother would always serve ham on Fridays, "so she could offend the Jews and the Catholics in one fell swoop," she recalled with an ebullient laugh.

At the time of the housing incident, however, I knew the administrator was not truly concerned about what I could or could not eat. I may have been naïve, but I was no fool. I did not perceive his comment as having been born out of religious respect. It sounded, smelled and tasted like anti-Semitism to me.

"You should look for another roommate," I told my three friends resolutely.

All three of them simultaneously came forward and hugged me. "We're not interested in rooming with anyone else," they assured me. "We won't give you up."

It was a precious moment of friendship and loyalty, a moment I never forgot.

"No," I insisted, "You need to have housing, and I can't be the reason for you not to have a place to stay on campus. If you wait too long, you won't get a good choice. You take my number and use it for yourselves."

If truth be told, I was so traumatized by that series of events and the not-so-subtle anti-Semitic behavior of the administrator and my housemother, the next day I began to look for alternative universities. Why would I be interested in staying at a university that discriminated against students because of their religion or ethnicity?

When I analyzed the situation more carefully, I realized that by requiring each student to document his religious affiliation on the entrance application, the university could identify all of the Jewish students on campus. And by requesting a photo they could discover if a student was African-American or Asian, even if they couldn't determine that directly through the family name of the student, especially if a student came from a mixed marriage. That information is what enabled the Admissions Office to establish quotas and to discriminate.

I spent the next two weeks researching other schools nearby. In the end, I didn't transfer because I was on scholarship, and the other universities in the area couldn't offer equivalent academic opportunities. I continued my studies there, but I was obliged to move back home.

I channeled my frustration by joining a grass roots student organization for human rights. It was through my association with that group, most notably when I heard other stories from other students similar to mine, that I began to realize how pervasive the problem of discrimination was on my campus. It was truly my wake-up call. I also began to experience "the Gentlemen's Agreement" kind of discrimination at other places on campus, where prejudice was more covert.

I remember one day in particular. I entered a sorority house on campus, where I had been working part-time in their office for several months. Even though I was on scholarship, I did not receive enough money to cover my entire tuition. I was grateful to find a job at a Christian women's sorority. I knew they had no Jewish members. My boss, a woman in her late forties, noticed a flyer I was carrying that advertised an upcoming event sponsored by the Human Relations Committee. She expressed genuine surprise.

"Why would you want to affiliate yourself with an organization like that?" she asked incredulously. "What's wrong with the human rights students already have on our campus?"

"Because there are many official policies that discriminate against students," I responded. "Why would the university ask for a photo or need to know religious affiliation when a student applies to study here? That's not necessary to determine if a student has merit. The university already has access to their SAT scores, grade averages, details about their extra-curricular activities, and teacher recommendations. They don't need any more information than that to make a decision," I insisted.

"Well, of course they do," she countered. "Otherwise our campus would be overrun by a whole lot of Jews and blacks! Would you like that to happen?"

She didn't know I was Jewish. It had never come up, and I had never found a reason to mention it. I started to answer her but then held back. A fearful thought suddenly came over me. Was this the ideal moment to tell her I was Jewish? Would I be fired if I told her?

I was afraid to go any deeper into the subject. After all, she was my boss and I was dependent on the job to pay my tuition. In retrospect, I realize I didn't have the courage for full self-disclosure. I admit I was "gun-shy" after my painful meeting with the Director of Admissions, so I simply answered, "I don't think that would happen, but I think students who are qualified and talented should be accepted on their own merits, and the criterion for acceptance should be academic capability, not their racial or religious background."

My boss raised a manicured eyebrow in displeasure. She studied me more closely, and I suddenly felt naked. We both realized the conversation was over, even though the topic had clearly not been exhausted.

The university incident proved traumatic, but not only for me. My friend Mary Ann—a Protestant who had converted to Catholicism —was so horrified by the blatant religious discrimination she witnessed against me, she transferred in protest to another college. I did not realize why she left until she finally revealed her reason many years later.

Perhaps my only consolation was in learning a few years later that the Director of Admissions was fired, and the university was no longer allowed to ask for photos or religious affiliation on its application form. Small victories that became large victories on many campuses in America, earned one by one over the years.

There was one other noteworthy incident during my college years that bears reporting, because it concerned my own Jewish community. No community is immune to experiencing or practicing prejudice, I learned.

But first I should share a bit of background about myself. I grew up on the North Side of Chicago, only two blocks away from Lake Michigan. Most of my friends and schoolmates were Jewish. I recall that the public schools would always close on the holiest Jewish days. The few Christians among us often celebrated our Jewish holidays with us, and sometimes they would even attend Jewish summer camp with us.

On the spectrum of religious practice, our family would be considered Conservative Jews, somewhere in the middle between Orthodox and Reform Judaism. My mother, who was a Hebrew schoolteacher for forty years, never worked on the Sabbath. My father, a math teacher and lawyer, a universalist in his orientation, was non-observant, but he did respect my mother's kosher kitchen.

Regardless of the fact that the vast majority of our public school classmates were Jewish, we all knew about Christian holidays, because those holidays were always celebrated at school, and all of us—Jews and non-Jews alike—learned to sing the traditional Christmas carols for the Holiday Choir. I remember being especially moved by the haunting melodies of "Ave Maria" and "Silent Night," although the words troubled me because they seemed to be about someone else's God. My friends and I never discussed how we felt singing about Jesus as "our Lord and Savior." Much later I would learn that Jews had been persecuted by Christians for centuries for not accepting Jesus as the Messiah. At the time, however, we simply accepted the fact that we were in the minority in America, and we did not question the obvious incongruence about our singing Christmas songs.

Since I was considered a budding artist, I was often asked to paint on the local store windows at holiday time. As a result I had many opportunities to practice painting Santa Clauses, reindeer, Christmas trees, and angels—as well as Menorahs for Hanukkah, the Jewish holiday that usually overlapped with Christmas. I had learned to distinguish between "their holidays" and "our holidays." After all, we lived in America, the great "melting pot" of the world, according to our social studies book.

My older sister Leah and I faithfully went to Hebrew school three times a week after regular school from about the time we were eight until we were seventeen years old. We each celebrated a Bat Mitzvah, our Jewish rite of passage, when we were twelve years old. We were called up to the pulpit on a Friday night to read a portion in Hebrew, from the Prophets, to show we had mastered the ancient language of our ancestors, and to recite a speech and commentary that took us months to compose and then several more weeks to learn by heart.

As a teenager I continued to celebrate the Jewish holidays with my family and community, and I never experienced any form of anti-Semitism in my daily life until college, in the incident I described earlier.

While I was in college, my mother invited me on one occasion to a luncheon organized by several of her friends. I would be the only one of my age, but my mother was so persuasive, I agreed to come. She promised me the food would be great and plentiful, which it was! Lox and bagels, cream cheese, herring salad, smoked fish, noodle kugel, fruit salad and at least ten different deserts, including chocolate babka. How could I resist?

While I was sitting and socializing with my mother's friends, all of them Jewish, several women began complaining about two of the local ethnic communities in Chicago, the Poles and the Greeks. They began to make disparaging remarks, remarks that pierced me to the quick. I recognized them as ethnic stereotypes and I started to squirm in my seat. They continued speaking in the same derisive manner for several minutes and, finally, I couldn't tolerate it a minute longer. I stood up abruptly and, in a loud voice, interrupted their conversation.

"How can you speak that way?" I demanded to know. "Don't you know they say the same things about us Jews? Shouldn't we know better than to generalize like that? How can you condemn an entire group of people based on your experience with only a few people from that group?"

My voice grew more indignant. Everyone remained silent, shocked by my outburst.

"Haven't we learned anything yet? Don't we remember what the Poles were saying about us in Europe? Or how we were demonized by the Germans? Shouldn't we—of all the people on earth—know better?"

I paused for effect. The room was noticeably silent. I had created an incident.

My mother had not been among the women who had spoken so disparagingly, but these women were her close friends. I had embarrassed her in front of her friends. I saw her looking at me as only an aggrieved mother can look at her rebellious child.

"I can't sit among you if you are going to talk like that," I continued. I was on a roll. "It isn't right for us to be saying things like that, and I won't be a part of it." I was too afraid to look at my mother at that moment, so I picked up my pocketbook, turned on my heel, and made a grand exit.

I had created my own minefield.

Several days later, when I had a chance to consider in depth what had happened, and speak with my mother about it, I learned a very important lesson. Embarrassing people publicly and pointing out their prejudices does not result in their becoming less prejudiced. It only alienates them and prevents a civil discussion of ideas. Moreover, it doesn't actually afford people an opportunity to acknowledge their prejudices. It usually provides them with a perfect opportunity to disapprove of and find fault with the person criticizing them, which inevitably becomes the main topic of any further discussion. When people are embarrassed or made to feel wrong or bad, the real issues get subordinated, and the subsidiary issues become paramount. Morality usually takes a back seat to an injured ego.

How we speak about these matters, the language we use, is crucial. When we are on the attack, those attacked will inevitably become defensive, or then move into attack mode themselves.

I have come to realize that all nations, all peoples, all religions, and all tribes, have a tendency to stereotype and label those unlike themselves. That's probably how the expression "the other" originated. We continuously seek to distinguish and separate ourselves from "the other," as evidenced in our long and protracted history of war and bloodshed. Therein lies the core of our eternal dilemma of how to get along with one another. Perhaps we should rephrase it as "with one and other."

More than thirty years have passed since that explosive episode with my mother and her friends took place. Nevertheless, I am constantly reminded of what happened among members of my own tribe when I attend conferences on the Israeli/Palestinian conflict. How ineffective and futile it is, ultimately, to launch verbal attacks against those who view the situation differently. Those public forums often deteriorate into shouting matches, and the net result is that the audience becomes polarized and less interested in attending future Middle East dialogues, if they can even be termed "dialogues." What has been achieved? Certainly no area of trust or even neutral terrain to explore the subject has been established, and in such situations most minds cannot be changed. On the contrary, people harden their positions and sink deeper roots to fortify themselves from anything that might threaten them.

I see now that I didn't have the wisdom to behave otherwise when I was with my mother's friends. I was a young woman, passionate about justice and equality, heightened by my painful experience at my own university.

But if I could go back again to that moment in time, I think I would have approached the situation quite differently. Perhaps if I had shared my painful experience with them, describing my hurt and disappointment at being singled out and then denied housing because I was Jewish, perhaps they could have truly heard me. If I could have aroused their empathy rather than their enmity, I might have spoken into a space where they could listen to me rather than react to me.

This was a lesson that took me several decades to learn, and I continue to revisit that experience as I observe the minefields that we ourselves create.

(Center, front) With my high school newspaper colleagues.

(Standing third from left) With my fellow journalism school colleagues.

The traveler has to knock at every alien door to come to his own, and one has to wander through all the outer worlds to reach the innermost shrine at the end.

~Rabindranath Tagore

CHAPTER 2
My Latin American Immersion

Nineteen countries and fifty-four cities in eighteen months. That could be the headline, but certainly not the substance of my story.

I had studied Spanish in Mexico for three months in my sophomore year of college, and found myself deeply enamored of the Latin culture, its language and history. After graduating from college with a degree in journalism, a minor in Latin American political science, and an intermediate fluency in Spanish, I decided to tour the entire southern half of America. It seemed totally reasonable—anything a twenty-one year-old decides appears reasonable at the time. Mostly I hoped it would satisfy my appetite for travel and desire to learn about other cultures.

I was too young and definitely too inexperienced to get a job as a foreign correspondent, so I did some basic research on travel costs and found a temporary job as an administrative assistant in an office. I calculated that six months of frugal living and conscientious saving would be sufficient time to amass enough money to buy a round trip ticket with some extra cash for travel expenses. I planned to travel on a shoestring, of course. When you are young and hungry to know the world, you are even willing to travel third class with the chickens—but I didn't know about the chickens until I got there!

To save money, I lived at home with my parents. Though I was faithfully depositing each pay check, I decided I needed an innovative master plan to interest magazines in my on-the-scene reporting from Latin America. I came up with the idea of sending a mass mailing to all the Jewish newspapers and magazines around the U.S., offering them a young journalist's bird's eye view south of the border, and an intimate look at the Jewish communities in a part of the world that was rarely examined. I also approached several neighborhood newspapers and pitched them the idea of my being their correspondent in Latin America.

To my delight, several of them answered me and said, "We would welcome any articles you would like to send us, but on a free-lance basis only." Later on I discovered that was an indirect way of saying, "We won't offer you any money up front, but if we like what you write, we'll print it and then pay you as little as possible."

Clearly, a freelance arrangement would not be enough to support myself financially, yet it was encouraging. To my surprise, an editor of a Jewish magazine for B'nai Brith, an international Jewish organization headquartered in Washington, DC, also asked me to visit them before I left on my journey. Lily Edelman was so intrigued by my plan to research the Jewish communities, she agreed to write introduction letters to all of their representatives in Latin America, and arranged for me to stay with Jewish families throughout Central and South America. When she learned of my experience as a youth leader, she suggested I serve as an itinerant youth leader for their individual communities in South America. I was flattered by her proposal and also a bit relieved because it meant that I could give my parents an actual itinerary with names of individuals to contact if they wanted to reach me—just in case.

I took off for what would become a watershed experience in my life. At age twenty-one, with a degree in journalism, a round trip ticket, about $1,200 in traveler's checks, a list of contacts, and plenty of *chutzpah*, (the Yiddish word for cheekiness), I was ready and eager to conquer Latin America, single-handedly.

I must have offered an amusing sight, laden down with my two 35mm cameras, telephoto lenses, a portable typewriter, an old fashioned, clunky tape recorder, and a suitcase of dreams. My greatest assets, in retrospect, were my spirit of adventure and my optimistic attitude. But when I was on the plane leaving America, observing DC's night landscape grow faint as we ascended into the clouds, I couldn't help but think of my family. I especially remembered my mother's sad and worried face as we hugged goodbye.

She had been opposed to my trip from the beginning, and to thwart my plans during the six months I lived at home, she would regularly hide items that were stored in my suitcase. When her shenanigans didn't dissuade me from going, she tried talking mother-sense to me. "A daughter's place is at home. What kind of a profession is journalism for a girl anyway?" she would ask rhetorically. "You should stay here, with your family, get married, and become a teacher."

She was also very concerned my traveling alone as a young woman might be misinterpreted. It turned out my mother was right about that! My liberal-minded father supported me with his usual "my-daughter-can-do anything" enthusiasm, and wished me well, "but don't forget to write to your mother often," he advised me. "She'll be worried all the time. You know Mother."

The truth is when we feel confident enough to maneuver through the world's minefields on our own—if we are even aware minefields exist—we don't want our parents to be around.

There is a time for each of us to step into that field of pure potential, for better or for worse. While I realize not everyone takes that step, I did—without a backward glance—or maybe just one tiny glance out of the corner of my eye.

Mexico

My first stop was Mexico. One of my first discoveries was that the Jews of Latin America were divided by country of origin, not by degree of orthodoxy or religious practice, such as our Reform, Conservative, Orthodox, and Reconstructionist denominations in America.

Mexico City, for example, had five independent Jewish communities. They were founded by Jews who had immigrated from many parts of the world: Jews from Eastern Europe, the Ashkenazi Jews, spoke Yiddish; Jews from Germany spoke German; Jews from North America spoke English; and two communities of Jews from Syria, often referred to as the Sephardic Jews, spoke both Arabic and Ladino (also known as Judeo-Spanish, a hybrid language of Spanish and Hebrew with a smattering of other languages mixed in).

One of the Sephardic communities in Mexico City originated from Aleppo, the other from Damascus. They didn't get along, so they established their own separate synagogues and discouraged their children from "intra-marriage" with families from the other city in Syria—even though they were all Jewish. That last fact still makes me smile.

Much later in life I would learn that all of the major religions of the world—Christianity, Islam, Judaism, Buddhism, Hinduism and more—are subdivided and often at odds with one another internally. Their beliefs and rituals vary denominationally, as do ours, and often their leaders are unwilling to cross borders to dialogue with fellow clergy from their own religion. Many of my interfaith colleagues have acknowledged that one of their first important discoveries was the fact that other religions face their own internecine struggles.

At the beginning of my journey, however, this was a revelation to me, to discover the Jewish communities in Latin America were stratified and divided. Considering that in the post-Hitler world only about twelve million Jews were left, how could we be so divided and at odds with one another, I wondered, since our Torah was one, our God was one?

But even beyond my ability at the time to understand the great divide within Judaism, I wondered if there is something about human nature itself that leads us, time and time again, to plant our individual flags in the sand and proclaim: "This is ours, and that is yours, and don't you dare step over the line!"

Central America

As I continued south through Central America, visiting the Jewish communities, and interviewing their leaders, I also discovered how little contact each of the Jewish communities in Central and South America had with one another. I also came to a deep visceral understanding of the meaning of the word "Diaspora," the dispersion of the Jewish people throughout the world. In Hebrew this phenomenon is called *Galut*, which literally means exile.

I found myself not only interviewing the leaders of the Jewish communities, but giving informal talks to the communities on what I had just learned in the country "before" theirs, to the north. The Guatemalan Jews wanted to know about the Mexican Jews; the Nicaraguan Jews were curious about the Salvadorian Jews; and the Panamanian Jews were hungry for information about all of the Jewish communities between Mexico and Panama.

I began to lecture about my findings. My Spanish had improved considerably since I started my journey. I became aware that the countries of Central and South America were truly separate and proudly so. It wasn't like the United States where we have different regional cultures and accents, but are still united under one government. Because of my mobility, I found myself becoming an unofficial Ambassador, forming a link between the Jewish communities in Latin America, as I moved from one country to another.

When I met with local journalists in all of the countries I visited, the first question invariably asked of me was:

"With whom are you traveling?"

No one ever asked if I was traveling alone, because no one believed it was possible in Latin America. Then—and it is still true in some of those countries today—young women didn't travel without a chaperone.

As an unexpected consequence of my breaking with their tradition, the Latin Americans became overly-protective, surrogate parents. In each country they welcomed me into their homes, fed me, helped me navigate around their city, and made sure I was home at a reasonable hour. They also plied me with gifts when it was time for me to leave, begged me to write to them, and sent regards to my parents, with whom they clearly empathized (and probably felt sorry for, as well).

Inevitably we would all cry. I had become part of their family and they had become part of my extended global family. It was profoundly moving then and even today I am still in awe of their hospitality, and I still feel gratitude for the shelter and care they provided.

I traversed the continent—learning the latest slang expressions in Spanish in every new country I visited—traveling by plane, bus, boat, and even on horseback. What became very apparent to me was there were no real borders, except in the cartographer's renderings. Yes, I had to apply for visas and, yes, I had to have my passport stamped as I moved across national borders. But for me the human race could not be contained or limited by those artificial lines drawn in the sand.

I became a border crosser in the truest sense of the word, and I came to see my Latin American odyssey not as a visit to nineteen countries and fifty-four cities, but as an opportunity to see the beauty in people everywhere, by learning about people's customs and family histories, and by witnessing people's joys and sorrows. None of this was circumscribed by any geographic boundary or by religious differences. Simply put, the human condition was universal. I saw it. I lived it. I recorded it.

It was an amazing discovery, especially for a young Jewish woman totally out of her element, crisscrossing a continent where more than ninety-five percent of the people were Catholics and where, in some cases, people had never met a "real live Jew" in their entire life—until they met me.

Peru

Rogelio was a young seminarian, not more than fifteen years old, whom I met when I was traveling in a third class train in the interior of Peru. Yes, with the chickens I mentioned earlier.

My fellow travelers were primarily from small villages outside of Lima, the Indigenous women colorfully dressed in dozens of layers of ankle-length skirts, sporting their characteristic white bowler hats bedecked with a specially designed hatband and sometimes a feather to indicate their tribe. They seemed to be traveling with all of their possessions, gathered in big bundles that had been wrapped up in rainbow-striped serapes. They were traveling together with their children, their husbands, and their chickens.

This from an entry in my diary:

> *A journey of life, on the third class train: mothers changing diapers as they sucked on a sinewy pork tendon or picked their teeth with a bone sliver, all the while pressing their brown swollen breasts into eager, noisy mouths. They let their children play bare-bottom on blankets on the floor of the train as they alternately fed them warm breast milk, then*

Orange Crush from a bottle. Blanca, at my side, displayed an entire front row of gold fillings and every time she laughed, her mouth glittered and the sunlight danced.

Rogelio was sitting opposite me as the crowded train bounced along. His handsome brown face also revealed some gold teeth when he smiled. He took out his lunch. We had exchanged a few words together earlier when he asked me where I was from—as he studied my blond hair, green eyes, camera bags and typewriter.

I told him I was a North American journalist, a *yanqui*, and I learned he was on vacation from his Catholic seminary. It was his first trip to see his parents in two years. As the train bounced and jolted from side to side, Rogelio unwrapped a package of meat, opened it up, and extended it towards me. "*Por favor, sirvase,*" he said, offering me some of his lunch.

I looked at the meat and immediately went through a quick silent monologue. "I wonder what kind of meat it is. I don't think it is beef. It looks too white. It must be pork. I can't eat pork, but if I refuse, he'll be insulted. But that's a chance I'll have to take. He's obviously trying to be so hospitable to me because I'm a foreigner."

"What kind of meat is it?" I asked him, hoping I would be mistaken.

"*Puerco!*" he replied enthusiastically. "Do you like pork?"

I took a pause before I answered. My mind suddenly flashed back on a childhood memory and a favorite story my mother liked to tell about me.

When I was about six years old, I locked myself out of the house. Our upstairs neighbor invited me into her apartment and offered me a snack: a bacon, lettuce, and tomato sandwich, to be exact.

"Oh, no," I demurred, "I can't eat that. It's not kosher," I announced proudly with the aplomb of a six-year-old. I was smart enough to know bacon was *verboten* because bacon came from a pig.

"Well, then, the only other thing I can offer you is a ham sandwich," my neighbor replied.

"Ham? Oh, ham is OK," I assured her.

At that very moment my mother rang the doorbell looking for me. When she would relate the story, this was the part she especially relished—how she saved me from that ham sandwich just in the nick of time!

I found myself smiling when I reconnected with Rogelio's eager face and extended hand.

"No, I don't eat *puerco*," I told Rogelio.

"Why not?"

He refused to be dissuaded from his gesture of hospitality, and pushed his offering of meat closer to my face. "Smell it. It's really good. *Es bueno. Es muy sabroso.*"

I searched my brain but I couldn't find any way to tell him why I was refusing other than to say, "I can't, Rogelio, it's against my religion to eat *puerco*." I felt he would somehow understand, he being a seminarian, with strict religious practice, someone who must have been introduced to the concept of self-discipline and self-denial.

"Against your religion? What religion is that?" he asked.

"I'm Jewish," I said. "*Soy judia,*"

Rogelio looked at me and then uttered in the most ordinary and matter-of-fact tone, "Oh, the Jews are the ones who killed God."

I was speechless. I had no idea what I could tell this fifteen year-old seminarian, who had never met a Jew in his life. He had obviously learned that Jews were "God-killers" from the priests who were his teachers at the seminary where he, too, would one day become a priest and then teach his seminarians the same lesson.

For the Jewish people that has been truly one of the most painful legacies left by the Catholic Church in Latin America and elsewhere in the world, a legacy which would only be addressed and corrected many decades later, and is still a subject of debate.

For the moment, this was one minefield for which I was definitely not prepared. I truthfully didn't know how to respond to Rogelio. As I recall, I took out an orange and offered him some of my food instead. Perhaps I changed the subject, made light conversation, or asked if he had brothers or sisters.

I was acutely aware of being in uncharted territory. I didn't know what I could possibly say to Rogelio to enable him to view the world from a new and different vantage point. He had been entrusted by his parents to the Catholic Church at a very early age. They knew he would be fed and housed and receive an education. Their son would learn to read and write and have a chance for advancement. For poor families, that was a gift and a blessing. His teachers, all priests, were the lords and masters of his world.

Sitting together on that third class train in Peru, with the cackling hens scurrying underfoot, and the women feeding their babies, what could I possibly say to the young and earnest Rogelio as he extended his arm, offering to share his dinner which for me was forbidden food? Should I say he was wrong, that the Jews hadn't killed his God? Could I say that without threatening the foundation of his world and the bedrock of his education? What could I possibly say to him that would make any sense? I had no idea.

I remember studying Rogelio's young and appealing face, the color of mineral rich earth. His dark, expressive eyes and friendliness still dance in my mind's eye. What would I say to him today if I were to meet him again and hear him categorically state, "Oh, the Jews are the ones who killed God."

Little did I know within one year I would confront a similar situation in Venezuela. But for the moment, I had no answers for Rogelio.

I continued my travels south. Soon I would be leaving behind the countries made up primarily of Indigenous peoples and entering the countries whose populations were largely immigrants from Europe, countries such as Chile, Argentina, Uruguay and Paraguay. My personal experiences with families in those European-oriented countries would prove to be no different than those to the north. I was warmly received everywhere, and my suitcase grew heavy with gifts I couldn't use but couldn't discard because they were given to me with such affection.

Argentina

In Argentina, I entered from the north and first visited Tucuman—where I learned to eat soup as a final course. From there I made my way down through Mendoza, and Cordoba until I reached the city that never sleeps, Buenos Aires, the capital of Argentina. The cosmopolitan *porteños* (as the natives are called) were larger than life, with their boisterous Italian-tinged slang, their bravado, their passion for food, entertainment, and the Tango, of course. Buenos Aires, I discovered, also boasted the largest Jewish community in all of Latin America, numbering about half a million.

But shortly after arriving, I abruptly interrupted my stay in Buenos Aires because I learned about a very unusual centennial celebration of a small agricultural Yiddish-speaking settlement in the interior of the country, called Moises Ville (City of Moses). It was described as the home of Jewish farmers who had immigrated there after Baron De-Hirsch, a wealthy Jewish philanthropist from Europe, bought land and offered it to Jews escaping the pogroms of Europe. I was fascinated and determined to visit that settlement to write a story about it.

When I arrived there, I discovered Moises Ville was a town where everyone spoke Yiddish, the language of the Eastern European Jews, including the non-Jewish policemen, postmaster, firemen, and government officials. What a concept! An entire town—within the Catholic continent—where everyone spoke Yiddish! I was eager to interview the residents but my Jewish identity became suspect when they discovered I didn't speak any Yiddish at all, and they were reluctant to be interviewed. I knew a bit of Hebrew from my Hebrew school classes and Bat Mitzvah days but, for the people of Moises Ville, that didn't count.

"Are you sure you're Jewish?" they queried me, in their Yiddish-tinged Spanish, looking suspiciously at my blonde hair and green eyes. I was never able to convince them of my

Jewish pedigree even when I told them my mother was a Hebrew School teacher and had immigrated to Palestine from Riga, Latvia. In truth I mostly resembled the Argentinean German nationals they were used to seeing in their environment. Argentina was the only Latin American nation that failed to break off relations with the Axis during WWII, and after the war many Germans decided to make their home in Nazi-friendly Argentina, including some well-known Nazis such as Adolph Eichmann.

For a young Jewish woman, all too familiar with the statistics of the Holocaust, being mistaken as a German was an interesting irony I would only fully understand many years later. But for the moment, most people in Moises Ville—and elsewhere in Argentina—thought I was German, and would even address me in German. "Fraulein," they would often call out to me in the streets of Buenos Aires, rather than the "senorita" I was accustomed to hearing.

Brazil

I continued my travels and, at the end of 14 months, I rounded the tip of South America, passing first through Uruguay and then through Paraguay. I finally reached Brazil, the largest country in South America, affectionately known as the "Sleeping Giant." I had become so intimate with the Spanish language and Latin culture, I found myself wanting to be identified as a "Latina" rather than a *yanqui* (yankee).

Because I spoke no Portuguese, the national language of Brazil, my language of communication was Spanish, which the Brazilians all understood. In Argentina they thought I was German and in Brazil, because I was fluent in Spanish, they thought I was a Latina.

For sport I decided to tell the Brazilians I was from Chile, which they wholeheartedly believed! They liked the friendly Chileans enormously, preferring them to the *porteños* from Buenos Aires whom they often described as being too self-satisfied and overbearing. That was the prevailing stereotype about Argentineans at the time, and so it convinced me to assume a Chilean identity, just for the fun of it.

It was fun—until I found myself being introduced as a Chilean journalist in front of several million TV viewers during Carnival celebrations in Rio. I was visiting the huge sports stadium that was preparing to welcome the Samba dancers from neighborhoods across Rio. The energetic dancers, resplendent in their elaborate, glitzy costumes, had toured the city, dancing non-stop for eight to ten consecutive hours, and now they were coming to the stadium to be admired and celebrated by the public. The stadium was filling up quickly with thousands of spectators when the Brazilian journalist I had met earlier in the afternoon pulled me over in front of the camera and asked me "to deliver a message to the Brazilians from your own country, Chile." I hastily declined, and tried to move aside, desperate to make a quick exit. But he strong-armed me back in full view of the camera, and insisted I speak into the microphone he was holding. He held on to my elbow, moving me towards the camera saying "*Sí, sí, sí.*" I tried to disengage myself, responding with an equally emphatic "*No, no, no!*"

Finally, realizing I was figuratively and literally on the spot, I agreed to speak.

En nombre de todos los Chilenos… "In the name of all my fellow Chileans," I began, "I want to extend the heartiest greetings of my countrymen to our wonderful neighbors, the Brazilians, and to congratulate you on this magnificent celebration." I don't remember what other good neighborly phrases I invented to get myself off the hook. I only know, as I reminisce, I still find myself squirming but also laughing at my colossal audacity. I remember that exquisite moment of psychological nakedness, realizing I was an imposter on no less than Brazilian national TV. But I can also understand clearly now that I was boldly experimenting with border crossing, even before I could give it a name.

I remember wondering, after the Brazilian incident, what it would take for me to totally assume the identity of someone who came from a different cultural and linguistic background. Nobody knew me in Latin America when I first arrived. I was an unknown quantity. I had no history, except for what I was willing to divulge. I had nothing to live up to and nothing to live down. I was a free agent who could live out the novel of my choice. I was Jewish, but in Moises Ville they didn't believe I was a member of their tribe because I couldn't speak Yiddish and I "didn't look Jewish." In Argentina they thought I was German. In Brazil I was able to pass myself off as Chilean. Who was I really? Could I re-invent myself and my history, or would I eventually return to my source? What was my source? Was I only Jewish and American or did I have a source that transcended religion and ethnicity, country and family?

Those were some of the questions that raced back and forth in my young journalist's head as I was heading back north after sixteen months abroad. I hadn't planned on returning so soon, but I had learned my sister, Leah, my one and only sibling, was planning to get married in August. It was already April and I had not finished exploring the continent, but it was time to speed up my plans.

I left my Chilean disguise behind when I left Brazil and went back to being a *yanqui*, although that identity didn't seem to describe me any more either. I had crossed the border beyond *yanquihood*. I still had my birth name, Ruth Ariella Broyde, but other than that I was no longer willing to be labeled by my country of origin.

I found a kindred spirit and a guardian angel not long after my Brazilian escapade. I met him on a plane as I was flying from Brazil to Venezuela.

Venezuela

Pierre was my seatmate. A tall, ruddy man with a full head of thick white hair, Pierre appeared to be in his late fifties, old enough to be my father. He proudly laid out his border-crosser credentials. He was born in Italy, had a French passport, and he was the owner of a Brazilian soccer team. In fact, he was on his way to Caracas, the capital of Venezuela, because his team was about to play a crucial game that would determine if they were eligible for the finals. His team was already there, waiting for him to arrive.

Pierre quizzed me at length about my mission. What was I doing, traveling in Latin America as a young, unaccompanied woman? He expressed great concern. "You will be arriving in Venezuela when it is considered dangerous for tourists. Where will you be staying?" he wanted to know. "Do you know anybody there? Will anyone meet you at the airport?"

I was expecting to be met by a Jewish family in Caracas, with whom I believed I would be celebrating the first night of Passover. Their names had been supplied to me by the B'nai Brith organization in Washington, and I had written to them a month earlier to let them know of my arrival date. I had their name and phone number, I told Pierre.

But Pierre was still concerned. "I'll wait for you at the airport until you reach them," he promised me. "You can't be on your own here, not now."

We arrived in Caracas and, as promised, Pierre waited to see if someone would come to receive me at the airport. No one did. He waited patiently as I tried reaching the family by phone. No luck.

"I don't want you to take this the wrong way," Pierre assured me, "but I want you to come to my hotel with me. I'll arrange for you to stay overnight in your own room, and then the next day you can try to reach your contacts again. But I will do this on one condition only."

"One condition?" I was genuinely intrigued by Pierre's proposal.

"My condition is: if you see me later this evening in the hotel lobby, and my wife is with me, you act like you never met me. She's in Venezuela, expecting me at the hotel, and she is very jealous. I'll also arrange to get you a ticket for the game, but when you see me, don't acknowledge me, please!"

I accepted his condition, and thanked him profusely. I certainly didn't want to get him in trouble with his wife.

Pierre sat beside me in the taxi and instructed the driver to take us to his hotel. He then asked me to wait in the lobby before going to reception to check in. Later I discovered he had paid for my first night at the hotel, left me a ticket for the soccer game, and also a huge box of Italian Bacci chocolates.

In the hotel corridor that evening, I saw Pierre escorting his beautiful blonde wife. As he passed me, I said nothing, but he winked at me out of the corner of his eye.

I was unable to reach any of my Jewish contacts, and very disappointed not to be able to celebrate the Passover holiday with other Jews as I was accustomed to doing each spring. Two days later I found myself in the interior of Venezuela. I was the guest of two brothers, Antonio and Giuseppe, both in their 20's, whom I met at the soccer game. They had invited me to their home for a few days, to meet their family, originally from Sicily, and to introduce me to a friend from the American Peace Corps.

Antonio became an instant friend, as often happens when you are traveling alone and find someone who feels familiar and safe. He wanted to introduce me to his parents and family as his new "friend" from America.

I arranged to leave most of my luggage at the hotel in Caracas and, after a long drive, we reached their home in Barquisimeto. They took me to a spare bedroom in their family home, and waited for me to join them for dinner. I washed up and entered the dining room. Antonio motioned to the only empty chair at the large round table. I sat down and looked around at their friendly, welcoming faces. There were nine of us, including Antonio, Giuseppe, two other brothers, Angelo and Luigi, the sister, Sarina, their mother and father, and a Peruvian cousin who was also visiting. Antonio introduced me to each of his siblings in Spanish, but he used a Sicilian dialect which I did not understand to communicate with his parents.

I looked around their modest home. Everything was spotless, but aside from their furniture they had only one piece of art in the dining room. It was as large as a portrait from an art gallery, dwarfing everything else in the room. It hung directly above the heads of Antonio's parents, as I sat facing them at the dinner table. It was impossible to be present in the room and not be aware of this painting, especially for me, because it was a larger-than-life painting of Jesus—not on the cross—but as an all-encompassing beatific image, wearing a red robe and beaming love.

I swallowed hard.

Antonio's mother began to serve the meal. She passed out pasta to everyone at the table because, as in every good Italian family, pasta is always served at the main meal. I watched everyone else as they began to eat their pasta, but I did not touch the food on my plate. Since it was Passover I couldn't eat anything that had leavening in it, for eight days, a custom I had been keeping since I was a child. It included not eating bread, crackers, or pasta.

Antonio's mother noticed I was not eating my pasta. "*Non ti piace la pasta?*" she asked worriedly, fearing her cooking had not met with my approval.

I looked over at Antonio, his fork in mid-air. I consulted with him briefly in Spanish, and explained to him I couldn't eat pasta during the holiday of Passover because it was forbidden. He translated everything I said to his mother, a devout Catholic who attended Mass every day of her life. She looked at me very carefully, her eyes regarding me in a new way, and then said in a conversational tone, in perfect Spanish, "*Ah, sí, los judios son los que no creen en Dios.*"

"Oh, yes, the Jews are the ones who don't believe in God."

A year ago I had refused eating pork from a young Peruvian boy who insisted the Jews had killed God. Now, I was rejecting pasta from a Sicilian woman in Venezuela who told me Jews didn't believe in God. This time I was a little older, a little wiser.

"Oh, no, on the contrary…" As I spoke, Antonio translated carefully to ensure my words would be understood.

"We very much believe in God." I pointed to the huge portrait behind them. "In fact, Jesus was a Jew. Many people believe the Last Supper was actually a celebration of Passover, the same holiday I am celebrating tonight. And Jesus didn't eat pasta or any bread during Passover. He ate *matzah*, unleavened bread."

Antonio's mother leaned towards me as I spoke. When I finished no one uttered a word. No one breathed. Their lips were slightly parted in anticipation of her response.

"Well, can you eat chicken?" she asked her eyebrows lifted.

"Yes, I can eat chicken," I replied. A collective sigh resounded from around the table and no one spoke again until after my first bite of chicken.

Minefield neutralized. Full speed ahead.

Minefields & Miracles

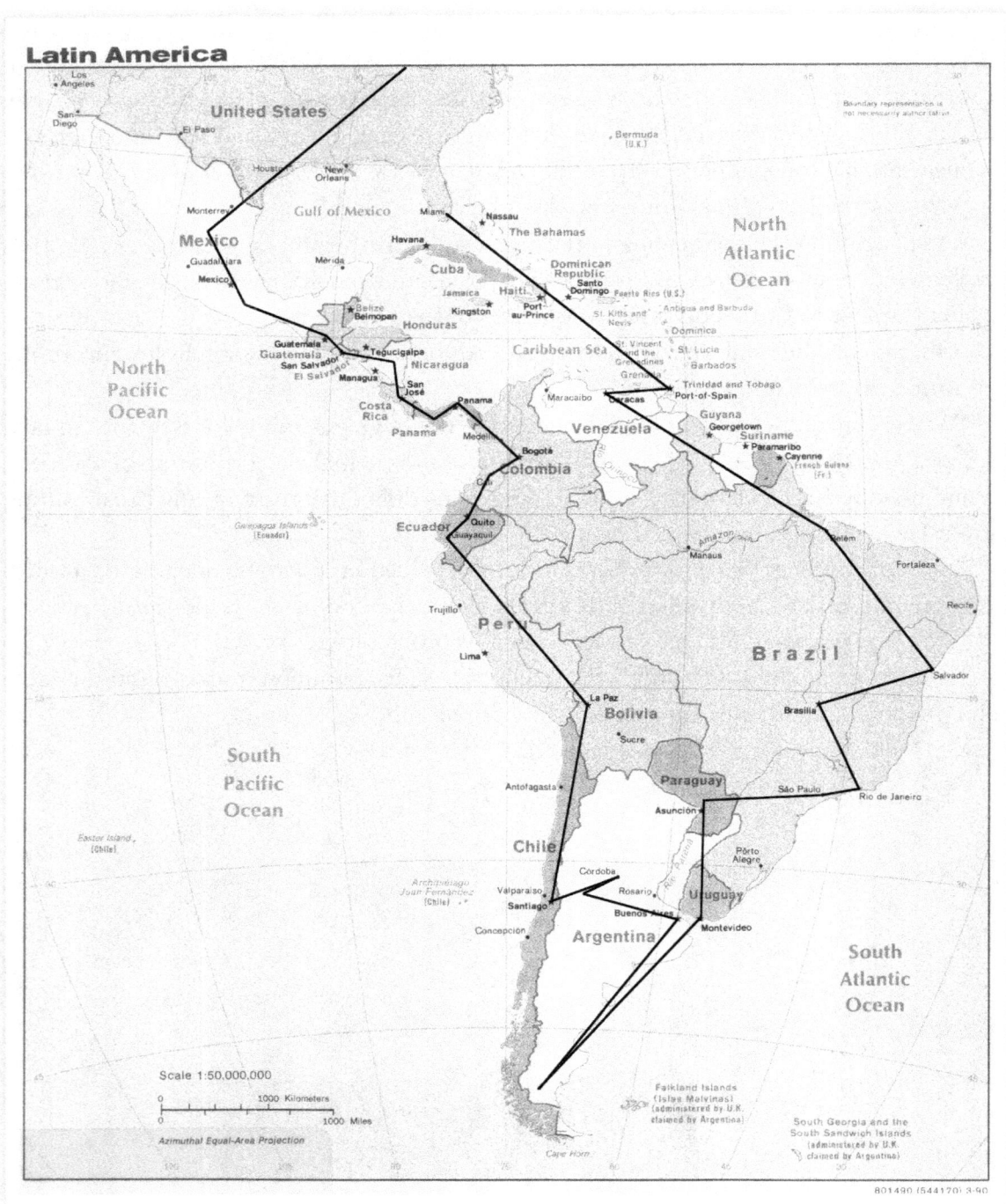

My 18 month journey to 19 countries in Latin America. (Source: University of Texas Map Library, UT-Austin.)

Indigenous women of Peru.

Brazilian women and children in the *favela* gather at the pump.

One of the densest *favelas* (slums) of Rio de Janeiro.

Brazilian carnival. (Mark Van Overmeire / Shutterstock.com)

Brazil: land of carnival

By RUTH ARIELLA BROYDE

"WHAT'S THE MOST important thing in life for a Brazilian?"

My Brazilian friend grinned at the earnestness of my question, held up four fingers, and began to enumerate. "Not just one, but four things are important to the Brazilians: carnivals, football, women and cachaca (a very potent alcoholic drink made from sugar cane)."

"In that order?" I demanded to know. "Well, that depends upon the Brazilian. With me it's women first," and he flashed me a dazzling smile that ended my questions for a while.

Carnival in Rio de Janeiro is without a doubt one of the most exciting, colorful and exhausting festivals in the world.

AFTER WITNESSING and participating in this year's special celebration, commemorating the founding of Rio 400 years ago, I began to understand why carnival keeps Brazil happy despite her millions of undernourished, illiterate, indolent, unemployed and homeless.

And I understood why in the April revolution that ousted President Joao Goulart and his administration rife with loud-mouthed communists, not one shot was fired. It was the most bloodiess coup in Brazil's history, and the next day the Brazilians were back at the Maracana, the famous football stadium in Rio, cheering their favorite players, caring little for political intrigues and manifestations of violence that are so characteristic of Latin American uprisings.

IN BRAZIL, carnival is the poor man's panacea. For 361 days out of the year, the poor man and his family are crowded together in the filthy, worm-infested, degrading "favelas" (slums) where in Rio, for example, one fourth of the population are reputed to live. The poor man and his family usually includes six to eight barefoot children with grotesquely swollen bellies which, ironically, are the result of a lack of food.

These Brazilians of the favelas eat a monotonous, insufficient diet of "arroz y fejon"—rice and beans—and bananas, the poor man's fruit. If they can afford it, and they usually can't, they may buy bread or oranges for variety's sake and, once in a very great while, a slab of greasy pork.

WHAT PLEASURE does this life give him and his family? Is he an outspoken malcontent? Jealous of the propertied class? Unsatisfied with his paltry, bottom-of-the-barrel existence?

If he is, he doesn't show it. He and his family rarely leave the favela, but on carnival, bedecked in the most lavish array of silks, satins and glittering sequins, he is the rich man out on the town—not for one but four consecutive days and nights of marathon celebration.

He and his family scrimp and save all year long, eating less rice and beans, sacrificing bread and bananas, in order to be able to dress like kings and queens on carnival. This year, for instance, it was estimated that some residents of the favelas who took part in the costumed processions, paid out one million cruzeiros (about $500) for their royal disguises.

The "Escuelas da Samba" (Samba schools) which represent different neighborhoods in the city, spend 361 days practicing, planning and preparing for the four-day extravaganza.

THE PROCESSION OF the poor kings and queens of Brazil is a vista-vision, technicolor pageant that Twentieth Century Fox would find difficult to duplicate—not the lavish costumes or Rio's night landscape, but the spirit of the people; the whole year's priva-

and poverty

tion and longing transformed into four days of tireless dancing, singing and jubilation.

Every year at carnival time, the streets of Rio are inundated by the vivid sea of costumes and decorations. But this March, in addition to her population of 22 million, Rio played host to 18,000 visitors: 8,000 Brazilians who live outside of Rio and 10,000 foreigners: Russians, Swedes, Italians, Argentinians, Mexicans, Czechs, Japanese, French, Americans.

The masses turned out in the most luxurious and garish getups, as well as the most simple and tasteful. Many donned only a mask with their street clothes.

DOWNTOWN RIO WAS ablaze with endless chains of street lights, draped in parallel rows like a necklace, of golden beads. Between the rows of lights swung gay Japanese paper lanterns in bold reds, greens, yellows and blues.

Avenida (avenue) Presidente Vargas, the site of the all-night costumed pageants, stretched for miles in a Brazilian version of Broadway at night.

No night hour was silent. Only the following day, from dawn until noon, the less spirited carousers would return to their homes for "forty winks." Those who were too tired to return home, or who lived too far away, chose a convenient street corner or building entrance or park bench, curled up, and slept far into the afternoon. The streets, still littered with confetti, streamers, posters and discarded food wrappers, were almost deserted until midday.

THEN SLOWLY THE CITY came to life; the drums began to pound out the hypnotic, inescapable carnival rhythm and by 8, 9, 10 in the evening, the city was throbbing with movement and sound. Rio was a giant heart beating aloud, her pulse in the streets, under lampposts, in the parks, in private clubs, on the beaches, aboard buses, a giant heart consuming the city and her people.

Men, women, children; old and young; rich and poor—all were caught up in the relentless tom-tom of the city; in the frenzy of half-naked bodies shiny with sweat; in the syncopation of bright eyes and painted mouths, of flashing hands and feet; all possessed by the music, possessed by a spirit that could only drive them harder, harder, faster, faster, until they were the spirit, until they were carnival.

For 361 days out of the year, the poor Brazilian dreams of velvet-robed, golden-crowned kings. For four days out of the year he is that king.

(EDITOR'S NOTE. In the following article, Ruth Ariella Broyde, a North Side resident, explains her impression of the Brazilian people during her recent trip to that South American nation.)

After spending most of the year in squalor, Brazilians enjoy their annual fling at Carnival time.

Article I wrote for the Lerner Newspapers of Chicago describing Brazil as a "Land of Carnival and Poverty."

Conducting an interview with a group of young Jewish men in Buenos Aires.

Jewish youth group practicing Israeli dancing in Buenos Aires.

The tables get turned...

Buenos Aires newspaper clipping.

Maracaibo, Venezuela newspaper.

And the journalist gets interviewed.

"The people of North and South America know almost nothing about one another," I told the Brazilian press.

Interviewed by Brazilian TV.

If we have no peace, it is because we have forgotten that we belong to each other.

~Mother Teresa

CHAPTER 3

American Homecoming, European Detour, and the Call of Israel

    I was in a state of culture shock. I became aware of it on the last leg of my trip from Curacao to Florida to Chicago, returning home after 18 months in Latin America. My seat mate was a pleasant American woman who was eager to hear details about my adventures south of the border.

    I told her when I was in Trinidad, people commented on how good my English was. I laughed heartily, thinking she would get the joke and laugh along with me.

    But her response was not what I had expected. "Yes, I was noticing your English is quite good. Where were you born?"

    "In Chicago," I replied, puzzled by her question.

    "No, I don't mean where you live now," she insisted. "Where were you born?"

    "In Chicago," I repeated again, growing a bit impatient with her line of questioning.

    "Then why do you have a Spanish accent when you speak English?" she wanted to know.

    It was at that moment I realized how fully I had been immersed in Latin American culture. Even the shape of my mouth had changed. I was now speaking my native English with a Spanish accent, without realizing it. And so it went, as I tried to reorient myself to my homeland. I felt like a stranger among my friends and family. On the one hand I was brimming with the excitement of the rich cultural experiences I had absorbed for 18 months, but I found no easy way to convey the totality of what I had experienced. I had crossed a familiar border back to a world that no longer felt familiar. I would awake in the morning, even in my parents' home in Chicago, and I would find myself in a state of bewilderment.

"What country am I in and in whose house am I living?" I would ask myself at the first light of morning. It was a strange question, to be sure, but it became my daily mantra. I also noticed I was dreaming in Spanish.

Who am I? Where do I belong? What language is my language? When do I no longer belong to a country or to a language? I reviewed the same questions I had asked of myself during my trip, but now I was asking those questions in my own home, in my own bed.

My family had no answers for me. Everyone was busy with wedding plans for my sister, Leah, so I put my questions of identity on the back burner.

I visited with my sister and her husband briefly after their wedding, but then felt the urge to move on to continue my explorations.

I sold an article about my travels to the *New York Times* Travel Section. A good sign, I told myself. I informed my parents I was moving to New York for what I believed would be an exciting career in journalism. My mother didn't put up a big fight this time, because she knew New York was a lot closer to Chicago than Latin America!

Finding work as a journalist wasn't quite as easy as I had imagined. Instead, I found a temporary job as an Administrative Assistant at a private school in Manhattan, and I convinced Lorraine, an old childhood friend from Chicago, to move to New York and share an apartment with me on West 86th Street.

While I was waiting for Lorraine to arrive, I spent the Jewish New Year alone. I didn't go to synagogue. I didn't seek community. In fact, I decided not to fast on Yom Kippur (the Day of Atonement) for the first time—and what became the only time—in my life. I see now I was still testing my identity. I was trying to strip away the accoutrements of my persona and discover who I was without my family, my language, and my tradition. In retrospect I realize the culture shock I experienced with my family in Chicago was a result of over-identifying as a "Latina." That feeling of alienation led me to become an outsider in my own country and culture. Although I was lonely, somehow I felt safe in New York, a city of multiple cultures and languages. I was able to disguise my feelings of being a foreigner by living among foreigners.

Six months later things started looking up. I was enjoying New York and its many charms. I lost my Spanish accent and nobody asked me any longer about my country of origin. A well-known international news service hired me to write headlines for TV and radio announcers. I worked the night shift, from midnight to nine in the morning, but I was optimistic I would work my way up quickly, and then be able to pursue a career as a foreign correspondent.

My first personal encounter with another journalist who worked at the news service, however, proved deeply disturbing. It illustrated how poorly Americans have been educated about the rest of the world, and how sheltered we are as a nation. When I told my twenty-four year-old colleague I had spent eighteen months traveling around Latin America, he let out a huge belly laugh, slapped his leg, and exclaimed, "Who would want to spend a year and half with a bunch of Puerto Ricans!"

I was horrified by his prejudicial remark, and astounded by his ignorance. But that paled by comparison when a few weeks later I heard the comment of one of my other colleagues, a man in his late forties, who didn't know I was Jewish. After writing a headline about Israel's conflict with the Arab states, he complained in a loud voice, "Too bad Hitler didn't finish the job and get rid of all of the Jews in the world when he had the chance."

My face turned very red, but I didn't respond. The night editor said nothing. Did he agree with him, I wondered.

Some minefields were not worth detonating, I decided.

I left my job after six months, for a variety of reasons, including my progressive disillusionment with my colleagues. I no longer wished to be a foreign correspondent for that news service and, besides, I had begun to study filmmaking in New York. I became more and more enamored with the idea of becoming a filmmaker. Perhaps I could study filmmaking abroad…

I made a decision that would have profound consequences for my life and my identity as a border crosser. Europe would be my next destination; an opportunity to test my restless wings on the continent that had produced some of my treasured heroes: Shakespeare, Jean Paul Sartre, Michelangelo, Leonardo Da Vinci, Bach, Simone de Beauvoir, and Federico Fellini.

A group of friends accompanied me to the dock in New York to say goodbye. It was winter time. My friends and I huddled together, stamping our feet and shivering in the cold. I had managed to secure passage on a Belgian freight ship staffed by a Scandinavian crew, and I was ready for my next adventure, even though I was told the seas would be rough. My high school friend Bob surveyed five bulging suitcases lined up beside me on the dock, and he quipped, "For a free spirit, you are awfully encumbered."

"A genuine problem for border crossers," I acknowledged with a mischievous grin.

Once in Belgium, with my meager French, I managed to buy a used Volkswagen Beetle in a small town near Antwerp. My silver-gray car was so antiquated it didn't even have the requisite flashing lights to indicate a left or right turn. Instead it had little white flags, like artificial arms, that would shoot up on the left or right side of the car when I signaled. It was definitely a conversation piece. Maybe if my French had been better, I could have made a better deal, but I didn't care. I had wheels now, and I was crossing borders, sometimes even daily, moving from Belgium to France to Switzerland and then to Italy.

My not-so-secret long-term plan was to visit all of Europe, including Eastern Europe and then travel to the Soviet Union, where I had first cousins from my mother's side. From there I would make my way around the Middle East and visit the Arab countries and eventually end up in Israel, where I had uncles, aunts, and first cousins from both my mother's and father's side, family I had never met. I didn't know how long it would take, but I was going to cross a lot of borders before I slowed down. I had three bulging notebooks of maps from AAA showing my planned itinerary in red. The maps alone must have weighed ten pounds.

I ended up spending eight months in Rome, where I worked for a while as a photographer and reporter for the English language daily, *The Italian Chronicle*. I was hoping to find a job in the Italian film industry and, in the meantime I was also flirting with the idea of studying film at the national film school in Rome. For one of my audition assignments, I was asked to prepare an essay about my favorite Italian film director, Federico Fellini. When I completed my assignment, I found a way to send a copy to Fellini himself through a friend, Gideon Bachman, who had worked as Fellini's still photographer.

For me Fellini was the ultimate cinematic border crosser. He created a sumptuous, fantastical world in which people of diverse nationalities would suddenly appear and speak in their own languages—which he never translated. He had a unique style of seamlessly integrating everyday, homely people who had never acted in a movie with the most glamorous movie stars. He defied labels and stereotypes, but he also launched a stereotypical model that soon would become known as a "Fellini character." Yes, he was my favorite Italian director, hands down, and my dream was to find a way to work on one of his films.

But my dream was about to be challenged.

When I was told I would only be able to have the status of an observer—and not of a full-time student—at the Italian film school, I gave notice on my rented room and bought a one-way boat ticket to Israel.

The truth of the matter is I had been experiencing a special urgency to meet my Israeli family, especially after the 1967 Six-Day War in the Middle East. With the shadow of the Holocaust hovering nearby, I had begun to worry some tragedy would befall Israel and I might never get a chance to know my relatives. Though it seemed paradoxical, I was developing a deep nostalgia for a land I had yet to visit. I was a Jew who had been hearing about the Jewish homeland all of my life, and I wanted to see for myself what it could mean to live in a land where the majority of the people were Jewish and where every Jew was guaranteed the right of return, regardless of his or her country of origin. I decided I could put Europe, the Soviet

Union, and the rest of the world on hold for the time being.

However, just days before I left Italy, I had an extraordinary encounter with my hero, Federico Fellini—something I could never have foreseen. I met him serendipitously at Cinecitta, the largest film studio in Rome. Recognizing my name from the essay I had sent him, Fellini invited me to go on location with him that very evening. Within minutes, I was riding in the car of Fellini's production manager, and three hours later I was on location outside of Rome with the Master Ringleader of Italian Cinema.

What a joy it was to watch him plan every camera angle. He directed his crew and his cast with great expertise and effortless grace. I marveled as he practiced each camera move on the dolly before he surrendered it to his cameraman. I relished his charismatic personality, his joking manner, and his attentiveness to everyone present, including me, his unexpected but warmly welcomed American guest. He came to chat with me several times during the night shoot, and he even asked me to read his palm. He made me feel I was part of his inner circle. His cast and crew also were warm and welcoming. Suddenly, after eight months of waiting in vain to find work in the Italian film industry, I met my hero and, before the morning light, his production manager had invited me to stay and work on Fellini's next film. Production was scheduled to start in a couple of months, they said.

It was another watershed moment in my life. What should I do?

I had given up my apartment in Rome, packed my bags, and written to my relatives in Israel to announce I was on my way. And now I was being offered an opportunity to fulfill my dream, to work with the film director I most admired in the world.

The ticket to Israel weighed heavily in my pocket, and I felt the hand of destiny pulling me towards the Holy Land. I left Italy behind and sailed for Israel. Many times since I have wondered what I would be doing today if I had stayed.

In front of a travel poster designed by my friend Lorraine.

(Antwerp, Belgium) The very first car I ever purchased: an antiquated 1956 silver Volkswagen Beetle that had no electronic turn signals.

With Lorraine (left), on a balcony in Rome.

Article I wrote on evacuating Americans during a crisis in the Middle East, published in the English-language newspaper of Rome, *The Italian Chronicle*.

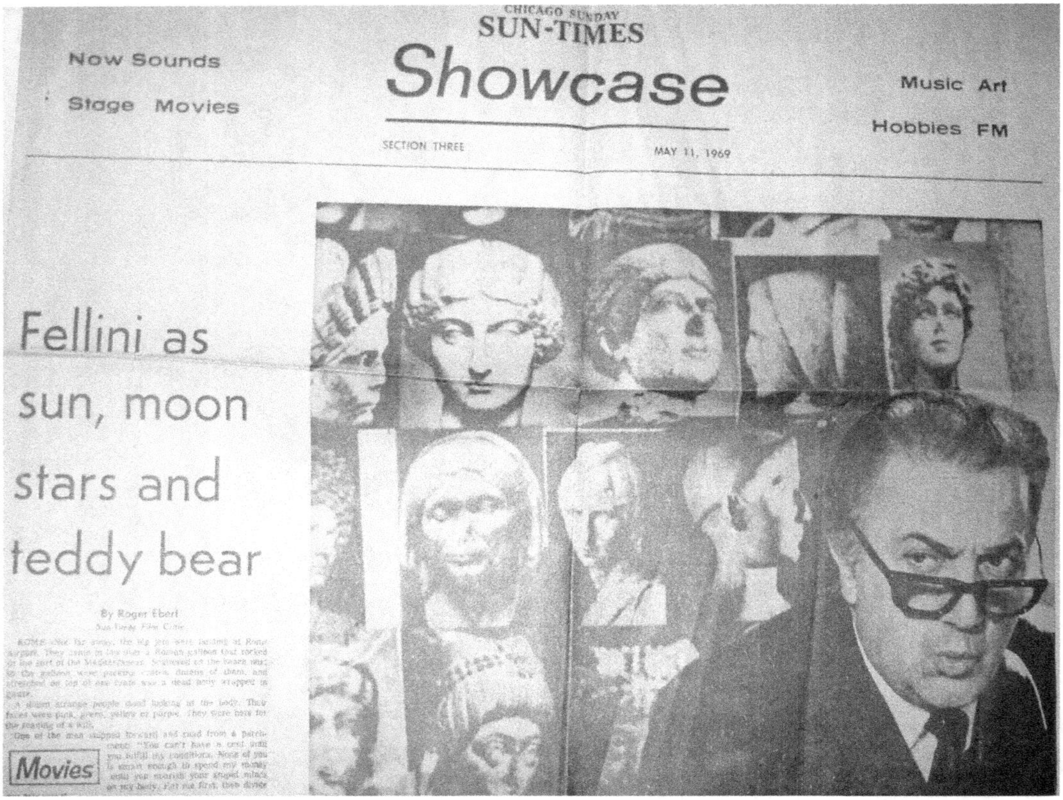

CHICAGO SUNDAY
SUN-TIMES
Showcase

Now Sounds
Stage Movies

Music Art
Hobbies FM

SECTION THREE
MAY 11, 1969

Fellini as sun, moon stars and teddy bear

By Roger Ebert

Movies

Article about Fellini, my cinematic hero.

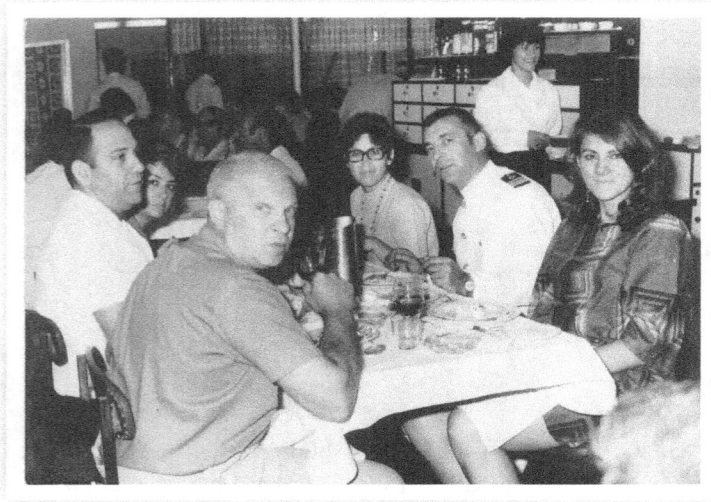

On the boat to Israel, sitting next to the captain and opposite the bursar, an auspicious beginning.

American Homecoming, European Detour, and the Call of Israel

ISRAEL IS "THE PLACE" to make westerns and documentaries and also a good place to adopt as home, according to Ruth Broyde. The young filmmaker is the daughter of Samuel and Raya Broyde, 6130 N. Kimball.

Also, seek the peace and prosperity of the city to which I have carried you into exile. Pray to the LORD for it, because if it prospers, you too will prosper.

~Jeremiah 29:7

CHAPTER 4
The Holy Land

For many Jews in the world, Israel is not just a state, but also a state of mind.

Since 580 BCE, the destruction of the First Temple, dispossessed of our land, imprisoned and persecuted, forcibly converted and expelled, ostracized and despised, dehumanized and exterminated, the Jews of the world have not known extended periods of peace, safety, or brotherly love.

The aspiration and longing to return to our homeland comes with a backdrop of thousands of years of history during which time, again and again, we have been shown that Jews are the most unwanted group of people to walk the earth. For someone who was born Jewish, and who knows Judaism was the parent religion for both Christianity and Islam, it is often incomprehensible and always painful to realize that Jews have been "the sacrificial lamb" for so many successive generations. We have been persecuted by the very people whose most sacred traditions and beliefs originated in the wisdom of the Book, especially since we have always been known as "the People of the Book."

There is no way for Jews to visit Israel casually, just as tourists. We cannot explore the hills of ancient Jerusalem, or pray at the Western Wall without the specter of history and of millennial yearning at our back. I imagine it must be similar for Muslim pilgrims making their *haj* in Mecca, or for Christians following the Via Dolorosa, or Sikhs visiting their Golden Temple in India.

During a sacred journey, everything and every moment counts. I have heard first-person accounts of modern-day pilgrims, and noted how their voices change timbre, their chests expand, and their eyes dilate as they recall their pilgrimage to their holiest shrine.

So it was when I went to Israel in the early seventies, I was not merely visiting another country on my AAA map. I was coming to experience what it means to be on land sacred to my forefathers and precious to my own family. I had uncles and aunts who had helped to build Israel into the modern miracle it is, and I had cousins who had been born and raised there. My connection to Israel could never have been casual. The Israeli-Palestinian conflict was clearly defined even then but the dialogue at the time was at a very different stage than it is today, and I myself did not have a well-defined position about the politics of the region. I did understand, however, there were enormous differences of opinion and a clash in historical narratives between Israel and her neighbors, and that one day those differences would have to be addressed and resolved if peace were ever to be achieved.

As a Jewish journalist, I also came to Israel bursting with an enormous curiosity about the nature of the new state. I wanted to know more about the native-born children, called *sabras*, who were having a totally different experience than their parents' immigrant generation. After more than 2,000 years of being dispersed among the nations of the world, what was it like to have a homeland? Had the experiment worked? Were we now a different people because we had a home of our own and somewhere to go in times of danger? What was it like to live in a country where the policemen, the teachers, the artists and farmers, the judges and the criminals, were all Jewish? And what was it like to hold discourse in Hebrew, an ancient language that was now modern and malleable, a classical language that had been lifted from sacred scriptural texts and transformed into a living, breathing lexicon?

And how would I relate to Israel's Arab neighbors? Would they ever accept Israel's right to exist in their midst? Starting with the war of 1948, after the UN partition of Palestine, and after the UN declared Israel a state, there had been no cessation of hostilities. Wars had been fought in 1948, in 1956, in 1967, and would occur once again in 1973 while I was in that part of the world. In a country as tiny as Israel, the Palestinian refugee camps—the painful legacy of those wars—were only miles away, not across the ocean.

The recurring question of how to achieve mutual co-existence never changed or lost its bite. How would it be possible to meet the demands of the stateless and homeless Palestinians while assuring Israel's security? The security fence, or "the Wall" as it is now called by the world at large, had not yet been built when I lived there. Nevertheless, I experienced a virtual wall, even in the seventies, keeping us separate by the way we privately regarded and referred to one another.

These were complex political/historical/geographic/religious issues I found myself dissecting and reviewing endlessly. For me there was no obvious way to resolve the conflict once and for all. No matter what position I would take, there was always "the other side" to consider. That was understandable from my basic training in Judaism. Jews love debate and the intellectual excitement of examining and dissecting the finer points of any issue, top to bottom, left to right, inside out, front to back. It would be no different for this thorny issue of Israel's rights versus the Palestinian rights, but at the moment, as a first-time visitor to my historical and spiritual homeland, both a state and a state of mind, Israel became the center of my world.

Israel was not going to be an easy place for me to live, I concluded. But it was destined to become a profound crucible for my learning about our Palestinian cousins, our partners in both the ongoing conflict and also our potential partners for a negotiated peace. I intuitively understood that in the end it wasn't going to be just about boundaries or practical applications of a peace treaty. It would have to be resolved as much in our hearts as on paper. In short, for me it was going to become a homeland for minefields or for miracles—perhaps both.

Jerusalem, the eternal city.

Jewish women praying at the Western Wall.

The Holy Land

Narrow streets of Jerusalem.

Peace may sound simple—one beautiful word—but it requires everything we have, every quality, every strength, every dream, every high ideal.
~Yehudi Menuhin

CHAPTER 5
My Palestinian Heritage and My First Palestinian Friend

My heritage is intimately connected to historical Palestine. To understand my inherited connection to the Israeli-Palestinian conflict, I myself had to go back to my family tree from the early part of the twentieth century.

Born in Riga, Latvia, my mother, Raya, was the youngest of four children. She lost her father, Abraham Friedman, when she was only nine years old, and being the youngest she didn't enjoy much time with her older siblings either. Her eldest sister, Zipporah, joined a Zionist youth group as a teenager, and immigrated to Palestine in 1917 where she volunteered on Kibbutz Degania, one of the first cooperative settlements. Then their older brother, Nicholas, took off for St. Petersburg, Russia to study engineering, leaving behind my mother, still a child, her sister, Luba, and their mother, Sara, in Riga.

The rising climate of anti-Semitism was palpable, my mother would tell us, and like hundreds of thousands of other Jews, from all of Eastern Europe, they knew it was time to leave. Many managed to come to the United States, and many made their way to Palestine.

Because of British quotas on Jewish immigration, it was extremely difficult to secure a visa, but my mother's eldest sister, Zipporah, somehow arranged for immigration visas to bring her mother and sisters to Palestine in 1926. Zipporah was one of the first nurses to graduate from Hadassah Hospital, and she was excited to welcome her family to a land she now called "home."

My mother acclimated quickly. She picked up conversational Hebrew with ease—she was already fluent in Latvian, Russian, and Yiddish, along with a brief exposure to Esperanto.

After she matriculated from high school, she was accepted as a literature student at Hebrew University on Mt. Scopus in Jerusalem, and then received a degree in education and became a teacher.

She met my father, Sam Broyde, a lawyer from Chicago, in Jerusalem. He had come to Palestine with his mother, Leah, who was ill with cancer and wanted to be buried in the Holy Land. My grandmother was also seeking a wife for her only child, Sam, a brilliant man who was also a dreamer and an idealist—I come by my idealistic traits honestly! She wanted to make sure he would marry a practical, down-to-earth, clever woman. (She recognized my mother as just such a woman, which my mother always liked to remind us when she reminisced.)

I learned that my father, when he first arrived in Palestine, already had a large group of cousins living there, who had emigrated from Russia, which meant Palestine figured significantly on both sides of my family tree.

Shortly after my Grandmother Leah died, my parents married. They lived in Jerusalem for a while but sensing the impending war in Europe, decided to return to my father's hometown, Chicago. They managed to embark on the last boat leaving Paris for America, literally on the eve of World War II. My mother said she realized she might not see her birth family again when she left Palestine and traveled to Chicago, her third home during her lifetime. (In fact, she never saw her mother again, and she didn't return to visit Israel until 27 years later.)

When my parents left for the States, my mother traveled on her Palestinian passport, the only passport she had—which I still have and like to peruse. Ironically, my early family history has provided me with a great ice breaker for Palestinian-Jewish dialogues because when I introduce myself, I can truthfully say: "I'm Jewish, and my mother was a Palestinian."

My first encounter with family in Israel took place three decades after my mother left Palestine. I spent a great deal of time with my Aunt Zipporah and her husband, Matityahu, and my two first cousins, Avi and Mochi. I also met Aunt Luba and her husband, my Uncle Butchy, and members of their extended family. In truth, I had more family in Israel than I did in America. I had never considered that before. I was just beginning to realize how deep my genealogical connections to the Holy Land were.

Uncle Butchy had been a police officer during the time of the British Mandate, and I had a chance to catch up on both family history and Middle Eastern history when I was with him. He spoke seven languages fluently, including Arabic, and was a very popular and beloved figure among Jews, Arabs and the British. He respected his Arab friends greatly, he told me, and appreciated their kindness. When he was away from home for long periods because of work, he recounted, his Arab neighbors would look in on my Aunt Luba, to make sure she was OK. For me, today, as someone deeply engaged in Muslim-Jewish dialogue and reconciliation, my uncle's story means even more to me now than it did when I first heard it, over 30 years ago,

On my father's side, I discovered relatives who were also intimately connected to pre-Israel history. My cousin, Ephraim Broido, his brother, Alexander, and their parents arrived in Palestine in 1925. Ephraim grew up in Palestine, and later founded a highbrow literary magazine, called *Molad*. He was well-known as a translator of Shakespeare and Yeats. An extremely erudite man, he also translated many other great works of literature from English, German, Yiddish, Italian and Russian to Hebrew. Ephraim's passion for the Hebrew language was legendary among his family and colleagues. I was always on my toes when I spoke to him in my newly acquired Hebrew, because I knew he would correct me immediately if I erred, and I actually looked forward to it. I was truly proud of the fact that, as a member of the Academy of the Hebrew Language—still in existence today—my cousin Ephraim helped to coin some words that are now part and parcel of contemporary Hebrew, words such as *darkon*, which means passport, and *etgar*, the Hebrew word for challenge.

My other cousin, Alexander Broido, Ephraim's older brother, was the head of the Dvir Publishing House. He played his own illustrious part in Israel's history. He fought in the War of Independence as an aide to Col. Mickey Marcus, the famous American officer whose military genius helped the ill-equipped Israeli army break the siege of Jerusalem in 1948. Alexander's wife, Rifka Griffel, was a piano teacher and composer (known in Israel as Rivka Gvili). Born in Hungary and raised in Vienna, she arrived in Palestine in 1930 and became a founder of Kibbutz Afikim. Rivka served in Washington, DC as a pro tem diplomat for Israel in 1947 while waiting to see if the UN would approve Israeli statehood. This history, as I learned it, became a part of my family heritage.

After spending several weeks with Aunt Luba and Uncle Butchy in their home in Tivon, a small town near Haifa, I traveled south to Jerusalem. There I would begin my studies at an *Ulpan*, an intensive five-month study program to learn Hebrew and speed up the process of integration and assimilation into the larger society.

My classmates hailed from more than 20 countries around the world. There was no one language to serve as the *lingua franca* for all of us, so our primitive Hebrew became our unifying tongue, comically so, because we all managed to make the most egregious mistakes. But no one among us seemed to mind or even notice, except for our elegant teacher, perfectly coiffed, silver-haired, Vienna-born Sarah Rotbard, who guided us, chided us, encouraged and admired us, as we became Hebrew speakers.

I had studied Hebrew as a youngster, knew the alphabet, and had learned to read prayers and master my Bat Mitzvah Torah portion. It had been a language to access my Jewish heritage, but certainly not a language to be used on an everyday basis. So although I realized I had certain advantages over the true beginners, I still toiled for hours over the vowel-less Hebrew newspapers and I struggled with Hebrew syntax and grammar along with the neophytes. Nevertheless, I was placed into an intermediate class.

That's where I met Vida, a strikingly beautiful girl from Bethlehem, and the one person in our class who breezed through all of our assignments and conversed quite comfortably in Hebrew. With large expressive dark eyes lined in black kohl, thick auburn hair that fell to her shoulders, and a deep voice that could effortlessly produce the guttural sounds we all struggled over, Vida was a star. She always sat in the third row, on the right hand side, and I felt drawn to her and began sitting next to her almost from the first class.

Vida was Christian, not Muslim, which meant she lived as a minority member in her predominantly Muslim environment. She knew English, almost as well as her native Arabic. She had graduated from university in Lebanon. In fact she was the first young woman from Bethlehem to become a college graduate and also the first to get her driver's license—which triggered considerable envy among the other young women in her town. Five mornings a week for five months, in order to learn Hebrew, she would drive her car from Bethlehem to the *Ulpan* in Jerusalem—about a 20 minute journey—and then she would return home every afternoon. The rest of us lived in the dormitories provided for us by the *Ulpan*. We always socialized at meals and in the evenings, so the only way to get to know Vida outside of the classroom was to visit her in Bethlehem.

She invited me to her home several weeks after we started becoming friendly. It was a large, airy home, made comfortable by warm colors and the hospitality of her family. In one of those remarkable jokes of the universe, I discovered I could converse with her parents in Spanish, because they had lived in Honduras for many years. So Vida and I would speak in English, Vida and her parents would converse in Arabic, and her parents and I would communicate in Spanish. I finally understood why she had been given a Spanish name rather than an Arabic name. Vida, I knew, was the Spanish word for "life."

It became especially amusing when I would joke with her parents in Spanish and notice Vida was not laughing. She had suddenly become the stranger in her own home. We would then have to translate the joke to her, either in English or in Arabic, but there was never one single moment we could all simultaneously comprehend what was being said. And yet, somehow, miraculously, we all were able to understand one another. When people don't have a common language, as I had experienced traveling in Latin America and in Europe, there is another language of communication that will triumphantly come to the rescue, the language of good will.

Vida's parents often invited me to stay for dinner, which I genuinely appreciated. It was an opportunity to enjoy the camaraderie of a home-cooked, family dinner, rather than a cafeteria style meal in a dormitory. Her brother, a few years her senior, and her younger sister would usually be present as well. I would look around the table from face to face, listen to the Arabic, English, and Spanish that were now our constant companions, merging, melding, and overlapping. I was content.

Soon Vida began to invite me over for the weekends as well, including sleeping in her family home. We would giddily immerse ourselves in girl talk. I recall how once we compared notes on how to deal with dry hair. Vida taught me how to concoct a nourishing hair conditioner out of olive oil and then wrap my hair in a turban for 12 hours. We would also discuss our dreams for the future. Her dreams were not unlike mine. She wanted to work professionally, as well as get married and have children. We also liked to discuss the personality traits of the different students in our Hebrew class, especially the one young man from Belgium, who was obviously and hopelessly in love with Vida. He followed her about like a devoted puppy and would respond with enthusiasm to her slightest comment or the quick turn of her beautiful head. She laughed and blushed as I described my version of the scene in detail.

Vida was Vida. She was also a Christian and also a Palestinian, and through her I began to learn of the difficulties Palestinians were experiencing under Israeli rule. She introduced me to other Palestinians, families I would have tea with, tailors whom I hired to sew clothes for me, and Palestinians whose shops I frequented in the center of Bethlehem. They were always extremely hospitable to me, and at times I could even forget there were substantial differences in our political points of view.

But, ultimately, it would come back to a place where I was aware that they were looking at me not just as an individual but, on some level, as a representative of the Israeli people. Even though I was American-born, they knew I was Jewish, that I was living in Israel, and that I considered Israel my homeland. I sensed that all their warmth and friendship towards me might be summarily threatened if, suddenly, we would be facing each other across military borders. Perhaps the borders were already there. Perhaps the barbed-wire was there too, even though I was too naïve or too much of an optimist, like Candide, to see it.

These were some of the thoughts going through my mind while I was living in Israel, especially when I just narrowly missed being in a supermarket in Jerusalem that was bombed one Friday afternoon, killing five people. It occurred less than thirty minutes after I had completed my shopping there. Later it was determined by Israeli security that the bomber was from Bethlehem.

I couldn't help but think of Vida and her family whom I had come to love. If I had been one of the five victims, how would they have felt if they discovered one of their townsmen had been responsible for killing the person who had sat at their dining room table, slept in their guest bed, and was a good friend of their daughter?

And what if I had discovered that a bomber who had killed an Israeli relative or friend of mine was a member of Vida's family? Or a relative of one of the many people I had met and befriended in Bethlehem? Or, how would I feel if one of my Israeli cousins, serving in the Israeli Defense Forces, had been responsible for harming someone in Vida's family?

Oh, the places my mind would go with those mental minefields! In America, I could be denied housing in my university because of anti-Semitism, and I could transfer to another university, if I so desired, but in Israel I could be killed for being considered "an enemy."

As I was writing these lines, I remembered a passage from a book written several years ago by an American Jew who was serving in the Israeli military. In *Prisoners: A Muslim and a Jew Across the Middle East Divide*, author Jeffrey Goldberg writes about his experience guarding Rafiq, a Palestinian prisoner accused of terrorism:

> *I had consoling thoughts about Rafiq—thoughts about the thickening possibilities of peace, a peace that could be made first by two inconsequential soldiers. If Rafiq Hijazi could somehow extend the border of his compassion to take in Jeffrey Goldberg, then why should peace be impossible?*

Goldberg details how the two become improbably close friends. However, the author admits he was devastated when, on one occasion, he tried to determine if Rafiq was really his friend. He invented a hypothetical situation in which Rafiq, once released, would have an opportunity to kill him. "Would you do it?" Goldberg wants to know. "I probably would," Rafiq answers, "Look, it wouldn't be personal."

Somehow, the stakes were much higher in the Middle East than I had ever imagined, and that further underscored the importance of establishing a foundation of ongoing trust. Good will could sometimes take the place of language, but good will in the realm of local politics and international "chess games" was definitely not enough. What was crucially needed was evolving structures for ongoing collaboration: economic, cultural, and interpersonal. Without those, all the good will in the world would not be enough, I decided.

In Goldberg's book, he describes how he wishes to continue his relationship with Rafiq after Rafiq had been released and had become a professor in Gaza.

I wanted to reestablish our friendship for its own sake, and I wanted to see the Israeli-Palestinian conflict through his eyes, in order to answer a crucial question: Could the Arabs finally accept—accept, not merely tolerate—the presence of Jews in their midst, and not just Jews, but a Jewish state? Or would we forever be viewed as invaders?

Rafiq asks in return: "Could the Jews live with the Palestinians without fear, without guns?"

To my deep regret, I lost contact with Vida and her family. I began to work for the documentary film department of Israel TV after I graduated from the *Ulpan* and, shortly after that, I returned to the States where I received a commission to produce and direct my first professional film for Encyclopedia Britannica, entitled *Israeli Boy: Life on a Kibbutz*.

During subsequent visits to Israel, I tried to contact Vida, but in vain. I later learned she had become a journalist, like me, that she had married and moved to Nazareth, and that she had two daughters.

I honestly don't know where she stands politically today. I don't know if—because of Israeli rule for more than sixty years, the subjugation of the Palestinian people, and the unfulfilled desire of the Palestinians for nationhood—she has become more radical in her views. I wouldn't blame her if that were true.

In 2010 I visited Israel briefly and spent time with my honorary "son," Shimon Katz. I have known Shimon since he was one year old, when I befriended his mother, Dr. Ellie Katz, an American-born psychologist, who has continued to be a dear friend for more than thirty years. A former officer in the Israeli Defense Force, Shimon invited me to attend a meeting in Tel Aviv sponsored by a group he has been active in for several years, called "Combatants for Peace." Shimon also toured America with his Palestinian counterpart on behalf of that group, to demonstrate that many Israelis and Palestinians are totally dedicated to non-violent co-existence, something we might never know from our daily newspapers and local and international TV coverage.

When I arrived in Israel this time, Shimon was very eager to take me to visit Husan, an Arab village on the road to Bethlehem, the same road I had travelled many times to visit my friend Vida, thirty-five years earlier.. This time it was to meet Ziad Sabatin, an extraordinary man whom Shimon had met doing research for his thesis, which was built on a series of interviews with Palestinians who had served time in Israeli prisons, had subsequently been released, and had foresworn all violence.

Ziad, Shimon told me, had a pet project to promote peace that he wanted to discuss with me. Many people in his village were opposed to the project for political reasons, but he was steadfast and believed it could be achieved.

I immediately liked Ziad, a tall, lanky man in his forties with a full head of thick black hair, bushy eyebrows, a winning smile, and an air of determination. I also noticed he was a chain smoker.

Shimon and I were taken to Ziad's home and introduced to his cousin, his wife, his children, his nephews and nieces, and several of his good friends. Immediately we were offered tea. The seven children jammed themselves together on the couch opposite me, giggling and smiling. They were obviously curious about the nature of my visit. After a while, when the adult conversation began, they left, and I heard them playing outside.

Ziad laid out his plan to us, in Hebrew, and when he lacked the Hebrew word, he would say it in Arabic, which was then translated by his cousin. He had a dream, he told us, to build a community house for peace on an abandoned and dangerous plot of land in his village that was riddled with mines, left over from frequent wars. Even though there was barbed wire surrounding that plot, several children had lost limbs exploring it or retrieving a ball. The mines would be professionally removed, he explained, and then, with the help of his villagers and residents from the neighboring village of Jewish settlers, they would build a house of peace together. The building could be used for classrooms during the day, as well as for cultural and artistic activities in the evenings and weekends.

What a wonderful idea, I said to Ziad, and my mind immediately took off in a thousand directions. I suggested that people from around the world —especially young men and women—should be invited to help construct the building and, while they were visiting and working, they could also attend seminars on non-violence. Ziad nodded excitedly as we explored options and possibilities for making it an international house of peace. What if each person who came could decorate a ceramic tile with his/her name, and then those tiles could actually be incorporated into the building itself? I was getting more and more enthusiastic myself as I realized Ziad literally wanted to transform a minefield into a miracle.

I embraced his dream and we began to discuss it in even greater detail. How many *dunams* (acres) would it occupy? How much would it cost for construction? How long would it take to build? How many rooms would it hold? I was trying to get him to be as concrete as possible because I had learned from my experience as a life-long dreamer that the act of supplying details to a dream helps further the realization of the dream itself.

He was able to answer many of our specific questions on size and cost. He wasn't sure of all of the architectural details, but in his mind's eye he saw the building as an edifice with flower gardens encircling it on all sides. He described it to us lovingly, with details about the gardens, while he continued to smoke throughout his description. He also told us he had already discussed his idea with Jewish settlers who lived nearby, who often came to his village to repair their cars. Many of the Jewish settlers said they would collaborate and help with the construction, he told us animatedly. Furthermore, the mayor of his village—who was his relative—had agreed to help with the project.

"How much do you want to realize this dream," I asked Ziad?

"With all of my heart and soul," he replied, his eyes alight with hope.

"What would you be willing to sacrifice to realize your dream?" I asked him.

"My daughter," he said without a beat.

"No more child sacrifice," I told him with a smile.

"No, I didn't mean that, of course," he said earnestly, "but I just wanted you to know how important this dream is to me." He drew on his cigarette and exhaled.

"I knew you weren't serious about your daughter," I said. "But would you be willing to stop smoking?"

Ziad became solemn and said. "Yes, of course," taking another drag, "but I hope I won't have to," he added mischievously. We both laughed. We both knew he would give up his cigarettes, if needed.

Shimon and I told Ziad we would be happy to meet with the mayor in a few days and, if the project were feasible, we would try to raise money in Israel and abroad to help him achieve his dream. He smiled continuously throughout our conversation and throughout the translations.

A few days later, we returned, this time accompanied by Shimon's father, Michael Katz, a very talented artist and architect. We were taken to the mayor's house and offered plates laden with cold sweet watermelon and strong tea in beautiful crystal glasses.

Jamal Sabatin was hospitable but didn't seem especially enthusiastic about the project. We sensed Ziad's enthusiasm was enough for two people, but we also realized that without the mayor's help and support, the project would never be realized.

The Israeli government would have to approve the clearing of the mines, which was the first hurdle, Michael explained to me, which would involve a lot of red tape, he continued. Also, the mayor wanted to know why they should build a house for peace if they really needed classrooms for their children. He smoked continuously throughout our visit and seemed impatient for the visit to end. I could sense Ziad's discomfort and disappointment that the mayor was not showing enough support for his dream. Ziad spoke to him rapidly in Arabic and I intuited Ziad was trying to convince the mayor that his project would ultimately prove valuable to the village and to the mayor himself.

"I don't really think there is enough interest here for us to continue," Michael said to Shimon and me, and he suggested we not pursue the conversation any further, "at least for the time being until the mayor demonstrates greater interest," Michael added. I could see Ziad's dream slipping away. I also felt a profound sense of disappointment because I, myself, had bought into the dream. I also understood why the mayor might be critical, even hostile, towards my involvement, considering I was an outsider, an American, a Jew, and a woman.

After some further conversation in Arabic between the mayor and Ziad, we were told we were going to visit another plot of land, not the minefield, but a plot of land on the outskirts of the village. Perhaps, Ziad offered, something could be built there instead, especially if clearing the minefield proved too difficult bureaucratically and from an economic standpoint.

We drove in two cars over a long stretch of bumpy road, and at last we stopped. We climbed out of the cars and turned to face a breathtakingly beautiful area of rolling hills and vast expanse of sky. The air was so fresh it was intoxicating to inhale. The wind was also a welcome visitor on that hot afternoon.

We all surveyed the land in silence. I noticed the occasional olive trees dotting the landscape, and rows and rows of stones and boulders that must have been there for centuries. Ziad spoke first. He said perhaps they could build a peace park on that site. The mayor's dour look indicated he was not yet convinced. Suddenly, I found myself approaching the mayor and standing only a few inches away from him, looking directly into his eyes in what I realized was a total a breach of cultural etiquette in Palestinian society. Women did not initiate that kind of intimacy with a man.

He was startled by my approach. I said to him, "Mayor, if you could do anything you wanted here on this land, anything you could imagine, what would you do?" He averted his gaze from my eyes, but then looked back at me again. My glance did not waver. Again, looking deep into his eyes, I asked him earnestly. "What would you build here, if you could do anything, with no limitations? Anything at all…"

He looked away and up at the hills, sighed, turned to me and then replied.

"I would plant one thousand olive trees."

"And so you should," I said to him in full agreement. "And so you should. One thousand olive trees! I can see them. Can you see them?"

"Yes," he said, smiling for the first time. "I can see them." He had a far away look in his eyes, and I knew he was seeing himself in the midst of his virtual olive grove.

From that moment on, his relationship with us and his manner of speech changed. He told us the land belonged to one of his relatives from his tribe and could be easily purchased. "No problem," he said. (Most of the Palestinian villages still have tribal connections, and sometimes the tribe will own the entire village and then sell individual plots to families who live there). Ziad was reanimated. He had been drooping earlier, like a thirsty plant, but when the mayor began to show interest, Ziad suddenly came to life. He straightened up and moved closer to us, to listen.

Our conversation continued and the mayor and I took photos together and chatted like old friends. He had bought into the dream. He could imagine walking among his one thousand olive trees.

They took us back to the main road. We said we would continue our conversation about the project through Shimon and the internet since I was leaving shortly to go back to the United States. Michael purchased several watermelons and grapefruit from their fruit stand on the side of the main road, and we all took photos together in celebration of our encounter.

What will happen with Ziad's dream still remains to be seen. I hope he will realize his dream one day and, if I could be instrumental in making that happen, I would be delighted to be part of that miracle.

As Shimon, Michael, and I were returning to Jerusalem, on the Bethlehem road, I was reminded once more of my first Palestinian friend, Vida.

I don't know what she has taught her daughters about Israelis and about Jews. I would hope she remembers our friendship and the borders we crossed together. And one day, I hope to meet her children, to tell them about their mother, and how special she was to me as Vida, my girlfriend, and also as Vida, my first Palestinian friend.

And I also hope one day to introduce Vida and her family to Ziad, and invite them to take a walk with me in the Peace Park, built side by side by Arab villagers and Israeli settlers.

Photos of my mother, Raya Friedman, as a young woman in Riga, Latvia, her birth city.

My Palestinian Heritage and My First Palestinian Friend

Standing (l. to r.) my mother, Raya, her eldest sister, Zipporah, and two first cousins; Seated (l. to r.) My grandmother Sarah and her sister. (This photo was taken in 1929, the night before my mother, her sister and my grandmother left for Palestine. The other three women died in the Holocaust.)

My mother's eldest sister, Zipporah, was one of the first nurses to graduate from Hadassah Hospital in Jerusalem.

Aunt Luba (my mother's other sister) and her husband, Butchy.

My Palestinian Heritage and My First Palestinian Friend

(Above) Uncle Butchy is on the far right. (Left) Uncle Butchy is in the middle.

Uncle Butchy served as a Jewish policeman in Palestine for three consecutive governments: Turkish, British, and Israeli.

My cousin, Alexander Broido, (r.) serving as assistant to Col. Mickey Marcus (l.) during Israel's 1948 War of Independence.

My father, Sam Broyde, as a young man.

My paternal grandmother, Leah Broyde.

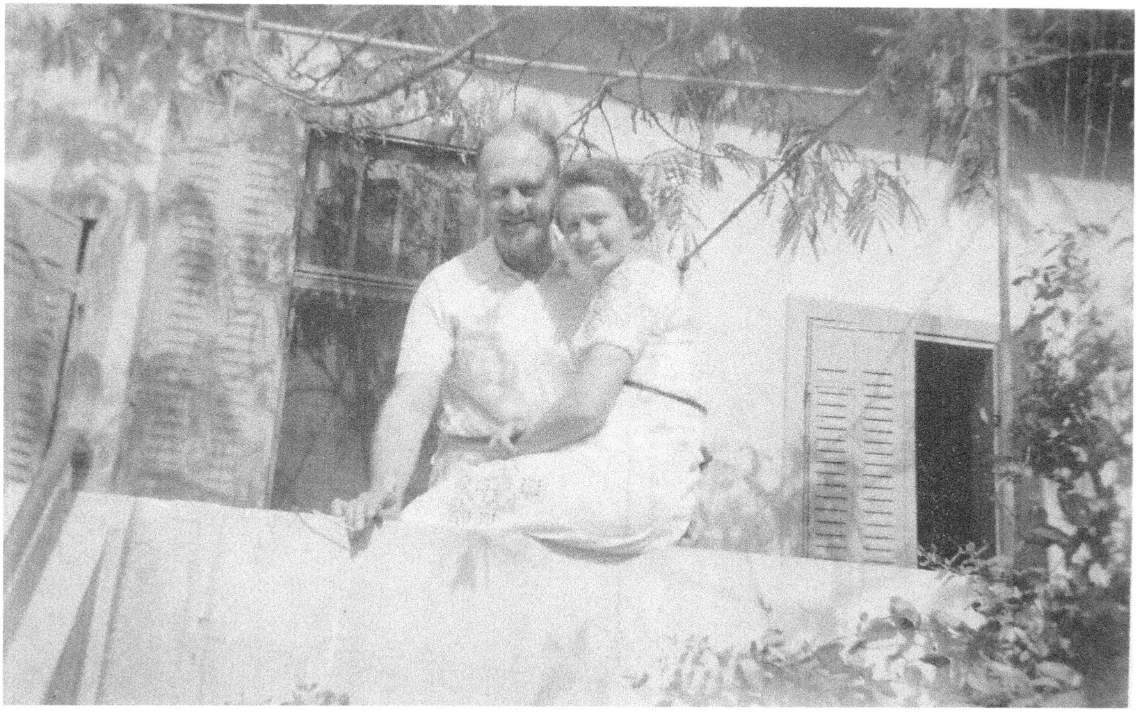

My parents, Sam and Raya, newlyweds in Jerusalem.

No. 2715

IDENTITY
AND
TRAVELLING
DOCUMENT.

Name of holder Mrs. Reichele (Raya) Broyde
Nom du titulaire

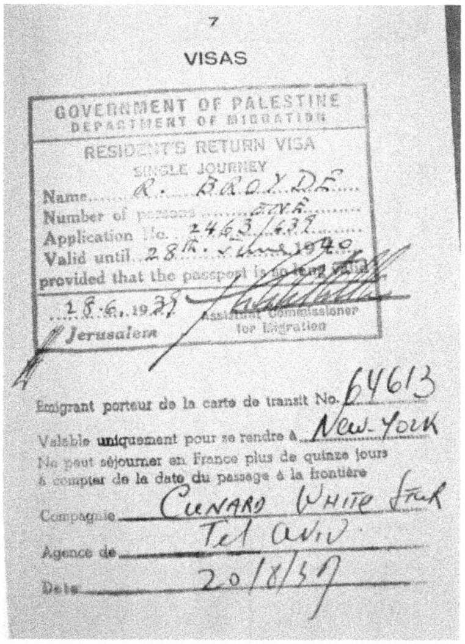

7
VISAS

GOVERNMENT OF PALESTINE
DEPARTMENT OF MIGRATION
RESIDENT'S RETURN VISA
SINGLE JOURNEY
Name R. BROYDE
Number of persons ONE
Application No. 2463/439
Valid until 28th June 1940
provided that the passport is so long valid
28.6.1939
Jerusalem
Assistant Commissioner for Migration

Emigrant porteur de la carte de transit No. 64613
Valable uniquement pour se rendre à New-York
Ne peut séjourner en France plus de quinze jours à compter de la date du passage à la frontière
Compagnie Cunard White Star
Agence de Tel Aviv
Date 20/8/39

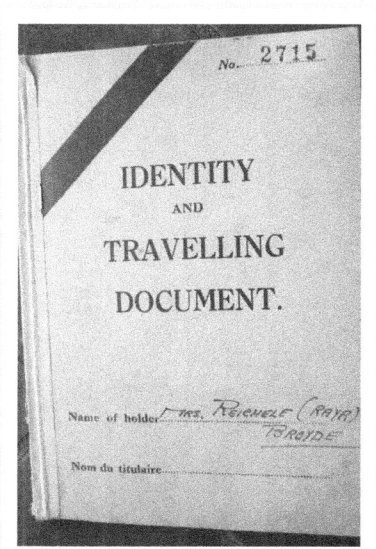

My mother's Palestinian passport.

My cousins Rivka (l) and Alexander (r) Broido, among the founders of the modern State of Israel.

My cousin Ephraim Broido, Hebrew poet, literary magazine editor, and translator.

My ulpan Hebrew class in Jerusalem. I am seated in the front row, third from the left; Vida, my first Palestinian friend, is the sixth from the left.

With my Ulpan teacher, Sara Rotbard.

Ziad's children, nieces, and nephews.

Ziad describes his dream to the Mayor.

My Palestinian Heritage and My First Palestinian Friend

With Ziad, the "Peace Park Dreamer."

With Mayor Sabitin, after he has shared his own dream of planting 1,000 olive trees.

Ziad Sabatin (l.) the Arab dreamer of Husan Village, with Shimon Katz (r.) a former Israeli army officer now active in "Combatants for Peace."

(L. to R.) Michael Katz, Ziad Sabitin, village vendor, Shimon Katz, village vendor.

Beyond any technique, relationships are what heal.
~Lewis Mehl-Madrona

CHAPTER 6
German-Jewish Encounter: Another Time, Another Place

In 1975 I went back to Chicago from Israel to visit my parents and to pursue my filmmaking career with Encyclopedia Britannica Educational Corporation (EBEC). My very first commission and the first commercial film I ever made, *Israeli Boy: Life on a Kibbutz,* was to be part of a Britannica series of films on children from around the world. It was selling well and had been selected to be shown at a UNESCO conference on children, and the head of the film department at EBEC was willing to entertain another film proposal of mine. What good news!

My choice of themes, as a Jewish filmmaker, was unexpected and perhaps daring at the time. But now, thirty-five years later, as a Jewish interfaith activist deeply involved with the Muslim community and promoting interfaith engagement through the Arts, it does seem perfectly logical. I proposed to make a series of five children's films based on the Arabian Nights. I had carefully selected and expurgated some of the racier elements from five adventure stories that could convey both the exotic and fascinating character of the Arabian world while simultaneously affirming their great moral principles. My idea was to teach values through adventure, art and culture.

It was while I was researching the Arabian Nights material and preparing budgets for submission to EBEC that I met Karl.

He was introduced to me by his friend, a young Polish filmmaker who had asked me out on a date. Karl was tall and slim, with an angular face and body, blond hair, and crystal blue eyes. He was more than ten years my senior, but we both experienced an immediate and profound connection we later confirmed with one another. I remember seeing him in a glow of pulsating light, and the rest of the room disappeared from view, a bit unnerving since I was on a date with his friend. Karl found a way to contact me within the next twelve hours, cleverly pretending he knew someone living on my street. He asked for my exact address, and then left me a note in my mailbox. I waited two days before I responded because somehow I instinctively knew a continuation of our relationship would change me forever.

Karl was an architect and divorced. He had three daughters who lived nearby with his ex-wife, and he saw his girls several times a week.

Karl was German and Christian.

That combination was not a simple matter for me. As a Jew who had read history, and the daughter of a woman who had experienced and fled from persecution, I was only too aware of my people's suffering, often at the hands of Christians, and most recently at the hands of the Germans during World War II.

Nevertheless, Karl and I fell in love, although I think we both realized at the outset it would never be a simple *boy-meets-girl-and-they-fall-in-love-and-live-happily-ever-after* script.

Karl told me a highly personal story after we had been dating for several weeks. When he was just a boy, his father decided to leave Germany because he despised Hitler and the political agenda the Fuhrer was forcing on Germany. Karl's relatives in Germany, as he described them, represented the entire spectrum of human behavior. On one end was his uncle, who joined the SS and was actively involved in rounding up and murdering Jews. On the other end of the spectrum was Karl's aunt, who refused to abandon her friendship with a Jewish neighbor. While trying to protect her friend, the Nazis caught her, and she, too, was sent to a concentration camp where she perished. Today his aunt would be considered a "righteous Gentile," but at the time she was considered a fool and a traitor by her countrymen.

In the middle was Karl's father, an interesting and complex character *vis-à-vis* Nazi Germany. He wanted nothing to do with Hitler or the Final Solution, so he extricated his wife, his son, Karl, and his daughter and moved to Canada. Regardless of his political stand against Hitler, Karl's father had no great love either for Jews or Catholics. In fact, he forbad his children to marry either one. This, Karl assured me with a smile and a wink, was probably why he, Karl, married a Catholic and his sister married a Jew!

We laughed together about his family story, but the shadow of recent European history was still hovering nearby.

Our life together in Chicago was idyllic for a while. Every morning before he went to work for a local architectural firm, Karl would write me beautifully illustrated love notes, in English, Italian, or French. I would be busy during the day writing my proposal for the "Arabian Nights for Children" and, in the evening, we would come together, spending hours talking and sharing stories of our lives. Karl especially loved when I would tell him stories from my Jewish heritage.

On Friday nights he would expectantly wait for me to come back from synagogue. Then he would ply me with questions and ask me to give him a synopsis of the Torah portion and the rabbi's sermon. I found it strange but also endearing that he would be so fascinated by my religion and my heritage.

At the time, I never shared any details with my mother about my relationship with Karl because I thought that information would be too painful for her to bear. The last thing she would want—as was true for many Jewish mothers around the world—was for either one of her daughters to be involved romantically with a non-Jew or, even worse, a German non-Jew. The Holocaust was still too fresh and raw for most Jews to be able to pardon the German nation or individual Germans for the decimation of six million Jews. And so my mother never learned about my relationship with Karl. That was one minefield I was not willing to step into.

Karl understood my position and never questioned my reasons for not wanting to introduce him to my mother. My father did meet Karl and they liked one another. I counted on my father's liberalism and universal philosophy, and I knew in advance he would never make a disparaging comment about Karl's German background.

I can't remember exactly how or when it began, but in a bizarre reversal of roles, Karl began to bake *challah* (Jewish braided bread for the Sabbath) every Friday morning, the traditional role of a Jewish woman. On Friday evening I would go to pray at my synagogue, fulfilling the traditional role of the Jewish man, while Karl would wait for me to return to eat the *challah* and a Sabbath meal he had prepared for us.

Somehow it worked. We were content and planning a way to continue our relationship in the future, most likely in the Middle East where I would hopefully be shooting films in Israel based on the Arabian Nights. He said he would accept an architectural job in Lebanon he had already been offered, and he assured me we could successfully commute between Israel and Lebanon. Our love would heal the Middle East conflict, he predicted optimistically, his blue eyes twinkling.

One night, however, our plans were irrevocably interrupted.

We were sitting opposite each other at the kitchen table, as we had so often done, drinking tea and sharing stories. Karl casually mentioned that once, when he was a little boy, his father took him to a neighboring town to visit some relatives. On that very day, Hitler arrived at the same town for a visit. I began watching Karl's face, both in fascination and in horror, as he recounted the incident.

As Karl reconstructed the scene for me, I felt my body grow cold. Karl described how he began playing on the running board of Hitler's car with some local children. At that moment in his narrative, I inadvertently covered my eyes with my hands and slowly my head dropped forward until it touched the kitchen table.

"Oh my God," I whispered over and over again. "Oh my God, oh my God!"

My mind was still reeling at the image. The man I loved had played on the running board of Hitler's car. The image of my kind and loving Karl juxtaposed with the image of the twentieth century murderer of six million of my people created a maelstrom of emotion in me that I had never before experienced. I felt I could not breathe. Neither could I bear to look at Karl.

Karl jumped up in anger and fled to the living room. He began pacing uncharacteristically, and shouting.

"Ruth, you can't blame me for what happened. I was just a boy." He glared at me while I was still sitting at the kitchen table.

"Everyone blamed us Germans," he continued, fiercely poking at his chest, "even though my father denounced Hitler and took us to Canada. Ruth, I was just a little boy, but they all made fun of me at school. They called me *Kraut* and tormented me for being a German. It was horrible." All of his pent-up childhood hurt spilled out like hot lava.

I can still hear his voice in my head even as I write these words today.

"Ruth, it wasn't my fault what happened to the Jews."

I rose from my chair in the kitchen to follow Karl into the living room. Tears streamed down my cheeks as I faced Karl whose pale skin was now ruddy with rage, his playful blue eyes now flashing with anger.

"It wasn't my fault," he repeated over and over again. "It wasn't my fault!"

That nanosecond of a moment between us as we faced one another was as long a moment as I had experienced in my lifetime.

We were both caught up in our individual histories of loss, pain, hurt and alienation brought about by the great forces of history for which neither of us was responsible. I sensed it might be impossible to cross that great divide.

Eventually we did cross the divide, and grew even closer, although we never referred to that minefield again. The love between us became a soothing balm for our psychic and historical wounds. I would never again be able to view the entire German nation as a monolithic country of murderers, or label each German I met as a co-conspirator to eliminate my people.

It also became clear in those coming months, because of our career plans and due to other geographic logistics, that we were not destined to share a life together, in spite of our love for one another. Our separation was not pleasant or easy but, somehow, through our encounter, a miracle had taken place.

In that small Chicago apartment where my German-Christian boyfriend had baked *challah* bread for me, and I had taught him the Hebrew blessing over the Sabbath candles, somehow we were healed.

Do not be daunted by the enormity of the world's grief. Do justly, now. Love mercy, now. Walk humbly now. You are not obligated to complete the work, but neither are you free to abandon it.

~ *The Talmud*

CHAPTER 7

Multiple Narratives, Multiple Truths, But Still One Dream of Peace

Israel became my home for almost ten years. Although I zigzagged back and forth between Israel and the States, I lived in Israel long enough for me to feel I had a stake in the country of my ancestors and my relatives. My Hebrew was now fluent and I felt totally at home. In fact I was considering becoming an Israeli citizen and living in Israel indefinitely.

During this period I worked in the feature film industry as a Script Supervisor and Assistant Producer, and soon I began to produce and direct documentary films, for an American producer and for Israel Television. I also edited a magazine about the local feature film industry, and penned feature articles for *The Jerusalem Post*, with a stint as their film critic. In that capacity, I had the good fortune to interview, among many celebrities who came to visit Israel, two well known French directors, Francois Truffaut (*Four Hundred Blows, Jules and Jim*) and Marcel Carne, the director of the classic film *Children of Paradise*. Unfortunately, Federico Fellini never visited Israel while I was there.

One of the more fascinating film projects I directed for Israel TV indirectly had an influence on my future as an interfaith activist, but I did not recognize it at the time. Along with three other free-lance directors, I was invited to make a personal film about Jaffa Gate, one of the thirteen entry gates leading into the high-walled Old City of Jerusalem.

Built by Suleiman the Magnificent in 1538, Jaffa Gate was the main entrance to the Old City, and it marked the end of the highway leading from the Jaffa coast. It now leads into the Muslim and Armenian quarters.

In 1898, during the time of the Ottoman Empire, the Turks opened a wide gap in the wall in honor of an upcoming visit by Kaiser Wilhelm II of Germany. The opening was to make sure the German Emperor would not have to dismount his carriage to enter the city. Today the same opening provides entry for cars and trucks, while the original Jaffa Gate nearby, with its huge, powerful wooden doors, is used for pedestrians and street vendors only.

The film I made became a kaleidoscope perspective of Jaffa Gate as related by the engaging and colorful characters I interviewed in each of the four main quarters of old Jerusalem: Christian, Armenian, Jewish, and Muslim.

Depending upon who was telling the story of Jaffa Gate, the historical details differed greatly. Which family had the historical right to keep the keys to Jaffa Gate was one disputed topic. The reasons given for the political hangings that took place at Jaffa Gate during Turkish rule also varied from interviewee to interviewee. It was a clear case of multiple narratives somehow managing to co-exist in parallel worlds, just like the four neighborhoods.

I decided not to prove anyone wrong. I would concentrate instead on weaving the disparate and conflicting stories together, to show how myths were created and maintained. It was clear I was not going to be able to budge anyone from his version of history about Jaffa Gate, or her family's unique role in the city's history. In the end, what emerged was as much evidence of human bravado as well as the nature of personal belief, i.e. the stories we tell ourselves.

It reminded me of the Japanese film, *Rashamon*, where the same incident was witnessed and then described by five different individuals who played a part in the event. None of their testimonials coincided. In fact some accounts were totally contradictory, leaving the viewer with two provocative questions: What had really happened? Who was telling the truth?

Jerusalem seemed to be a Middle-Eastern *Rashamon* with her own multiple and divergent narratives. Jaffa Gate, with its huge, heavy wooden doors, remained intact and immutable, a charismatic, but silent witness to Jerusalem's chaotic history. And perhaps it was the perfect preparation for me, for a later period in my life, when I would have to confront the distinct and conflicting narratives describing a modern day history of the Holy Land, as told by Palestinians, versus the stories I had absorbed from my family, my teachers and my Jewish history books.

But for the moment, historical discrepancies aside, life was full, rich, and exciting. I was feeling at home and even considering remaining in Israel when I met Isaac. An Israeli psychologist who had been living and working in the States, Isaac returned to his home in Israel for a brief one year assignment. My next door neighbor, Roni Carmel, introduced us and within nine months we were married.

As in my family, Isaac's parents and grandparents were intimately involved in the establishment of the state of Israel. I was fascinated by the stories of his parents' courtship, their devotion to the socialist movement, and his father's stint as a Jewish freedom fighter against Franco and fascism in Spain. Both were European in origin—his father was from Romania and his mother was from Poland. Like Isaac, they considered themselves atheists, although they had dedicated their lives to the land that provided the crucible for monotheism, Judaism, and the Torah.

Their atheism and lack of connection to religious traditions never failed to amaze me, as an American Jew raised in a Conservative Jewish environment. This was especially perplexing for me as I came to realize the majority of Israelis were secular Jews, who frequently visited holy sites, not for spiritual or religious inspiration, but as historical landmarks. History, geography, and religion were merged into a familiar, comforting backdrop for many Israelis. Many preferred not to lead a religious life or profess a belief in God. What an eye-opening discovery for me!

Israel was a country that always seemed to be in transition and on the verge of a new look. The western part of Jerusalem morphed daily, its landscape punctuated by expanding, multilane highways, skyscraper hotels, sprawling *Yeshivas* (schools for the advanced study of the Torah), new parks, art galleries and museums. In some ways it reminded me of Alex Toffler's prophetic book, *Future Shock*, when he described the changing Middle-American landscape. If you were gone for more than a couple of years, he wrote, you would do a double take, because the old familiar stores and neighborhoods had been replaced by identical shopping malls and updated communities. He tells a story of a little boy who was sent by his mother to buy some bread at the nearby supermarket. The boy came back empty handed. When questioned by his mother he said, "I couldn't find it. I guess they must have torn the supermarket down."

The same was true of West Jerusalem. If you were gone for even one year, when you returned you would have to reacquaint yourself with the modern part of Jerusalem. But if you kept your eye on the Judean Hills, the Mosque of Omar, the Russian Orthodox Church, the Via Dolorosa, the Mount of Olives, and the Western Wall, you would never lose your bearings. It was history. The religious fervor provided by the thousands and thousands of pilgrims who arrived each year kept Jerusalem from becoming a metropolitan shopping center, like so many of the other dynamic cities of the world.

But there were other aspects about Israel that never changed or morphed, no matter how long I lived there, no matter how attached I felt to my historical roots, and no matter how many relatives I could produce, to claim authentic modern roots to the land.

What never changed during all of my visits were the painful issues revolving around the Palestinians, their intolerable lives in refugee camps, their despair, and their resolve to liberate themselves. Those aspects remained in my immediate field of vision, when I lived in Israel and would travel to Bethlehem, Ramallah, Hebron, or Kalkiliya, for work or for pleasure. And those same aspects were never absent from my peripheral vision even when I lived in the States, where I also made friends with Palestinians, Israeli Arabs, Israeli Jews, and with American Jews who wholeheartedly supported Palestinian rights and the Palestinians' desire for self-determination.

I don't think there is any other modern issue as contentious and as troubling for Jews as the Palestinian-Israeli conflict. And like most complex problems that confront us, there are many ways to view it and many ideas of how to resolve it.

I was living in Israel during the extraordinary and unexpected turn of Middle East events when Egypt's President Anwar Sadat courageously announced Egypt was through warring with Israel. He said he was ready to initiate diplomatic relations and would even visit Israel. That historic visit took place on November 19, 1977. I remember the high volume of excitement and hope Sadat generated—on the radio, TV, in the newspapers and in the streets—when his feet touched Israeli soil!

Sadat's initiative would forever alter the course of Egyptian-Israeli history and the Middle East map. Israel agreed, in exchange for peace, to give up the Sinai territory it had acquired during the Yom Kippur War in 1973.

Peace negotiations between Jordan and Israel followed, and like many other optimists in the region, I was convinced peace could also be achieved between the Palestinians and the Israelis. On so many successive occasions, however, I watched sorrowfully as the best laid plans of Israeli, Jordanian, and Palestinian visionaries—partners in peace—were dashed to the ground. They were visionaries who had collaborated together in anticipation of the dawning of a new era, men and women of all political stripes, Israelis and Arabs, Jews, Christians, and Muslims. Many were entrepreneurs who had brainstormed together to come up with innovative methods to share water and agricultural resources, and to build collective grids for electricity to supply the energy needed for the entire region. They had also come up with new and exciting economic models that they hoped would transform the entire fertile crescent into one of the most prosperous and productive enterprises of modern times.

But, alas, none of our dreams for peace materialized. We watched, sighed, and then lamented as we saw each new peace effort between the Israelis and Palestinians evaporate. "Why is this particular conflict proving to be insoluble?" I would ask the heavens. I couldn't help thinking God had presented us with this political conundrum for a special reason, a reason that over time grew to be obvious to me, but certainly not to everybody.

The Palestinians were considered among the most industrious, shrewd, resourceful, and talented people of the Middle East, traits often attributed to the Jews as well. The Palestinians also resembled the Jews in other ways, in particular, in their yearning for a national homeland, and in their desire for self-determination. They were, as some pointed out, outcasts among their own Arab brothers and sisters—in fact, they were sometimes called the "Jews" of the Arab world. As the Jews before them had been, they would also become a forgotten and invisible people, yearning to be free. As refugees, they were not helped by their wealthy Arab neighbors and fellow Muslim countries, or given shelter or possibilities for a new life, just as Jews were denied entry into the United States and other countries during World War II.

Historians tell us twenty-five million European refugees were settled successfully after World War II. But since the Israeli War of Independence, more than sixty years ago, the Palestinians have been forced to keep their refugee status, enforced by the UN, pending resolution of the conflict. That status has been continually exploited by many of the countries in the region and elsewhere around the world. It still remains a thorny issue, exacerbated today by the debate surrounding their right of return to the homes and lands now occupied by Israeli families. The Palestinian refugees were the casualties of war, as many peoples have been throughout history, but their plight is still far from being resolved. It became obvious to me when I lived in the Holy Land that Israel's past and future are conjoined to the Palestinians' destiny, in as intimate a dance as can be imagined between two nations or two peoples.

The similarities between the Palestinians and Jews were simply too great for me to ignore. And knowing what we Jews know—as I had impertinently pointed out to my mother's friends many years ago—having experienced three millennia as a persecuted and despised nation—it behooves us as people who were once strangers to help find a solution. Even the DNA markers between Israelis and Palestinians match, according to recent scientific findings. Israelis and Palestinians—no matter how you want to dissect, bisect, or deflect the issue—are cousins.

I acknowledge the human geology of this conflict is complex and multi-layered. I don't pretend to have the solution in my pocket. There are so many factors to consider such as the politics of the region, including the Arab rulers' determination to maintain their governmental status quo and avoid a coup d'état (to wit, the revolution in Egypt and the other flare ups in the Middle East that began in 2011). Other factors I duly noted were Arafat's inability to forge a Palestinian State while he was alive and at the helm of the PLO (Palestinian Liberation Organization); the competition among the world superpowers jockeying for oil and hegemony; the internecine conflict of the Palestinian political factions; Israel's mistrust of Arab deal-making; and Israel's expansionist desires.

These and other explanations for the failure to make peace between the two peoples have been written about in depth by experts and by a long stream of American career diplomats who have seen their own hopes for peace in the Middle-East dashed, time and time again. I could not deny or gloss over any of these many factors when examining the entire picture. Nor could I minimize the long-range effects of Palestinian suicide-bombing, and perpetuation of hate towards Israelis in mosques, in Palestinian *madrassas* (religious schools), in Palestinian literature, and on Palestinian TV stations. For me, the cult of martyrdom achieved by murdering Israeli civilians, encouraged and financed by Arafat and more recently by Hamas, was a boomerang policy that ultimately has harmed the Palestinians and their own children more than the Israelis.

Neither could I, in good conscience, ignore the inability of Israel's leadership to resolve its schizophrenic status as a lover of peace and as a conqueror/occupier after sixty years. Added to that was Israel's confiscation of Palestinians lands to build new religious settlements in the disputed territories after promising to curb their growth. Finally, I noted the enormous psychological damage caused by humiliating Palestinians at the border check points. There was more than enough blame to spread around on all sides. But pointing fingers was not bringing peace any closer to the region. Something beyond the ordinary was needed to resolve this situation.

These were my reflections, even when I no longer lived in Israel. Like many Jews around the world, I still feel compelled to keep my finger on the pulse of the Middle East and the Israeli-Palestinian conflict, measuring its temperature daily. Even now, almost thirty years since I left Israel, every day I still check the headlines for the latest Middle East developments—without fail. I realize how profoundly my own existence and well-being are caught up with the outcome of an ongoing struggle halfway around the world.

It also became clear to me while I was living in America in the nineties that I would need to find an outlet to invest my passion for peacemaking. From filmmaker to activist, I found myself drawn into the arena of interfaith engagement as a result of wanting to understand and repair the brokenness of the world. To be completely honest, perhaps I was also looking for a way to compensate for the sorrow and disillusionment I was experiencing in my own marriage during that period, due to irreconcilable differences.

We all have our own personal minefields that can unexpectedly explode, showering us with shrapnel, but hopefully, also with sparks of understanding.

Feature-film crew for an English/American/Israeli production starring Peter Ustinov (back row, third from the right). I am kneeling on the far right, in the first row.

Interviewing French director Francois Truffaut (left) for *The Jerusalem Post* while he was visiting Israel.

Interviewing Marcel Carne, director of the film classic, *Les Enfants du Paradis*.

Directing a documentary for Israel TV.

Clipping from Israeli newspaper: "Director from Head to Toe."

Multiple Narratives, Multiple Truths, But Still One Dream of Peace

With three pantomime artists while directing *An Israeli Fashion Tale*.

Directing an Israeli actor in an historical re-creation of early Palestine for the documentary *An Israeli Fashion Tale*. (I was 7 months pregnant at the time.)

Ad designed for my newly established film company, Ariella Films.

Street sign of Jaffa Gate in Jerusalem.
(Credit: Alexander Sharone)

Multiple Narratives, Multiple Truths, But Still One Dream of Peace

Contemporary photo of Jaffa Gate.
(Credit: Alexander Sharone)

(Left) Artist's rendering of Jaffa Gate.

(Right) Archival photo of tents erected outside of Jaffa Gate for Kaiser Wilhelm II of Germany.

People interviewed for documentary on Jaffa Gate, illustrating multiple narratives:

Shoshana Halevy, Jerusalem historian.

Armenian resident and store owner near Jaffa Gate.

Jewish resident whose family owned a hotel near Jaffa Gate.

Muslim resident whose family members were caretakers of the keys to Jaffa Gate.

Multiple Narratives, Multiple Truths, But Still One Dream of Peace

At my wedding, June, 1978, (l. to r.) Aunt Luba, Uncle Butchy, Ruth, Isaac, and my sister, Leah.

Famous headline: Egyptian Prime Minister Anwar Sadat signs historic peace treaty with Israel.

There is no time left for anything but to make peacework a dimension of our every waking activity.

~*Elise Boulding*

CHAPTER 8

Let There Be Peace on Earth and Let It Begin with Me

Our son Alexander was born in 1980, in Tel Aviv, a truly joyous moment in our lives. He was named after Isaac's father who, unfortunately, died several months after we were married. We left Israel when Alexander was eleven months old because my mother was seriously ill with cancer in Chicago, and we wanted to introduce Alexander to her and my father. Two months after our visit my mother passed away. I was comforted knowing she had savored the pleasure of meeting her Israeli-born grandson and feeding him his first piece of solid food, a piece of toast with jam.

But we didn't return to Israel. Isaac had decided for the time being he wanted to stay in the States to practice psychology. We moved to California where he had lived for twelve years before we met. Thus began a long period of pushes and pulls between Israel and the United States, trying to make up our minds where we would establish roots and where our children would grow up. In 1983, our daughter Leora Raya was born in Los Angeles, another blessed addition to our family, but our deliberations to stay or go back to Israel became a constant source of friction between Isaac and me. We seemed to be living with one hand in our suitcase, trying to decide if we would bring our children up as Israelis or as Americans with a strong emotional tie to the Jewish homeland. It was also a challenge for our children as they sought to understand their own identities *vis-à-vis* their parents' vacillation between two homelands.

Isaac's and my predicament always reminded me of a joke I had heard when I first arrived in Israel. A particular immigrant from Romania was known by his friends for being a serial complainer. When he was in Israel, his new home, he complained about the food, his work, his neighbors, and the bureaucracy. For hours at a time he would berate his new country and then conclude with a sigh of longing, "Ah Romania, Romania…"

One of his friends, who often visited Romania with him, pointed out that he said the exact same thing when he was in Romania. Suddenly Romania became the source of his displeasure and he had only the highest accolades for life in Israel, the excellence of Israeli food, and the quality of his friendships there.

"Ah, Israel, Israel…" he would say with nostalgia.

"So, I don't get it," his friend confessed. "When you're here, you want to be there, and when you're there, you want to be here. So, tell me, where is it good?"

The Romanian Israeli responded without missing a beat. "*En route!*"

And so it was with us, as we tried to figure out what place would be just right for us professionally, and to raise our children. And so it has been for many Israelis who live in America but who are irrevocably tied to their homeland by an invisible umbilical cord.

Wherever they make their new homes in America, within a short amount of time Israelis establish Israeli restaurants and grocery stores specializing in imported Israeli cheeses and beer, olives and *hummus* (chick pea spread), and even packaged mixes for Israeli chicken soup. (The chickens of Israel obviously produce better chicken soup mix than American chickens!) Even if they have lived in the States longer than they lived in Israel, they continue to read their weekly Israeli newspapers, which faithfully arrive each Friday at the international newsstands. They use Amazon to buy novels in Hebrew by the latest Israeli authors; they buy CD's of their favorite Israeli singers and poets and always attend the annual Israeli Film Festivals to see what is happening in their "motherland." And since the advent of the Internet, they can hear the latest news in Hebrew directly from the Israeli broadcasts every night, in their own living rooms in America. Their bodies may be in America, but their hearts are pulsating in Israel.

This phenomenon, I noticed, is not particular to Israelis. Many immigrant groups in America cling to their roots long distance. It gives them comfort in a world they do not totally understand nor identify with, even if their material situation has improved. Creating their own miniature country-in-exile gives them a way to remain who they are, on their own terms. However, it also makes it enormously difficult for their children who cannot quite figure out to what culture or homeland they belong. When my son was a teenager he explored the theme of identity for a homework assignment. He confessed he wasn't sure if he was culturally American or Israeli.

Our custom was to visit Israel every summer with our children, to keep trans-continental family ties strong, but for the rest of the year Isaac's constant yearning to live in Israel created a wedge in our marriage. I did not want to live in limbo, and I had come to the conclusion it was best for us to stay in the US. However, there was never full agreement between us on that matter.

After my mother died, my father came to live with us in 1981, and the dynamics of our household changed. Much of our world was wrapped up in working, earning a living, caring for our children, and then caring for my father when he became ill. He died three years later.

We continued to make our annual pilgrimage to Israel to maintain our bonds with Isaac's family and my cousins there, hoping our children would appreciate having two homes. Aside from Isaac's and my constant debate about where we should be living, however, a different kind of minefield was developing in our marriage, one I had sensed when we first met but had discounted because I didn't think at the time it was significant enough to come between us.

When we were a young couple, people would often comment how compatible we were. "Don't you ever argue?" they would want to know. I would always respond with the same sentence, "Yes, but we only argue about one thing and always the same thing: the existence of God."

They would always laugh and I would join them in laughter because it seemed like a bizarre reason for us not to have a good marriage. After all, we were both Jewish, we both came from middle-class Eastern European backgrounds, we both had parents who prized education and good family values, and we loved one another. Wasn't that a foolproof recipe for a successful marriage?

But as we entered more deeply into our shared lives, the minefield of basic theological differences began to erupt, first in small bursts, and later into major conflagrations. I am convinced we both knew, subconsciously, sooner or later we would have to confront the ogre in our midst.

I recall that, after we first met in Israel, I experienced a manifestation of what I could only describe as *historical osmosis*. I sensed a deep bond with Isaac's deceased grandparents whom I had never met, but who I learned had attended synagogue and followed Jewish traditions. At the time I felt I had more in common with them than with Isaac's parents or even Isaac himself—truly a strange generational leap. Raised in a tradition of socialism rather than Judaism, Isaac was a non-believer. And he was not alone. Many of his generation, especially among the Eastern European population, were raised as secular Jews.

As our children grew up in America, and became more sophisticated in their ability to understand the subtleties of their parents' relationship, they noticed Isaac and I were often in conflict about religion and ritual. As I became more and more disenchanted with our marriage, I found myself becoming more involved in outside activities and causes, as often happens in troubled marriages.

Our thorny situation became one of the major conundrums of my life. In defense of our marriage, when I felt the most vulnerable, I would repeat my mantra: Isaac is a kind man, a good father, and we both deeply care about family life. He was certainly interested in his children learning Hebrew, and he totally supported their having a Bar and Bat Mitzvah. However, by his own account, he wasn't drawn towards religious observance or regular synagogue attendance, which was important to me.

My parents' marriage had been very rocky with periods of physical separation between them. I was determined to do better. One day, however, our son, who was then about eleven years old, told me abruptly he knew we were going to get divorced.

"How could you know something like that, Alexander?" I asked, totally taken aback. Isaac and I had never discussed divorce. "What makes you say that?"

"I just feel it in my bones," he answered, with an incredibly sad face.

Five years later, his prediction proved accurate. In an agonizingly painful family therapy session, we announced to Alexander and Leora we would be getting a divorce, assuring them that we loved them as deeply as ever, that they were not responsible for our divorce, and that they would continue to see both of us regularly.

Shortly after our family session, Alexander, then sixteen, approached me. Without mincing words, he asked: "Mom, are you divorcing Dad because he doesn't believe in God?"

I looked deeply into the blue-green eyes of my son, so young and yet so mature. He was obviously dreading the future of a broken home.

"You know, Alexander, because you are so perceptive and understand so much," I began, "I know you yourself have witnessed what has been happening between Dad and me over the last few years. If someone feels very passionately about something, and his or her partner is neutral, it is not necessarily a problem," I elaborated. "But when both people feel passionately about something, but in opposite directions, it can be very painful to stay together and keep the peace—even when you have children together."

Alexander looked at me earnestly, first in silence, and then responded with a voice full of authority. "God doesn't want couples to divorce. God wants couples to stay together and work out their problems."

"I know, I know," I agreed sadly, nodding my head. "I think God much prefers for couples to stay together, even in difficult times. But your father and I have grown too far apart, and we are on different journeys now, so we can't stay together any more. As difficult as it is to accept, it is the truth."

"Did you ask God for permission to divorce Dad?" Alexander asked bluntly. He was not about to let me off the hook, for even a minute.

I paused for a moment before I answered. "Yes, I did, Alexander. I asked and God granted me permission," I assured him, in a trembling voice, recalling my own profound experience a few months earlier as I had asked that very question of God, my face on the ground.

"Then, it's OK with me," Alexander replied. He turned and left the room.

"Let there be peace on earth and let it began with me," are the lyrics of a favorite song that still bring me to the verge of tears. There are all kinds of peace, I told myself. There is the peace of understanding, the peace of wholeness, the peace of mutual separation, and the peace of reconciliation.

But there can be no lasting peace without forgiveness.

After our divorce Isaac remarried, and our children had to deal both with the brokenness of their home and their family life, as well as accepting Isaac's new wife. This is a very common occurrence in a country where about half of the population is divorced. But statistics don't heal. Time and contemplation may.

About five years after our divorce, Isaac and I were able to fully forgive one another and be healed. Today we are good friends as we parent our two children together. Isaac continues to be a loving, supportive father. I honor him for that and I also know the children have benefitted greatly from our reconciliation. I acknowledge the efforts each of us had to put forth to come to a place of peace, and I am grateful to God it was possible. The joy of reconciliation, after dwelling in a place of great emotional pain, endowed me with greater clarity than ever before. "Let there be peace on earth and let it begin with me" was now more than just an idyllic song lyric.

I found myself rushing headlong into the minefields of interfaith engagement with confidence rather than trepidation. I was seeking a way to create peace among the religions, and peace even between believers and non-believers of the same religion!

Grandpa Sam (my father) holding Alexander and Leora, 1983.

Let There Be Peace on Earth and Let It Begin with Me

Alexander and Leora grow up in America, 1986.

Our family at Alexander's Bar Mitzvah, 1993.

Alexander and Leora as young adults, 2005.

We must see that peace represents a sweeter music, a cosmic melody that is far superior to the discords of war.

~*Rev. Dr. Martin Luther King, Jr.*

CHAPTER 9

I Have A Dream

In the spring of 1991, while I was still married, I decided to organize a Passover Seder, but not just for our immediate family. I wanted to include many people, Jews and non-Jews alike. My grand obsession grew daily, and I found myself at odds with my husband who preferred we have a more intimate Seder just for our family, which would also include my sister and her family who had agreed to come from Green Bay, Wisconsin for the holiday.

I could not be swayed from my missionary zeal to create a community Seder. In addition to the traditional Seder feast with its culinary symbols, and the retelling of the story of the Exodus, I was planning to include arts and crafts projects for the children, musical performances, personal anecdotes of liberation, and a dramatic skit to reenact the Moses/Pharaoh confrontation. My family teased me, calling it a happening, not a Seder. They were not wrong.

Why Passover? Passover was unequivocally my favorite Jewish holiday. It is the holiday that reminds Jews wherever they are in the world that we are connected by a common heritage and a common struggle, the struggle for liberation from oppression. It is rated the most popular holiday among Jews. Even when Jews no longer attend synagogue or participate in any other Jewish traditions, they still like to attend Passover Seders. Simply put, Passover is the Master Story of the Jewish people. All cultures and peoples have their Master Stories, and this is ours, but not exclusively, as I was about to discover.

"We were slaves in the land of Egypt and, with an outstretched arm, the Lord delivered us from Pharaoh." We are enjoined to repeat this phrase of affirmation every year, and to view ourselves as if we—not just our ancestors—are about to leave Egypt as free men and women. Lest we forget we were once slaves, and strangers in another land, we are required to tell the story of the Exodus to our children, as a sacred task every year.

Because I was a filmmaker, and because I believed I would probably never organize such a large Seder again (little did I know at the time), I decided it would have to be filmed. My family and friends were used to my ever-present video camera and my compulsion to document significant life events and holiday celebrations. However, since I would be leading the Seder, I couldn't film it as well, so I hired two cameramen to video the event for me.

The evening was a great success. Even my husband, who was originally skeptical about the scope of the project, and had asked me not to go through with it, got into the spirit of it and agreed to help out. When the night was over, we were all pleasantly exhausted.

At the time, although it looked like I was in charge, I felt the event had been orchestrated from above and not by me alone. Today I recognize that sensation of being directed by a force greater than myself, but I couldn't explain it to anyone then. It would have sounded too spooky to my family and friends, too much like a Rod Serling episode from *The Twilight Zone*. In retrospect, and considering the chain of events that unfolded following that evening, I see a clear trajectory, marking the 1991 Seder as my official entry into interfaith engagement. It indeed turned out to be a "mega" event for ninety-five people, many of whom who still remember their Passover experience and its impact on their lives.

A few weeks later when I had a chance to view the footage, a new thought emerged. There must be a lot of wonderful Passover stories circulating in the world, I surmised. I'm going to find them and put them all together and make a film, not just about my Seder but about many Seders.

What happened next was miraculous. I became a witness to and a documentarian of the most extraordinary Passover Seders. A casual trip to the library one evening with my daughter became a landmark of my project. I overheard three African-American women discussing a video about the *afikomen*, the name of the dessert *matzah* used in the Passover celebration.

I couldn't hold myself back. "Are you Jewish?" I asked boldly.

"I see you are interested in the holiday of Passover," I hastily added, to soften what may have been interpreted as a rude inquiry.

"No, we're not Jewish, but our pastor, Dr. Charles C. Queen, has been conducting a Passover Seder with our church for the last five years," one of them answered, "and this year we're studying about the *afikomen*, which is actually a Greek word for the dessert eaten at the end of the Seder," they explained.

Dr. Queen and his wife, Phyllis, I also learned, had made many visits to the Holy Land and the Pastor was teaching his congregation both Hebrew and Greek. He wanted them to get a better understanding of their own Christian religion and of Jesus, who was Jewish and who also celebrated Passover.

I couldn't believe my luck!

"Take me to your leader," I said excitedly.

They gave me Pastor Queen's contact information and within a few months I found myself filming a Seder of six hundred African-Americans. I stood in amazement, watching them recite the ceremonial blessings in Hebrew, and faithfully following the rites of the Seder, as they read from the *Haggadah* (the book which tells the story of the Exodus and explains the symbols on the table).

I was bursting with curiosity. Why were they celebrating my people's Master Story?

Afterwards I interviewed Pastor Queen and his wife who knew exactly why they had to celebrate Passover. For them it was also their story, a story so powerful and evocative they could easily imagine themselves as the Israelite slaves, calling out to God for their own liberation.

Seen through African-American eyes, their explanation reinforced my appreciation of the Passover Master Story, and made me even more eager to capture all the varieties of Seders being held around the city.

Shortly afterwards, I heard about a Seder conducted annually by the LA Catholic Workers. It was celebrated as a traditional Jewish Seder—rather than an interfaith Seder. I was fascinated to learn nuns and social workers led the Seder with no mention of Jesus. They had been celebrating Passover for almost twenty-five years when I contacted them and they agreed to let me film their Seder. The homeless and disenfranchised were included as equals around their Seder table as well as members of their religious community and Jewish friends.

Leads about other Seder celebrations in Los Angeles quickly came my way, almost magically: Seders for feminists, for the hearing-impaired, for battered women, for drug addicts and alcoholics, for the gay and lesbian community. In Chino prison, the Christian and Muslim inmates were allowed to attend the prison Seder with the Jewish inmates and their families. I even filmed a Seder organized on behalf of Hispanic garment workers struggling against exploitation of our modern-day sweat shops! They immediately identified with the Israelites and their inhuman work conditions in Egypt.

I was also introduced to individuals with fascinating personal stories about Passover. One such story was narrated by Edgar Maas, a man in his eighties, who had served in the French Foreign Legion. Edgar had helped to organize a Seder among a few Jewish soldiers serving at a remote location in the Algerian desert. He even arranged to have *matzah* flown into the desert for the Seder meal.

Passover was like a time machine. Entering the ancient story capsule of the Israelites, each person could identify a current struggle in his/her own life, be it emotional, physical, psychological, economic, political, sexual, or religious in nature.

That recurring theme of liberation from oppression emerged each time I filmed, and I reveled at my discovery. True, it was our Jewish story, our Master Story, but also a universal story. When people who were not Jewish joined a Seder table, they could enter the time warp with us, and take their place alongside the Hebrew slaves, as they confronted their own circumscribed lives. They, too, could leave Egypt behind—not the country, but rather a state of mind that keeps all of us trapped in narrow places. They could all make that journey together with us, because it was the human journey, not just the Israelite journey.

Filming all these disparate and creative Seders, with members of so many other faiths participating, I began to understand that it doesn't matter how we address God, or how we name the Creator. What we hold in common supersedes our differences. We can all share the journey from slavery to freedom, and in the sharing we can marvel at the similarities of our lives.

In 1991 the idea to use Passover as a uniting experience for people of all faiths was a true eureka moment for me. Not until I interviewed Rabbi Arthur Waskow in 1994 did I learn that he was the first to organize a Freedom Seder for blacks and Jews in Washington, DC in 1969, marking the one year anniversary of the assassination of Rev. Dr. Martin Luther King, Jr.

My epiphany occurred while visiting the Strait Way Church in 1992. I was listening to the sweet devotional music of the service when Pastor Queen called me to the pulpit. He spoke about the film I was making, blessed me for my work of conciliation, and then gave me a chance to speak to his congregation.

I looked at the upturned, welcoming faces, not knowing what to say, and suddenly I heard myself begin to speak. I was as eager as they were to know what I might say.

"I have a dream," I said in a firm, clear voice.

A loud noise of approval erupted from the audience. Instantaneously they recognized the iconic words of their hero, Dr. King, when he stood before hundreds of thousands of freedom marchers at the Washington Mall in 1963. His voice rang the bells of history.

"I have a dream," he had begun.

"Tell it, sister. Tell it, sister," the congregation urged me to continue.

I Have A Dream

"I have a dream that one day people all over the world will come together to celebrate freedom. I can see the pyramids in the background. I can see Mt. Sinai. I can see President Sadat of Egypt standing nearby, smiling with contentment. I see the people assembling, people of all colors, of all nationalities, of all religions, sitting down together to break bread and celebrate what we have in common."

I was on a roll, and the church congregants were with me every step of the way.

"Don't stop now, sister, you're getting there. You're almost there," they assured me.

"I see all of us celebrating freedom together at the table of humanity, because freedom is something precious to each and every one of us. We may not pray the same way, or call God by the same name, but we can sit together side-by-side and be brothers and sisters in the cause of freedom."

"Tell it, sister, tell it, sister," they chimed in unison.

"We were all slaves," I continued, suddenly seeing my ancestry and theirs woven together in one common swath of history, "but now we are free men and women."

A man in the congregation shouted out, "You're there now, sister. Tell it to us. Bring us home."

"And one day I foresee we will have an international holiday of freedom, and our gatherings will be telecast around the world. I can see us now, all sitting together, wherever we are, in America, Japan, India, and Europe and in countries all over the world. And then it will come to pass. We will experience it simultaneously, a moment in time when we will celebrate freedom as one people."

As I concluded, they erupted into wild applause and loud "amens." Moments later I found myself sitting down in the church pew, still lost in my reverie of the pyramids and Mt. Sinai, still witnessing people of all nations and religions seated around a huge dinner table, breaking bread or perhaps even *matzah* together, celebrating freedom as one enormous human family.

The service ended. I rose and found myself facing a tall, statuesque black woman who introduced herself as Delores.

"So, how many people do you think you'll have with you on that trip to Egypt?" Delores asked me, sharply bringing me back to reality.

"How many people will I have?" I asked blankly, staring at her. "How many people?"

"You know, on the trip to Egypt, when you bring all those people from all over the world," she explained, smiling at the obviousness of her question. "Do you think you'll have people coming from Philadelphia as well as from New York and California?" She continued along the same line of questioning while I stared at her in disbelief.

"That was just a vision," I assured her, feeling a bit annoyed at her practical questions.

"Oh," she said in a surprised tone. "Well, when you're ready to go, I want to be on the trip with you. In fact I can help you organize that trip. I'm a travel agent."

We exchanged phone numbers, because it seemed the only plausible way to gain some time to consider her comment. It seemed totally bizarre to me. While I was describing my vision of an idealized world, she was worrying about points of origination for an actual itinerary.

Delores called me a few days later and a week later again, asking me the same questions. I liked her, even though I couldn't quite plug into her literal take on my vision for world peace, so I just decided to invite her to a Friday night dinner at my home with my family and some other friends who were working with me on my film about Passover.

Delores arrived exactly on time and I noticed she was truly excited to be at our home celebrating a Friday night Sabbath dinner with a Jewish family. She watched closely as I kindled the Sabbath lights and said a blessing over them. She seemed to know some of the Hebrew words herself.

After dinner, my kids and Isaac left the table because they suspected we were going to talk about my Passover film. No one else in my family shared my Passover obsession, so they usually excused themselves when the subject came up. "Oh, there goes Mom again about Passover and all of those Seders. . ."

My two friends, Hanna and Luba, regaled Delores with stories about my latest adventures in filming Passover Seders. Delores, in turn, indicated she was one of the people at the Seder of six hundred African-Americans I had already filmed. She said she had recited one of the opening blessings in Hebrew. I hadn't recognized her.

I told her how moving that experience had been for me to see African-Americans celebrating my Jewish holiday. I recalled how their gospel choir had sung a passionate chorus of "Let My People Go" and their pastor had brought them to their feet as he reenacted the story of the Hebrew slaves. "They were at last going to leave Egypt," he declared. "They were going to be free people!" The audience responded with thunderous applause and jubilant affirmations. Delores nodded her head enthusiastically as she, too, recalled the audience excitement generated by the Seder.

As the four of us continued to sit around the dinner table, Delores and I began to reminisce about the stories told of the freedom marches in the sixties. Rabbis and other Jewish leaders marched side by side with Dr. King and his people from Selma to Montgomery to protest against segregation. Rabbi Abraham Joshua Heschel even went to prison with Dr.

King in Alabama to protest the oppression of blacks in the South. Blacks and Jews became a familiar sight as they marched in step, arms locked together in solidarity.

"It's too bad we're not close like that any more," lamented Delores. "We have a natural bond, but there were black leaders later who tried to separate us," she acknowledged, "like Rev. Louis Farrakhan."

"We could help heal that chasm by organizing interfaith, interracial pilgrimages to the Holy Land," I responded. "Blacks and Jews traveling together, retracing the steps of the Exodus together. Can you imagine that?"

Suddenly Delores grew pale. She began to pound her chest and we all thought she was having a heart attack. Delores suddenly sat up straight and said in a clear and unfaltering voice, "Now I understand what they meant."

"Who are they? What are you talking about?" I asked her.

"Three different preachers who didn't even know me made the same prophesy about me. They all told me I was going to lead the most unusual trips to the Holy Land, and it would be trips of blacks and Jews together. But until this moment I didn't realize what they were talking about. Now I understand." And she fell silent.

The four of us looked at one another. The room was absolutely still. I shivered and felt the presence of something pass over us, something I could only describe as "the Holy Spirit." Would people understand what had transpired and not belittle what all four of us had experienced?

Delores and I looked at each other again. We knew what we had to do. We had been selected to make an interracial, interfaith journey together. God had a plan and we were both part of that plan.

Within two months Delores and I had laid out an itinerary for an interfaith pilgrimage beginning in Cairo, Egypt, continuing through the Sinai desert, and then culminating in Israel where our group would celebrate a Universal Freedom Seder in Jerusalem, sitting side-by-side with people from all over the world—just as I had envisioned during my reverie.

Delores and I knew there were no coincidences. We had been "hand-picked" for this assignment. And from that moment on there was never a question of God's intentions for us, as interfaith, interracial emissaries. She was black and Christian. I was white and Jewish.

We were about to become sisters.

The original Festival of Freedom Seder I organized for 95 family and friends, 1991.

Pastor Charles C. Queen leads a Seder for 600 African-Americans in Los Angeles, 1992. (Credit: Morris Kagan)

To my left, Marty Steele, my cinematographer, and to my right, Ike Magal, my soundman.

With Pastor Queen and his wife, Phyllis. (Credit: Morris Kagan)

Chino inmates celebrating Passover, 1992.

25th annual Seder held by the Los Angeles Catholic Workers, 1992.

Hispanic garment union worker (left) bonds with Rose Freedman, the last living survivor of the New York City triangle fire.

The late singer/composer Debbie Friedman (left) with Rabbi Sue Elwell at the first Feminist Seder held in Los Angeles, 1992.

With Edgar Maas, one of my interviewees, who celebrated Passover in the desert of Algeria while serving in the French Foreign Legion.

With my new "sister" Delores Gray.

Article published by the the Atlanta Jewish Times.

Speaking at the Strait-Way Church in Watts, Los Angeles.

Strait-Way congregants cheer me on.

One little person, giving all of her time to peace, makes news. Many people, giving some of their time, can make history.

~*Peace Pilgrim*

CHAPTER 10
Two Women One Journey

"I'm afraid to say this to you, but I have to ask you something important before we leave on our trip together," I whispered to Delores. We were scheduled to leave the following week on a reconnaissance trip to Egypt and Israel in the winter of 1992, to map out the itinerary and speak to the people who would be assisting us on our first interfaith pilgrimage. We would be sharing hotel rooms and probably be with each other 24-7, so I knew I had to ask the question I had been putting off for weeks.

"Go ahead. You can ask me anything you want," Delores said in earnest, beaming her beautiful Queen-of-Sheba smile.

"You're not going to try to convert me while we're on the trip, are you?" I blurted out.

"Why would I want to do that?" Delores responded, looking surprised.

"Because almost every born-again Christian I have met has wanted to convert me. They want my Jewish soul. That has been my experience in the past, and I'm telling you now, in advance, I am not interested in converting."

Delores laughed enthusiastically, but I didn't join in her laughter. I was very serious. I needed her to tell me unequivocally she wasn't planning to proselytize while we were on our trip together. I recalled and reminded her of an episode that happened outside of her church when I was visiting. A young man named Cohen, who had converted to Christianity, approached me and began testifying for Jesus, hoping to "save" me. What many evangelical Christians don't understand about Jews, I told Delores, is we don't believe in the notion of "original sin," and therefore we don't feel a need to be "saved."

"I would never do that," Delores assured me. "I have such respect for the Jewish people and Jewish history. I don't want to change anything about you. You don't have to worry," she assured me, growing serious herself. "I have visited Israel over ten times myself, I have known Jewish people all of my life, and I have never tried to convert any Jew."

"Well, then," I concluded, "let's make our final arrangements and begin the Festival of Freedom." We had chosen the name Festival of Freedom to describe the world interfaith movement we were about to launch the following spring. Over a two-week period in the spring we would bring together people of diverse religious, racial and ethnic backgrounds, to retrace the steps of Exodus, beginning in Cairo, continuing on through the Sinai desert, climbing Mt. Sinai together at dawn, and then arriving in Jerusalem. As a finale we would celebrate a Universal Freedom Seder during the holiday of Passover, also known as the Festival of Freedom.

We agreed, from a tactical point of view, we should first contact the Foreign Ministry in Israel when we got there, to let them know about our plans for bringing interfaith groups to the country, and to enlist their support. Just how we were going to arrange that was as yet unclear, but it was one of our first priorities.

I remember the thrill I experienced the first time I examined our royal blue and white Festival of Freedom business cards, fresh and crisp from the printer. I was listed as the Executive Director, Delores was the Travel Coordinator and, although we didn't print it on our cards, we both understood God was in charge and we were just following orders.

Our encounter with El Al airlines became the first test for us. I breezed through the check-in process—my passport had at least a dozen stamps showing I had visited Israel many times and I was able to converse with the attendants in Hebrew. I waited and waited for Delores to complete the security check for what seemed liked an inordinately long time. I saw she was being questioned by at least three different airline employees. El Al security was always tight, but it seemed unreasonable she would have to undergo such a length interrogation. I appeared at her side and interrupted the El Al security checkers.

"Why are you questioning this woman for such a long time?"

"What business is it of yours?" they countered, clearly annoyed by my audacity to question their authority.

"She is my sister," I explained, with a deadpan face.

I watched them look back and forth between us several times, noticing Delores's chocolate skin, her dark hair and dark eyes, and then looking over to my light skin, blond hair, and green eyes. We were both the same height, both of us had been born in Chicago, and both of us lived in California, but those facts would not have budged them anyway, I decided, so I didn't add any additional information to my statement.

"Oh, so you're sisters," one of them said, with noticeable irony. "I see, sisters. Uh huh. On which side, your mother's side or your father's side?" he quipped sarcastically, expecting to trip me up.

"On both sides," I immediately answered, and scooped my arm into hers. "Can't you see the resemblance?"

After a moment of stunned silence, we all laughed and Delores explained that we were "sisters" in our interfaith project. We were going to Israel to set up our first pilgrimage, and we didn't want to miss our plane. The ice was broken and they let Delores through the security barrier within moments.

We giggled as we walked arm-in-arm down the ramp to the plane, pleased with ourselves for having sidestepped our first "minefield." When people saw us together, as we would learn over the next few years on our shared journey, they immediately grasped our mission in a visceral way that never failed to amaze us. Sometimes we didn't even have to speak. We were *poster girls* for Two Women One Journey.

We boarded the plane and, as God would have it, we sat next to Yaacov, who worked for the Israeli Foreign Office in Jerusalem. We told him about our project, and he grew extremely animated and wanted to hear more details about our plans. Finally he said, "Well, you'll have to meet with Bruce Kashdan in our office when you get to Jerusalem. He's an American and he will genuinely appreciate what you are planning to do, and he'll be very helpful. You can use my name," he said, and took out his card and wrote Bruce's telephone number on the back.

Delores and I exchanged looks, like co-conspirators. We had just landed an important contact with the Israeli Foreign Office without even leaving the States. We were beginning to see the journey had already been planned for us. Our task was to find where to point our feet to coincide with that plan. As long as we remained eager, open and willing to meet our destiny, our destiny would be searching for us just as eagerly.

Our experiences the next day when we arrived in Jerusalem confirmed our belief we were on a sacred mission. We were able to reach Bruce Kashdan at the Foreign Office immediately and set up an appointment the same day. As Yaacov had predicted, Bruce was delighted to hear about our plans and when he learned about our intentions to have a Universal Freedom Seder in Jerusalem at the end of our interfaith trip, he urged us to contact Rabbi David Rosen, "the ideal Rabbi to lead your Seder," he assured us. "He is Modern Orthodox, he is extremely articulate, he already has considerable experience in interfaith engagement, and he will be a wonderful leader for your Seder."

We contacted Rabbi Rosen and met with him two days later, on Friday afternoon before the Sabbath. Although we hadn't planned it, we ended up spending four full hours in his office, telling him how Delores and I met, describing the Seders I had filmed and our discoveries about Passover, explaining why we had decided to organize Festival of Freedom, and how important it was to end the pilgrimage with an interfaith Passover Seder.

"Who's behind this project?" he wanted to know, midway through our elaborate descriptions. "What's the name of the organization sponsoring it?"

Delores and I looked at one another, laughed out loud, and answered in unison, "God."

"You will lead the Universal Freedom Seder for us, won't you?" I casually asked, at the end of four hours of discussion.

Rabbi Rosen looked at both of us, his face alight with both amusement and admiration. "Do I have any choice in the matter?" he quipped.

"No," Delores and I chimed in unison.

Rabbi Rosen would remind us of our first encounter as we called upon him, in the years to come, to be not just our Seder leader but also our main interfaith advisor for the Festival of Freedom, and to help us navigate the minefields as we encountered them. Along with the miracles, we invariably encountered minefields on each and every trip we undertook, and those minefields actually became the landmarks of our journey.

For the moment, however, we were deeply grateful for Rabbi Rosen's willingness to participate in the first Festival of Freedom. Originally from England, Rabbi Rosen had served as the Chief Rabbi for Ireland after a stint in South Africa where he managed to bring together clergy from different faiths and races along with their communities—much to the distaste of the apartheid authorities.

"I was probably kicked out of South Africa for being too successful," he acknowledged with a grin.

When we met him, he was Director of Inter-religious Affairs for the Israeli office of the Anti-Defamation League. Later he would become a member of Israel's negotiating team set up to establish—for the first time in history—diplomatic relations between the Vatican and Israel. He was knighted by the Pope in 2005, and in 2010 he was made a Commander of the British Empire by the Queen of England for his interfaith achievements.

At the time we only knew we had been divinely directed to his office, through the earthly intermediaries of Yaacov on the El Al plane and Bruce in the Foreign Office. I was not surprised, however, when I learned recently that one of Rabbi Rosen's favorite passages about a Jewish perspective on interfaith engagement comes from Rabbi Abraham Isaac Kook, a highly venerated Jewish scholar from Russia who immigrated to Jerusalem and died in 1935. Rav Kook is definitely one of my interfaith heroes.

This is the inspiring passage Rabbi Rosen shared with me from *The Teachings of Rav Kook*, translated by Z. Yaron:

> *Despite the differences of understandings between the Religions and Faiths and despite the distinctions of races and environments, it is the right thing to (seek to) fully understand the different peoples and groups in order to know how to base universal human love on practical foundations. For only within the soul that is replete with love of all beings and (above all) love of humanity, is the love of (one's own) nation able to reach its full nobility and spiritual and practical greatness. Disparagement that leads one to see anything outside the parameters of one's particular people (for example, in the case of the Jewish people) even that which is outside the parameters of Israel, as only (consisting of) ugliness and impurity, is one of the most terrible forces of darkness that lead to general destruction of all the positive spiritual development for whose light every refined soul aspires.*
>
> *One must strive greatly to love other beings so that (such love) will fill every chamber of the soul, so that one's love of humanity will extend to every other human person.*

Again and again, Delores and I would be led to the realization that when God wants something to happen, the entire universe conspires to make it happen, but even more so when you're in Jerusalem. Something that could take years to develop and bear fruit in other parts of the world could be ripe for the picking in just minutes in the Holy City. We had our own name for it: "Jerusalem Time."

Our next experience with Jerusalem Time happened the following day. We wanted to get an article about our project in *The Jerusalem Post*, an English language newspaper published in Israel, where ten years earlier I had freelanced for them as a feature writer and film critic. We wanted their readers to learn about the Festival of Freedom, and we also needed to begin developing a press kit.

When we turned up unannounced at *The Jerusalem Post* the following day, we were told the daily editor was unavailable, and it was questionable as to whether they would include an article about our project. I was hoping my time working for *The Post* in the past would constitute enough clout to land an interview. I was mistaken.

Although we were both disappointed things weren't working out, as we had hoped,

Delores turned to me and said, "When God closes one door, another door opens."

We got up and began to walk towards the exit. We were just about to leave the newspaper offices when a tall, attractive woman came up to Delores and complimented her on her black patent leather high heels. "You look like you wear about a size 10 ½," she said to Delores.

"As a matter of fact I do," Delores responded.

"Well, so do I," said the young woman. "I've been living here for more than ten years and I have to go back to the States regularly to get shoes in my size," she complained. "Where did you get your shoes?"

We introduced ourselves to Johanna, the woman who turned out to be the editor of the supplement for the International Edition and, within minutes, after learning about our project, she decided she would like to have an article written about Festival of Freedom for the upcoming weekend international edition. That meant it would be circulated around the entire United States and abroad, not just in Israel. She made a quick call to Sasha, one of the journalists on staff. Within minutes we arranged an interview time with Sasha at our hotel for the following day.

I looked at Delores incredulously, as we were leaving the newspaper. "Jerusalem Time again," I marveled, "and all because of your shoes."

"When God closes one door..." she began, "another door opens," we said in chorus.

As our Two Women One Journey continued, time and again we would notice we were truly caught up in a whirlwind of synchronicity that had aspects of a miracle. Sometimes it left us dizzy with awe. When that happened, Delores would suddenly declare. "I have to lie down now. I just can't take any more miracles right now. I must rest. God will understand."

With Delores (l.) and Muslim tour guide (center), outside the famous Egypt Museum in Cairo.

"Interfaith Sisters" in matching Festival of Freedom T-shirts.

Los Angeles Times article featuring the Festival of Freedom.

Documenting the first
Festival of Freedom pilgrimage.

Peace comes from being able to contribute the best that we have, and all that we are, towards creating a world that supports everyone. But it is also securing the space for others to contribute the best that they have and all that they are.
~Hafsat Abiola

CHAPTER 11
Festival of Freedom

Festival of Freedom, 1993

The first Festival of Freedom pilgrimage consisted of thirteen people, eight African-Americans and five Jews. Several participants were members of the Los Angeles Strait-Way Church, including Pastor Queen and his wife Phyllis; both had visited Israel many times in the past. Dr. Queen's emphasis on and devotion to the study of Judaism frequently left him open to harsh criticism from other Christian pastors, he acknowledged, but he never let their perspective influence his ministry. I found him to be a man of great personal courage, and I realized that Delores, as a member of his congregation, had also been deeply influenced by his commitment to the principles of Biblical scholarship.

We began our interfaith journey in Cairo with group prayer the morning after we arrived. We formed a circle and joined hands. In moments it became obvious to all of us that the Jewish participants were not used to or comfortable with Christian prayer. As Pastor Queen invoked the name of Jesus, I saw all the Jewish heads involuntarily turn away from the circle, including mine. That turning away was not conscious. I perceived it as an automatic, involuntary reaction to two thousand years of Jews being accused of killing the Christian god, and as a survivor's response to the Crusades, the Inquisition, the pogroms and, of late, the Holocaust. The name "Jesus" was a flash point for Jews.

That also became the subject of painful interfaith exploration during one of our late-night dialogue sessions. The youngest member of our group, Eric Greene, 25 years old at the time, who was part African-American, part Native-American, and who had been adopted and raised as a Jew, became our unofficial mediator. He embodied all of our minority features as well as being a very wise and thoughtful young man. Very often he was the one who held the parameters of the container for our dialogue. He protected the space for all of us to divulge our most dearly held religious beliefs and our views about "the other."

On one occasion the air became particularly charged when one of the Christian participants told the Jewish participants that Jews hold themselves to be morally superior. "You take 'the chosen people' title literally," he charged. "You think we should watch what you do and then we'll know how to behave."

Jewish members of the group protested vehemently against that stereotype, and then one of the Jewish participants launched a counter attack. "You Christians are always trying to covert us. You even forget Jesus was a Jewish rabbi, not a Christian. If Jesus came back he wouldn't even recognize the Christianity you practice," he declared, "and he would not approve of how you have behaved towards Jews."

The air was electric. The pastor's wife, Phyllis Queen, then asked the question on everyone's minds. Until that moment no one had expressed it quite as succinctly and articulately as she was able to do.

"If for you Jesus represents oppression, persecution, and fear, if every time you hear the name of Jesus you want to take flight, and if for us Jesus represents our salvation, our hope, and our deepest connection to God, how are we ever going to be able to get along?"

There it was. The interfaith minefield was a huge, gaping crater in our midst. We looked around at each other, and no one answered. Her question was left hanging in the air like a storm cloud, overpowering and inescapable.

We ultimately went on to other issues, but soon decided we were all tired, and that it was too late to continue our discussion. Our group did not recover from the exchange easily, and the next few days were tense. During an informal evening walk, one of the Christian women participants was offended when a Jewish man praised the merits of Buddhism. She accused him of supporting a religion that was Godless. He cautioned her not to speak about something of which she was totally ignorant. Offended, she abruptly turned away and even crossed the street to distance herself from her adversary. The rest of us felt paralyzed and didn't know what to do, so we walked in silence.

The next day another incident further polarized the group, and I found myself going back and forth between the offended parties, pleading for an end to hostilities. I asked them to remember the larger picture, the reason for our journey together, and to find a way to forgive one another so that we could enjoy ourselves together.

Festival of Freedom

Tempers flared. Accusations were hurled. Tears were shed and hearts were bruised. I found myself, like the biblical Aaron, known for pursuing peace (called in Hebrew a *rodeph shalom*) rushing back and forth between the aggrieved parties until, at last, apologies were offered, hugs were exchanged, and words of forgiveness were uttered. We continued on our journey, lost and found, with God as our witness. Good will, we all agreed, is not enough to make it through the rough spots. What we needed was a foundation of trust, and it was obvious it would take time to build.

We prayed by the Pyramids of Giza and asked for God's blessings, wrapped in a communal prayer shawl we ourselves had inscribed with prayers for peace and affirmations for freedom. We attended a "trial by fire" ceremony in a Bedouin tent which served as a Court of Justice. We traveled to Sinai and climbed the mountain at dawn. We stood where Moses is said to have received the Ten Commandments, our hands raised in exultation. We gathered together side by side in the Church of the Nativity in Bethlehem, and added our private prayers on folded scraps of paper to the overflowing crevices of the Western Wall. We climbed to the hill where Jesus gave his Sermon on the Mount, and we crossed the sparkling Sea of Galilee on a ferry at dusk. We toured Yad Vashem, the Holocaust memorial museum in Jerusalem honoring the lives of the six million Jews who were herded and dragged to gas chambers and crematoria. We also spoke about the millions of African slaves who were chained and dragged and herded onto slave ships to the New World, and the millions who died on the way.

And at the end, we celebrated Passover together, in a moving Seder led by Rabbi David Rosen, who reminded us that the same admonition recurs thirty-six times in the Bible. "You were strangers in the land of Egypt."

"Why thirty-six times, you might ask?" His gaze panned the entire room. He looked and paused at every face. "Our sages tell us it is written thirty-six times," he explained solemnly, "lest we forget that we were strangers ourselves and become insensitive to the suffering of others."

At the end of the evening we joined hands together with our guests, Russians, Moroccans, Israelis, Palestinians, and two nuns from the Ecci Homo Convent in Jerusalem. Pastor Queen and Sister Queen led us in our final hymn, "Bind Us Together, Lord."

It is often said "if you want to know someone, travel with him." Nothing could be truer or more accurate, especially if you are on an interfaith journey. In our case, Delores and I had discovered that any difficulties we experienced working together were due more to our personalities and lifestyles than our religious differences. Delores was happiest reading from her Bible, praying out loud, and going to bed early. She knew entire passages from the Bible by heart and would often quote them in conversation. We had developed an amusing routine in which I would make a point and then turn to Delores for the official quote from scripture. One of our friends said jokingly she was convinced Delores could only speak in biblical quotations.

Delores noted I had more energy than she did. I worked long hours and often into the night, and I thrived on intense interaction with people. Too much activity with people would wear her out. Those were the details of our lives, and had nothing to do with our religious orientation. They could have become irritations or flashpoints while we were working together, but we decided we were not going to let that happen. Those issues simply dissolved, as our friendship deepened, and as we got to know each other's likes and dislikes. What was also developing between us was a sense of kinship and caring for one another as family members do.

Frequently, when we would make an appointment to get together after lunch, we would both come to our meeting carrying small brown paper bags. Without any pre-arrangement I would be bringing her half of my sandwich, and Delores would have saved the other half of her lunch to share with me. It was uncanny, and it happened so often we soon began to expect one another to bring half a sandwich to share!

In the years that followed, 1994 and 1995, as the Festival of Freedom grew and spread, miracles and minefields continued to define the contours of our daily landscape.

Festival of Freedom, 1994

One of the many miracles that occurred came in the form of Yosef Ben Shlomo Hakohen (of blessed memory), a Jewish educator and writer from New York, who had moved to a Torah-observant community in Jerusalem. After reading *The Jerusalem Post* article about our mission in January 1993, he wrote us a friendly letter expressing solidarity with our project, and said he wanted to meet us. For some inexplicable reason his letter did not make it to the States for more than a year. It reached us just days before Delores and I were about to return to Israel for our second interfaith pilgrimage in March 1994. When we arrived in Jerusalem, we tried in vain to track him down. Frustrated at every turn, not able to locate him through the phone company—the Internet in those days was limited—we were ready to abandon our search for him. In another stunning example of "Jerusalem Time," one of the editors of *The Jerusalem Post* mentioned he would like to publish an accompanying article about Passover alongside the story he was planning to write about our group. "Would we mind," he asked us.

We examined the article in question, a fascinating article that mirrored the message we ourselves were trying to convey through our pilgrimage. It was entitled "Is Passover Just for the Jews?"

At the end of the article it said: "Israel is the first, but not the last nation to recognize that it is a 'child' of the One God. Passover is therefore a reminder that the Exodus is the beginning of a process of physical and spiritual redemption which will one day embrace the entire earth. For on the night that we commemorate the beginning of our own national journey, we are to remember the goal of all national journeys. *And many nations shall join themselves to God on that day, and shall be My people (Zachariah 2:15)*."

Then we noticed the byline. It had been written by Yosef Ben Shlomo HaKohen, the same Yosef we were trying to locate. Delores and I rejoiced. We requested Yosef's phone number from the editor, called him, and arranged to meet at a Kosher restaurant in downtown Jerusalem that same day. Our meeting proved to be providential, all three of us later acknowledged. Until his untimely death in 2011, Yosef, author of *The Universal Jew*, and editor of an on-line newsletter, *Hazon – Renewing Our Universal Vision*, remained a close friend of ours and continued to serve both as a teacher and mentor to us and as an international educator to Jews and non-Jews alike around the world. I still find it amusing that our meeting with Yosef can be traced back to our first visit to *The Jerusalem Post* in 1992 when Johanna admired Delores' size 10½ patent leather shoes!

It was in 1994 that I also met His Holiness, the 14th Dalai Lama, for the first time. We had sent him various letters requesting he join us at the Universal Freedom Seder in Jerusalem, to be led by Rabbi Zalman Schachter-Shalomi. Rabbi Zalman knew His Holiness from a recent trip he had made to Dharamsala along with a group of American rabbis. Roger Kamenetz captured the mesmerizing details of the trip in his book, *The Jew in the Lotus*.

Two days before our Seder, I learned His Holiness would be receiving an honorary doctorate from the Hebrew University in Jerusalem. I made sure to attend that ceremony and, through some connections I had, I was also able to join the reception that followed. When it was my turn on the reception line to greet His Holiness, I told him Rabbi Zalman sent very warm regards and we were hoping he would join us, as our guest of honor, for the Universal Freedom Seder.

I knew His Holiness had already heard about Passover in great detail from the rabbis who visited him in Dharamsala. He was fascinated by the Seder rituals because he had been told that one of the primary ways Jews maintained their connection to one another for thousands of years when they were living in the Diaspora was the retelling of the Exodus story around the family table, while sharing a ritual meal together. His Holiness was known to be deeply concerned about how the Tibetan people might survive in exile as long as the Chinese government was not willing to recognize their homeland. Word had it the spiritual leader of the Tibetans had considered using the Jewish *Haggadah*—the book used at Seders to help retell the Exodus story and explain the Passover rituals—as a template to design a Tibetan ritual meal-in-exile. Naturally, to make it their own, they would select their own culinary symbols and create their own rituals to tell their unique story. (In fact, a "Seder for Tibet" was held in Washington, DC three years later, in 1997, in solidarity with the exiled Tibetans.)

But now I was facing His Holiness. We shook hands warmly, and I looked directly into his smiling, kind eyes. His shiny round face seemed illuminated from within.

"We would be so honored if you could join our Seder," I said in my most persuasive manner.

"When is the Seder going to be held?" he asked.

"The day after tomorrow," I responded eagerly.

"Oh, I am so sorry. I won't be able to attend," he said rather wistfully. "I have an appointment scheduled with the Prime Minister of India."

Knowing from media accounts that the Dalai Lama was a man of great humor as well as compassion, I took a chance and said, "Can't you postpone your appointment with the Indian Prime Minister?"

The Dalai Lama burst into laughter and chucked me playfully under the chin.

"Good try," he assured me, acknowledging both my humor and holy *chutzpah*.

I told him we would miss his presence and I expressed my delight at being able to meet him in person.

"Send Rabbi Zalman my warm regards," he said, as we parted. I instinctively knew I would be telling the story for many years to come of how His Holiness, the 14th Dalai Lama, almost attended our Seder in 1994, and how I tried to come between him and the Prime Minister of India.

But 1994 was also a significant year for the Festival of Freedom because we were obliged to cancel the Egyptian portion of our trip due to a series of terrorist attacks against tourists in Cairo. Instead we created a special two day-workshop on Passover in Jerusalem, led by Rabbi Zalman and his wife, Eve Ilsen.

That same year our Universal Freedom Seder was highlighted on *CNN World News*, singling out the participation of our featured guests, the Muslim Mayor of Jericho, Raji Abdo and his wife. In the CNN segment, the Mayor blessed our gathering and prayed for "the reconciliation of the cousins, the children of Abraham."

The seminar participants, representing multiple faiths and nationalities, had decided to include new culinary symbols on the traditional Seder plate, an olive branch for peace, almond milk instead of a Pascal Lamb shank, and interlocking chains of Hebrew, Arabic and English newspapers.

Rabbi Zalman spoke movingly about the innovative nature of that evening's Seder. "This is not a Seder of the past but a Seder of the future, dreaming the world as it could be," he predicted. We then shared stories of miracles from our own traditions, and lit over fifty memorial candles in memory of the lives lost in war-torn areas around the world.

Our multinational guests included Ethiopians, Italians, South Americans, Asians, Scandinavians, the black Jews of Dimona, and clergy from around the world. By evening's end, we had inscribed on our thirteen-foot prayer shawl almost one hundred prayers for peace in more than twenty languages. Delores and I exchanged glances frequently, acknowledging the enormous sense of gratitude and pride we felt as the organizers of that event.

The success of the evening was almost marred, however, when an Israeli TV reporter tried to unnerve our Muslim guest by asking provocative political questions about the current status of the "occupied territories." Rabbi Zalman rose abruptly from his seat, in righteous indignation, to defend the Mayor of Jericho. He reminded the television reporter that the Muslims were guests in our home, invited to our table for dinner. The chastised reporter withdrew his question and apologized. Later Rabbi Zalman offered an apology for his harsh tone when he rebuked the reporter, but he did not apologize for the rebuke itself.

It was a close call, a minefield averted just in time.

It also provided a great interfaith lesson: politics and interfaith engagement can be as incompatible as oil and water. What we need to combine them are skilled chefs, or even more appropriate, skilled alchemists. That skill requires time and experience to develop if one wishes to become an interfaith healer, and not just an interfaith activist.

But I learned another equally important lesson that night from Rabbi Zalman. He taught me there are times when righteous indignation is absolutely required. When you know a wrong is being committed, silent acquiescence is not an option.

Festival of Freedom, 1995

One particular minefield stands out in my mind as I look back on our third pilgrimage. It occurred during our final days together, after a very successful journey with twenty-eight participants from thirteen states, led by Rabbi Stan Levy, leader of the B'nai Horin Congregation of Los Angeles.

Our dinner conversation, on the night before Passover, moved to the issue of Black-

Jewish relations. Delores and I shared with the group how the initial idea for the Festival of Freedom stemmed from our desire to heal the rift between the Black and Jewish communities and to restore the good will and cooperation that was manifested during the sixties, especially during the freedom marches.

One of the participants, Tina Allen, an African-American sculptor from Los Angeles, was put on the hot seat suddenly when one of the Jewish participants demanded Tina explain why Louis Farrakhan was so blatantly anti-Semitic, and why he was turning the blacks against the Jews. Other Jewish participants chimed in and wanted to know what Tina was going to do about it?

When that situation occurred at the dinner table, Tina rose indignantly to face her accusers. She no longer felt comfortable sitting at the table, she told them. She would not accept responsibility for Farrakhan's comments, and she did not identify with his ranting, she declared. She could only speak for herself, and her participation in our interfaith journey, she insisted, should be sufficient to show everyone present where she weighed in on the subject. She finished her statement, turned, and left the dining hall.

Mouths dropped open. Forks froze in mid-air.

I ran after Tina, feeling devastated this had occurred two days before the end of our trip. By that time Tina and I had become very close friends, and my heart ached for the pain I knew she endured at the table from the accusations. So little time was left to mend this situation, I lamented.

I found her sitting alone in the lobby of the hotel. Tina was calm when we spoke. I explained to her those questions from the Jewish participants, as sharp and jagged as she perceived them, actually originated from great hurt and disillusionment. Many American Jews remembered the exhilaration of marching with the black community for the common cause of freedom, as minorities with a shared history of persecution, I told her. It is difficult for us, feeling as close as we did to the black community, to hear a prominent black leader vilify us, calling us "people of the gutter."

"We just can't understand what happened, and we are bewildered and angry," I explained. "We don't hold you personally responsible, but for that one moment for some people you seemed to represent the entire black community, and the members of our group who spoke to you like that were desperate for answers and an explanation of why our friendship had soured."

Tina understood. She was too wise and too sensitive not to understand. But she acknowledged she felt hurt and angry, because she had been put on the spot, and was being held responsible for someone else's actions.

As Tina later explained to me, she suddenly felt she had been placed on a witness stand, as if she had to answer in the name of all of the blacks of America for Minister Farrakhan's behavior. It was not the first time I had seen that happen in interfaith situations. I was also reminded of my German friend's passionate outburst when he felt he was being blamed for all the Nazis. When we feel we have been mistreated or misjudged, anger is often our natural recourse—especially when we are in adversarial situations with people of other religious, racial or ethnic backgrounds. We usually start by saying something as inane as "you people," and then—beyond the bounds of reason and even common sense—we make sweeping generalizations about the other group, placing all of them in league with the devil.

That learning would arise for me, again and again, many years later, when I began to work closely with the Muslim community after 9/11. Many of my Jewish and Christian friends would question the wisdom of my working with "terrorists," the way they chose to refer to all Muslims and, in so doing, lump all one and a half billion Muslims into what they viewed as a "dangerous" monolithic group. It seemed to be a never-ending, up-hill task to get them to see how ludicrous it was to paint all of the Muslims of the world with one broad swath of their limited paintbrush. "There are only fifteen million Jews in the whole world," I would say, "and I don't think any one can make one single true statement about all fifteen million of us, so how can you possibly generalize about an entire group of people numbering one and a half billion?"

Another great interfaith lesson was unfolding before my eyes after the incident involving Tina and our group. We can't heal ourselves by hurting others. The language we use to explore our pain is as important as the fact that we are willing to explore it. It means we must learn the language of "appreciative inquiry," of how to ask questions to stimulate exchange of information and to find common ground. And perhaps the most important lesson of all is: one person cannot be held accountable for group behavior, and groups can not be held accountable for an individual's behavior.

Looking back on the Festival of Freedom project as a whole, if I were to choose the most painful minefield Delores and I encountered, I would choose an incident that occurred in 1994 on Passover, in the holy city of Jerusalem.

We had arrived in Israel in the spring of 1994, for the entire holiday of Passover, which lasts for eight days. Our Universal Freedom Seder was never held on the first night of Passover—out of respect for the Orthodox Jewish tradition, and also so our Israeli participants could spend the first nights with their families. As a result, Delores and I were looking for a place for ourselves to celebrate the first night Seder.

Uri, a friendly young Israeli taxi driver, of Moroccan descent, spontaneously invited us to his home in Jerusalem when he learned we were looking for a Seder to attend. An Orthodox American family had also extended an invitation to us, but Delores and I decided it would be refreshing to experience a Passover with a Sephardic family. We wanted to learn how their celebration differed from the Ashkenazi celebrations already familiar to both of us.

Uri picked us up in his taxi and we made a brief stop to buy a holiday bouquet of fresh flowers for his mother. He was talking non-stop and expressed great excitement about our coming to his home and introducing us to his family. He said he needed to make one more stop, to call his home. When he returned to the car, we noticed a marked difference in his behavior, but Delores and I did not comment about it. He remained silent for the rest of the ride.

When we arrived at his home, he ushered us inside but then asked us to wait in the foyer. His sister was nearby in the dining room setting the table with elegant linens and plates. She saw us but looked away and didn't come to greet us, which seemed odd.

Uri approached me hesitantly and asked me to step outside with him. I sensed something was wrong, but I insisted on first delivering the flowers to his mother to thank her for her hospitality. She was in the kitchen, and she seemed genuinely embarrassed when I presented her with the flowers.

I went back to Delores and told her to wait for me while Uri and I conferred outside. She said, "Don't worry. I'm fine."

Once outside I found Uri looking at me with such chagrin I thought he was going to cry. He started to speak and stopped. He began again and stopped. "I don't know how to say this to you, Ruth. But you can't stay with us for the Seder."

"It's about Delores, isn't it?" I asked.

"Yes," he acknowledged. "Our rabbi is coming tonight to be with us, and we can't have a Christian at our Seder."

"Christians are allowed to be at Seders," I assured him. "Delores has been at many Seders in the past," I explained. "And rabbis have been there."

"I'm so sorry, I'm so sorry," he kept repeating. "But our rabbi won't come if Delores is there."

"I understand," I told him, not really understanding at all and wondering what I was going to say to Delores. But I didn't have to say anything. Delores intuitively knew what was going on when I went inside to speak with her. She said, "It's OK, Ruth. We'll go."

We climbed silently into Uri's taxi and we asked him to take us back to Beit Shmuel, a reform Jewish residence and conference center where we had been holding our Festival of Freedom celebrations, and where we were also lodged.

Delores was sitting in front, next to Uri. In an amazing reversal of roles, Delores spent our entire time in the taxi consoling Uri, concerned about his fragile state. She expressed how difficult it must have been for him to withdraw his invitation, after we had crossed the threshold of his home. He kept repeating he felt torn, and didn't know how to handle the situation. "He is my rabbi," he explained, "and I can't be disrespectful to my rabbi." I said nothing during the ride back to our hostel. I was still traumatized by being asked to leave their home. Delores, however, concentrated all of her efforts on soothing Uri's feelings and being kind to him.

Delores waited in the taxi while I went inside to call the American family that had invited us to attend their Seder. They were delighted we would be coming. I started to sob when I hung up. I felt such anguish that my interfaith soul sister had been exposed to rejection by my people, my tribe. I couldn't help but wonder if, as a black woman, she was re-experiencing rejection she had felt on other occasions because of her color. For her to be rejected because she was a Christian might have been an entirely new experience for her, but personal rejection is painful regardless of whether it is the result of racial, religious or social discrimination.

As I finished my phone call Dov, the director of Beit Shmuel, suddenly came into the office and saw me crying. When I explained, he put his arm around my shoulders and said with infinite tenderness, "That's why the work you and Delores are doing is so important. Promise me you won't let this incident affect your resolve to continue your important interfaith work."

I nodded my head, dried my eyes, thanked Dov for his encouragement, and went out to the taxi.

Uri took us to the American family's home nearby and we wished Uri *Chag Sameach* (Happy Holiday). Uri had a hard time looking us in the eye. We saw he was crying himself. Delores touched his shoulder and said, "You should know we don't blame you or hold you accountable. We appreciate your invitation. We are not offended. Please send our regards to your family."

We rang the doorbell of the Taubman home. American-born Yael, our hostess, ushered us into a large airy room where 30 people were exuberantly celebrating the exodus of the Israelites from bondage. Delores and I looked at one another, and wordlessly agreed we would not speak about what just transpired. I was able to keep my vow to remain silent until we got to the passage in the *Haggadah* which says, "Let all who are in need come and eat. Let every stranger enter."

Passover is known as a holiday when Jews actively look for strangers to invite to the Seder table because it is considered a *mitzvah*, the fulfillment of a holy commandment. "In the Bible we are enjoined thirty-six times to remember that we were once strangers in the land of Egypt—lest we forget that lesson when we become free men and women," Rabbi Rosen had emphasized at the first Festival of Freedom,

I suddenly experienced such a powerful urge to speak out, I couldn't resist. It was a primal call that demanded a voice. I described to the entire group what had just happened, that Delores and I had been invited and then uninvited to a Seder, because their rabbi said a Christian could not be present.

Verbal pandemonium ensued. The Seder ceremony stopped abruptly. People who were in the room—the majority Orthodox Jews—divided themselves evenly and independently into two groups: those who were horrified and angered by the fact that we had been asked to leave, and those who were defending Jews' rights to celebrate their holiday on their own, without having people of other religions present.

Those who defended the Moroccan family's position and the rabbi's edict made it clear they felt the story of Passover was the defining Master Story of the Jewish people, and that it was an evening for Jews, not for interfaith engagement. They questioned Delores' and my efforts to use Passover as a bridge for interfaith understanding. "It's our holiday," they insisted. "They have their own holidays. They don't have to celebrate our holidays as well."

The other side was equally vehement. "Our forefather Abraham was the role model for hospitality, and Abraham would never have *un*invited people who were already in his tent," they insisted. "It's inexcusable. We're not behaving as we would want to be treated ourselves."

Rabbi Joe offered an argument using *Halacha* (Jewish law). He said that originally the Pascal lamb was only to be eaten by Jews. "But since we no longer sacrifice the Pascal lamb, therefore non-Jews can eat with us."

The debate continued for more than half an hour. The seventeen year-old daughter of one of the rabbis present suddenly bolted, her face flushed with anger. She said she was leaving the room in protest against those who justified the family's behavior in asking us to leave.

The minefield had become the Seder table itself, and the sparks of the explosion were ricocheting back and forth over our heads.

Yael, our hostess intervened, and brought the argument to an end. "This is my home and Delores and Ruth are my guests. You must not embarrass a person since, as it says in the Bible, it is akin to murder. So let's get on with the Seder!"

Delores had remained unflustered throughout. She explained to the group how she, as a Christian, viewed the Passover feast. She expressed concern for the taxi cab driver, and she reassured everyone she herself had not been offended. She quoted from the Bible, "In Jerusalem, nothing can offend me."

I looked at Delores and saw it was time for us to go. We were both exhausted from the evening's events and we wanted to spend some time alone, processing what had just happened. We excused ourselves and left before the conclusion of the Seder.

The evening air was cool and fresh. We walked through the empty streets of Jerusalem, arm in arm. We observed the bright lights of the homes where Jews were still faithfully completing the Passover rituals. I apologized to Delores, for anyone or anything that may have caused her pain that evening.

I was a Jew who, both in my personal life and my people's history, profoundly understood the angst of being excluded and rejected because I was a Jew. I was a Jew who had heard about the signs openly displayed in American country clubs which warned: "No Jews or Dogs Allowed." I had heard about the graffiti scrawled angrily on Jewish businesses in Nazi Germany, which read "*Juden Rous*" (Jews Out), and about universities that maintained quotas to limit the number of Jews on campus. I was such a Jew talking to a black woman who knew about the signs that specified "No Colored People Allowed," whose people were rejected and stigmatized, enslaved and exploited, marginalized and ostracized because of their color. Who better than the two of us could really understand what had happened that night? We had stepped into the minefield of exclusivity and of tribalism.

I cried softly. Delores tried to comfort me as I kept trying to apologize to her. "Nothing can offend me while I am in Jerusalem," she repeated.

The repercussions of our experience didn't end that night. The next day we heard comments from many people who wanted to weigh in on the previous night's events. Word had spread and we heard there was a lively debate going around the city among many people, including rabbis and laypeople. Everyone had his and her own opinion of what was the "right" thing to do under those circumstances.

There were other important interfaith questions that arose as well. If you are an outsider, how much should you be allowed to participate in someone else's religious observance? The Druze community keeps their religious practice secret. Aren't they entitled to celebrate their holidays and keep their sacred traditions just for themselves, if they so choose? When Jews and people of other religions attend Catholic mass as observers, they don't go up for the Eucharist, to accept the wafer and the wine.

What is sacrosanct? What is allowable? What is exclusive?

We shared our experience with another Moroccan taxicab driver, named Shalom (the word for peace in Hebrew). While we were in the taxi, he called his rabbi, also an Orthodox rabbi from Morocco, to hear his view. Shalom reported to us that his rabbi did not concur with the rabbi who would not attend the Seder because of Delores. Wanting to make up for our discomfort and any residual bad feelings, Shalom begged us to take part in his community's famous Mimouna Festivities in the Valley of the Cross, near the Knesset (the Israeli Parliament). Every year, on the day after Passover, hundreds of Moroccan families gather together for the pure and unadulterated purpose of offering hospitality to strangers. They bring tents, chairs, tables, picnic baskets, etc. and create little enclaves dotting the entire hillside. The entire population of Jerusalem is welcome to attend.

The Jews of Morocco brought that custom from their native country to Israel, many decades ago. It was a national—not a religious—custom they shared with their Muslim neighbors in Morocco. On the night of Mimouna in Morocco, doors were flung open and stayed ajar. Delicious sweets and other delicacies were placed on the tables for all to enjoy, and people spent the evening going from one home to another, to greet their neighbors, to sample their neighbor's sweet recipes, and to receive friends and strangers in their own homes.

We decided to attend the Mimouna celebration. Shalom and his family received us like royalty. They were very proud to introduce us to all of their friends who had set up their own tents nearby, and to share their food with us. I'm sure it was also their way of wanting to make up for whatever hurt Delores might have experienced being excluded the night before. I was deeply grateful for their hospitality. After all, they were members of "my tribe."

Ultimately, the pain of the first night's Seder became a transformative experience for Delores and for me. We realized we were being trained as minefield specialists in negotiating religious traditions. Fortunately, we had enough miracles under our belt to know that, in Jerusalem, nothing could offend us.

1993 – First Festival of Freedom

Interfaith peace pilgrimage, 1993.

Sounding the Shofar (ram's horn) in the desert to inaugurate our interfaith journey.

Wrapped in our communal prayer shawl near the pyramids.

Pastor Queen praying for the "Peace of Jerusalem" on a Jerusalem rooftop.

(Above) L to R: Seder Leader Rabbi David Rosen, Pastor Charles C. Queen, and Phyllis Queen.

(Left) The late Yosef Ben Shlomo Hakohen (z'l), Festival of Freedom friend and mentor.

1994 – Second Festival of Freedom

(L. to R.) I am standing next to Rabbi Zalman Schachter-Shalomi, his wife, Eve Ilsen, and Delores Gray.

Israel TV film crew documenting the 2nd Festival of Freedom.

Festival of Freedom

Jewish guests socializing with Jericho mayor and his wife.

Guests of honor: Jericho Mayor Rajai Abdo and his wife sign the communal prayer shawl for peace and freedom.

(Above) Delores and I greet Seder participants, the "Black Jews" of Dimona.

(Left) Moroccan-born taxi cab driver, Shalom, who invited us to the Morrocan Mimouna celebration in Jerusalem.

1995 – Third Festival of Freedom

Rabbi Stan Levy discussing the symbolism of the round Shemurah Matzah.

The late Rabbi David Zeller (z'l).

Participants at the table.

Participants learning a Sufi dance.

Delores and I enjoy the 1995 Seder proceedings.

My 12-year-old daughter, Leora, a 1995 participant.

Peace cannot be kept by force. It can only be achieved by understanding.
~Albert Einstein

CHAPTER 12
Be Careful What You Wish For

The emotional and financial stress from launching and then sustaining the Festival of Freedom over a three year period took its toll. We were exhausted.

Since Delores and I did not have outside funding to hire staff to help us organize the event—which was very labor intensive—we decided to take a hiatus. Aside from that, Delores was no longer available to work on the project; she had decided to remain in Israel. We eagerly sought an organization that might adopt the Festival of Freedom, but we weren't successful.

I was also facing the prospect of a divorce. My children needed more of my attention, which I gave them. Even though I was embroiled in a very difficult home situation, I realized I wasn't quite ready to throw in the towel and abandon my Festival of Freedom "baby."

My daughter, Leora, had accompanied me on the 1995 trip, when she was twelve years old, before she celebrated her Bat Mitzvah. She finally had a chance to figure out what her mom had been up to for three years when I would disappear for a month each year to work in Israel and Egypt. She was the youngest participant, but she was mature for her twelve years. She also looked older because she was tall. My biggest concern about having her with us on the trip occurred when we were visiting a tourist shop in Cairo with our group. I noticed out of the corner of my eye one of the local men eying her lasciviously. He then approached me and brazenly offered to buy her. I was horrified by his proposition and hurried her out of the store. I also decided not to share that information with her for several years, until we could laugh about it together.

Leora never noticed because she was busy absorbing all the exotic sights and sounds around her, and enjoying the camaraderie of our group. She had a profound experience climbing Mt. Sinai with the other participants. In her Bat Mitzvah speech a year later she shared how empowering it was for her to reach the summit of that sacred mountain. She explained how that accomplishment gave her the confidence to pursue other difficult challenges in her life. I felt very gratified when I heard her acknowledge her insight about her personal growth, and I was grateful I had provided the opportunity for her to make the journey with us.

She also made an extremely perceptive comment about me, something I had never considered before. She said, "Mom, you took your mother's love of Judaism and your dad's universal spirit and you put them both together and made the Festival of Freedom." I was deeply moved by her mature observation, not only about how I had absorbed the teachings and values of my parents, but also by her ability to see me not just as her Mom, but as an individual with dreams and ideas to be realized.

The positive feedback from past participants also served as a powerful motivator for me to keep the project going. The actual physical journey from Egypt to Israel, as well as climbing Mt. Sinai, had provided an amazing landscape for interfaith encounters. The very act of traveling together became the catalyst. We spent our days in continuous engagement, first discovering our differences and then growing close to one another as individuals with profoundly distinct faith stories. None of this would have happened if we were just meeting from time to time in our individual home communities. Stretching ourselves in every direction, testing ourselves physically, emotionally, and spiritually, we learned as much about ourselves as we did about our colleagues. Even more interesting, our commitment to our own faiths deepened, even as we were learning to appreciate "the other." And suddenly "the other" had a name. The other was no longer a stranger, but a fellow traveler.

Each trip brought its own set of difficulties and triumphs, I observed, but the setbacks never soured me on the desire to continue the mission. It only added seasoning and flavor to the journey.

Five years later, in 2000, I decided to organize another Festival of Freedom interfaith pilgrimage. Just one more pilgrimage, I told myself. Symbolically, it turned out to be the same year I was to receive my final divorce papers.

I invited Rabbi Marcia Prager and her husband, Jack Kessler, a cantor and musician, to be the spiritual leaders. Marcia and Jack headed a Jewish renewal community in Philadelphia and were also deeply involved in interfaith work with the local Quaker community. They enthusiastically accepted my invitation.

Our joint searchlight led us to thirty-six participants from across America, and also from Canada and Mexico.

After our journey began, I learned one of the Jewish members of our group had been seduced into joining a religious cult when he was a young man. His parents arranged to have him kidnapped and then deprogrammed. Later he himself became a deprogrammer. Others had come from traditional religious backgrounds but found themselves embracing more liberal ideas, while some of the liberal members of our group seemed to be gravitating towards more ritual and greater observance. One thing was clear; none of us would return from the trip the same as we left.

Our tour organizer, Mohamed, was an Egyptian Muslim who had been living in Los Angeles for several years, heading a travel agency that specialized in trips to Egypt.

Mohamed—also known as Joseph by his American friends—resonated so deeply with the mission of our group, he decided to accompany us on the trip as a participant, and not just as an organizer. In a whirlwind of deft diplomatic grandstanding, he also arranged for us, upon our arrival, to meet with the highest ranking Imam of the Middle East, a prominent Sunni Muslim leader, the late Muhammad Sayyed Tantawi. He was the head Sheikh of the famous Al-Azhar Mosque in Cairo, also the seat of a very prestigious Islamic university in the Middle East.

Our meeting with the Sheikh of Al-Azhar was auspicious and had reverberations far beyond our expectations—which I shall describe later. Reb Marcia and I had prepared two gifts for the Sheikh. One was a framed T-shirt that had been designed by Marcia. Bright cobalt blue letters silkscreened on a black background spelled out three words: *Peace Shalom Salaam*. The other gift was a ceramic *hamsa*, a talisman shaped like a hand, pointing downwards, showing all five fingers. On closer inspection, one could discover the outline of a dove, the symbol of peace, forming the hand itself. We were photographed presenting both those gifts to the Sheikh—a great photo op for peace.

All the women in our group had received instructions to wear scarves, out of respect for the Islamic tradition which requires women to wear head coverings when visiting holy places. Not every woman in Egypt wore a headscarf in the street, but all women donned headscarves upon entering a mosque.

Every country in the Middle East has its own rules about women's garb, rules that are a cultural manifestation of what is considered politically and religiously correct for that country, but not necessarily for the country next door. In one country Muslim women may be covered from head to toe with only their eyes visible behind a swath of black fabric; in another Muslim country women may dress in modern clothing and not even cover their heads. That was another fascinating discovery about essential differences within the Muslim world, a world frequently and erroneously described by outsiders as being homogenous and monolithic.

As we entered the Al-Azhar Mosque, we were introduced to a coterie of dignitaries, including the proud head of a new Department of Interreligious Activities the mosque had recently established. The director of the new department pointed proudly to the shingle outside his new office, announcing their commitment to interfaith engagement. A good omen, if it is indeed true and not just for show, I thought to myself.

We were ushered into the main conference room of the mosque. Our group was seated in the audience along with about thirty other Egyptian guests and an array of press and TV people. Reb Marcia, Liz Kamphausen (our Quaker participant), Mohamed and I were invited to sit at the long conference table on the dais with the dignitaries. Seated in between the Sheikh and myself was the head of the Interreligious Department whom we had just met. He would serve as my translator and guide for the proceedings.

I was given an opportunity to address the Sheikh and the audience. I began by speaking about the courageous move President Sadat had taken by coming to Jerusalem to meet the Israelis and jumpstart an historic peace process. "In fact," I added, "President Sadat was an inspiration for me in organizing our peace mission." The translator nudged me urgently and whispered, "Don't forget to mention Prime Minister Mubarak as well." I immediately mentioned the new prime minister's name, fearing I might offend my hosts. As far as they were concerned, President Sadat had been assassinated and was "history." They wanted to be sure I realized that Prime Minister Mubarak—not President Sadat— was responsible for my being there—an important political and diplomatic lesson delivered by a sudden elbow nudge and a whisper. (The February 2011 popular revolution in Egypt reminded me of my earlier encounter with the government authorities in 2000, and the political importance of acknowledging who is in charge.)

Taking a deep breath to summon up my courage, I spoke openly and honestly about the fact that it had been difficult to engage Muslims to become participants in our peace pilgrimage. I emphasized that we were sincerely interested in having conversation with all three cousins, Jews, Christians, and Muslims, "because we are all children of Abraham," I stressed.

My words were translated to the Sheikh in Arabic, who nodded enthusiastically and then added his blessing to our group's mission. The translator said he supported all of the same principles I had outlined.

Reb Marcia spoke next, followed by Liz, who conveyed the principles of peace as understood by the Quaker community. Both Marcia and Liz underscored the importance of interfaith activity in a world of religious unrest, and they expressed their pleasure in being able to address the Sheikh. In a dramatic gesture, we then unfurled the thirteen-foot Festival of Freedom prayer shawl created during the previous pilgrimages of 1993, 1994, and 1995. We were eager to illustrate to the Sheikh and all of the people present in the audience the wide array of prayers for peace that had been inscribed on the shawl in more than twenty languages. Then we invited the Sheikh to add his prayers to our shawl. He wrote his blessing for peace on a separate paper in Arabic and promised it would be transferred to our shawl afterwards.

The flashbulbs continued to pop like staccato musical notes throughout the proceedings.

At the conclusion, Cantor Jack Kessler, Rabbi Marcia's husband and co-leader of the trip, stood up with several men from our group and, wanting to show solidarity, chanted in Arabic, *Allah Hou Ahkbar* (God Is Great).

The ceremony ended with our presentation of the gifts we had brought. We were then led to the lobby for more photos. Mustapha, a young Egyptian journalist, came up to me eagerly, and asked permission to come to our hotel later to interview us about our mission.

"Of course," we told him, "you are very welcome to join us at our hotel. We will wait for you this evening." We were excited about the prospect of the people of Cairo—and perhaps beyond—learning about our peace mission.

Our group was taken to the Ministry of Tourism next for more pomp and ceremony. The group was showing signs of restlessness, because the truth is they were eager to leave the dignitaries behind and get busy exploring the city of Cairo.

Finally we were able to leave officialdom behind and enter the boisterous, colorful, exotic central market of Cairo. We were willingly buffeted and jostled about by the huge crowds and by the sounds of animated bargaining coming from every direction. Our own conversations were drowned out by the strident, urgent voices of the storeowners hawking their wares. We were hypnotized by the pungent, exotic fragrances wafting out of endless rows of stores offering perfumes and essential oils. Then, in quick succession, our senses were pleasantly assaulted by the aroma of the hot, freshly baked sesame-rings of bread that young men whisked by on huge trays balanced precariously on their heads. Colorful embroidered *jalibiyas* (long kaftans worn by both Egyptian men and women) were eagerly snapped up by our group, as well as bracelets, leather goods, rugs, and *nargilas* (smoking pipes with long coiled hoses attached to ornate ceramic bases).

We navigated the narrow winding passageways trying to keep track of one another but not wanting to miss any bargains. This aspect of our trip, I realized, was an important part of the interfaith exchange, because many of the Egyptian storeowners invited us to sit down, join them for conversation, and enjoy a glass of strong, sugary Egyptian tea. The storekeepers were curious as well as hospitable. They queried us about our cities of origin, and our reason for visiting Egypt.

Having established my reputation as a good bargainer, I was called upon frequently to negotiate purchases for individuals in my group. I enjoyed every moment of the bargaining ritual, including the dramatic part when I would turn my back as if I was about to call off the whole deal. I knew full well the shopkeepers would try to lure me back to negotiations by shaving a few more dinars off the original asking price, and that I would eventually succumb. And they knew it, too. I could tell they appreciated my participating in the ancient, revered Middle Eastern custom of bargaining until the very last dinar was secured, and then consummating the deal with a glass of tea.

The shopping frenzy continued for several hours. We arrived at our hotel pleasantly exhausted, laden with packages and the vivid memories of our eventful first day. Marcia, Jack, Mohamed, and I agreed to meet after dinner in the hotel garden, to await the Egyptian journalist who had promised to come by that evening. Little did I know that our next encounter with him would become one of the most vivid memories of my interfaith experiences in the Middle East, even till today.

After an elaborate dinner of meat, chicken, fish, salads, hummus, warm pita bread, and many honey-drenched deserts, the majority of the group retired for the evening. They knew we would be leaving early the next morning heading for the Sinai.

Marcia, her husband, Jack, and two other participants joined me in the garden to await the handsome young journalist, Mustapha. He arrived at about 8:30 and we spent one and a half hours together. He plied us with many questions—as any conscientious journalist would—about our group, our mission, and about our private lives. He asked me about my work as a filmmaker and a journalist. I told him how, in the process of making a film about the holiday of Passover, I discovered many other people were interested in our Jewish holiday and the universal theme of freedom. Out of that discovery grew our peace mission. He was surprised to learn Marcia was a rabbi, because he had never met a female rabbi before. Our conversation was animated and exciting, as he delved deeper into our motivation for coming and our obvious passion for interfaith dialogue.

Marcia and I exchanged glances with one another several times, in appreciation of our interviewer. We recognized his intelligence and his ability to probe in depth.

Suddenly Mustapha said pointedly to Marcia, "Why can't the Israeli Jews and the Arab Muslims make peace?"

Marcia didn't respond immediately. She reflected while Mustapha waited for an answer to the seemingly unanswerable question so many journalists, writers, and pundits had posed before, and would probably pose for many decades to come. "Why can't we make peace?" he repeated.

"Because we are cousins," she replied. "We are family. We're not having any squabbles with the Scandinavians," she explained, with her inimitable humor. Mustapha and the rest of us laughed appreciatively at her improbable comparison. "But Israelis, Arabs, we are of the same origin," she continued. "Don't you have family squabbles?" she asked him. "Don't you have members of your family that can't get along? And aren't those fights loud and passionate?"

As he nodded, Mustapha seemed to be accessing some personal memories of discord in his own family. He nodded once again, but then asked with obvious despair, "Will it never end?"

Reb Marcia was silent again and then said to him, "The answer is within our own faiths. The Hebrew word for Jerusalem, *Yerushaliyim*, contains the word Shalom, which means peace and wholeness, and also our deep love for God. And I know the word for peace in Arabic, Salaam, is also found within the word Islam, the name of your religion," she pointed out. "So if our religions contain our love for God and simultaneously the word for peace, then that is the answer to your question."

Mustapha absorbed her response like a dry sponge hungry for water. He didn't speak for several minutes. Then he turned to me.

"What is your agenda for being here?" he asked in earnest. I was startled by his use of the word "agenda." It smacked of politics and propaganda.

"I don't have an agenda, unless it is the agenda for peace," I told him, savoring the phrase *agenda for peace*. "I hope that this opportunity for us to travel and pray together, to meet you and many people in your country will pave the way for peace in the Middle East and in the world," I said.

"We came as strangers, but now we know you, Mustapha, and we believe you understand us. In fact, you are like an angel that descended from heaven. We are so delighted to find a kindred spirit here in Cairo. How wonderful that you will be able to write an article about an interfaith group of peace pilgrims in your country! You are exactly what we wished for."

Mustapha grew very quiet and began to fidget in his chair. The evening was warm and humid and a welcome breeze stirred the trees nearby. I watched Mustapha's face as it shape-shifted and then returned to itself. I waited for him to respond. Finally he leaned forward and said, in almost a hush, "What I write may not be what is published in the newspaper."

I nodded, in total understanding. After all, as a journalist I had also been "rewritten" by my editors. Sometimes they took out whole paragraphs and once, to my horror, the headline they created for an in-depth article I wrote contradicted the entire contents of the article. So I was not troubled by his statement, because I was savvy about editorial red marks, journalistic deletions and enhancements. Just the usual inevitable edits, I assumed.

Months later, when I was back in America, an Egyptian friend sent me the published copy of his article. Only then did I realize how prophetic Mustapha's parting words had been.

"What I write may not be what is published in the newspaper."

My Egyptian friend, Mohamed, who sent me the article, was an interfaith activist who knew Eliyahu McLean, my Jewish interfaith colleague in Israel. Mohamed was a doctor whose passion for interfaith surpassed even his passion for healing the sick. Although dialogue with Jews and especially Israelis was and is still considered highly suspicious by Egyptians and government officials, Mohamed initiated a number of dialogue activities and forums that were very successful. He anticipated problems but he was not deterred by them, because his commitment to interfaith engagement fed his soul.

When Mohamed learned our Festival of Freedom group was going to be in Cairo, he called me at our hotel. We were on our way to the docks for a dinner cruise down the Nile. He agreed immediately to join us and arrived breathlessly an hour later, just as the boat was about to leave. Each of us came to know and genuinely appreciate Mohamed in the short time he spent with us on the boat. We all agreed our trip was greatly enhanced by his presence. Moreover, my friendship with him did not end with that trip down the Nile. Today, more than 10 years later, we are still in touch.

It was Mohamed who reluctantly sent me a copy of the article Mustafa had written—or perhaps had not written, although his byline was published next to the article.

Mohamed actually tried to persuade me not to read the article, because it would only upset me, he warned in an email. I insisted, and finally he relented and sent it to me by snail mail. I still have the original copy in my possession.

It took several more months before I was able to find a translator. I was visiting Jonathan, my Israeli cousin who lived in London, and he told me that one of his good friends, Armand, who was born in Egypt, lived nearby. Armand was a Christian Armenian, fluent in Arabic, French, and English—and some Russian as well.

After an initial cordial meeting with Armand and my cousin, Armand said he was more than willing to translate the article for me as a personal favor. He refused to receive any financial compensation for it. I left him the original clipping with the understanding we would meet in a few days when the translation was complete. I knew no Arabic, but as I handed over the newspaper, I peeked again at the front-page photo of our group. "Look at this," I said to Armand, opening up the newspaper. "I pointed at a prominent photo. Below our group shot, the Imam was prominently displayed, holding the peace plaque, our gift to him. Behind him, in an obvious photomontage, was an image of the Al-Azhar Mosque exposing a giant crack that seemed to rip through the mosque from top to bottom, carving the minaret into two jagged halves.

"Hmm, this looks interesting," Armand said. His comment proved to be a colossal understatement. The article, once translated, became one of the most unexpected minefields in my long career of peacemaking.

A few days later, Armand called me and asked me to come to his house. He ushered me in solicitously and offered me tea and cake. He introduced me to his wife, and then she left the room.

"I have to tell you frankly," he began, "if I hadn't engaged in dialogue with you the other day when I met you, I would not have recognized you from what was written about you in the article."

"What do you mean?" I asked, puzzled by the way he was regarding me as he spoke.

"Well, I guess you'll just have to read the translation of the article to understand," he said with a pained look on his face.

"May I read it here at your home?"

"Of course."

Armand busied himself with a book while I read through his translation. He heard me gasp several times, looked at me, nodded understandingly, and then let me finish reading.

"This can't be," I protested, still only half-way though the article. "These are flagrant lies. Perversions of what we told him. Half-truths and then invented stories."

"Just look at this headline," I said incredulously.

The "Shalom" Sheikh of Al-Azhar and a Jewish Delegation
Violate the Sanctity of Al-Azhar

"Yes," he nodded sadly. "That's what it said in Arabic."

Under the photo of our group the caption read:

In cold blood, they sat in the sanctity of the holy Azhar.
Who are they laughing at and who are they mocking?

The next headline read:

> *Zionist Prayers in the Heart of Al-Azhar.*

My lip began to tremble as I read the first paragraph.

> *A black day in the history of the Holy Azhar. We refer to last Wednesday when the Mosque-University was violated once again by Jewish Zionists invited by our greatest Imam who listened to them, talked with them and adorned their books and banners with his handwriting. Our Sheikh. …acted as if he had come from another world, as if he was not of this country and this history and as if he had been totally unconcerned with the thousands of men, women and children who fell, martyrs to the bullets, knives, bombs and rockets of the Zionist enemy for the last decades, and to this day.*

Anxiously I read further and located the first personal reference about me.

> *The delegation was headed by Ruth Broyde Sharone, the founder and Executive Director. She is a journalist, film producer for one of the biggest federally funded American TV companies, CDS.*

I laughed out loud, enjoying for a brief, ironic moment my newfound status as a producer for one of the biggest federally funded American TV companies, CDS. Did he mean CBS? But then I stopped laughing when I read the following paragraph:

> *Her work mainly consists in showing programs and film documentaries on Jewish history and civilization and on Arab terrorism. Ruth hosted a television program with representatives from the three religions to present the Jews falsely, as peace-loving people. In fact, most of the employees of this TV company and its subsidiaries are pro-Zionists, amongst others McNeal Lehrer and Frank McIntosh. The organization is well supported by American religious institutions and colleges teaching the Torah. Most of our Imam's guests were students at those institutions.*

> *Would our Sheikh like more?*

Could this have been written by our Egyptian "angel," Mustapha, I asked myself. I couldn't believe it. I wouldn't believe it.

The article continued to heap aspersions on me and the group for several more paragraphs. Suddenly, I discovered, I had a new husband!

> *Ms. Sharone is helped by her husband, Mr. Jacob Kessler, whose particular interest is the propagation of religious songs to light up the spirit of hatred, in Jewish hearts, against Arabs living in the occupied territories. He travels around the world, with his group of musicians, for that purpose.*

"Armand, this is ridiculous!" I erupted with indignation. "Jack Kessler, who is married to Rabbi Marcia—and who is definitely not my husband—formed two musical groups of Arab and Jewish musicians in Philadelphia to play music for peace. They were even invited to perform at the UN in New York because of their work for peace."

Armand listened sympathetically and remarked, "As I said earlier, if I hadn't met you personally, I wouldn't have recognized you in this article as you were described."

What was emerging from the article was a bizarre combination of truthful reporting interspersed with fictitious information. In fact, I could even tell which paragraphs were written by Mustapha and which, I assumed, had been added later by editors who wished to undermine our mission and convert us into the "enemy."

The Sheikh, for example, was quoted accurately. Mustapha had been at the mosque and obviously took notes and obviously this was one of the paragraphs Mustapha had composed that escaped the guillotine:

> *(Quoting the Sheikh) "Heavenly religions consider all people to be brothers. God creates us so we could know each other, visit each other and share the good things that we were given. Heavenly religions call for peace and happiness between nations. All the wise men know that the heavenly religions call for the belief in the one and only God, and the valuing of good morality. The two issues have been confirmed by all the prophets. Justice, honesty, co-operation, helping the unfairly treated and the needy, the sharing of the good between people, is why the prophets were sent. Undoubtedly, knowing each other and visiting each other are commendable deeds valued by all religions."*

What made the article so maddening was that when I was quoted, it was often accurate, such as when I said: "We are not diplomats. We are ordinary people."

He then quoted me accurately saying, "I have studied the names of God."

(The article was referring to the comment I made indicating I knew there were ninety-nine names for God in Arabic, and that I had studied those names and found similarities between the Arabic and Hebrew.)

My quote continued:

> *I have learned that man has names and qualities of a similar nature. God wants peace and the path to peace is the love of God who ordered us to love one another.*

Later the article quoted Rabbi Marcia, also with accuracy—obviously penned by Mustapha:

> *Some people translate the word "Shalom" as peace. "Shalom" is much deeper than the word Peace. Shalom means our complete love for God who leads us to our love for one another.*

The article itself served as a brilliant and cunning minefield. It disguised the carefully placed explosives by first leading the reader through flower-filled phrases which included our entreaties for peace. But suddenly, in the next sentence, our motives were made suspect, our intentions declared as evil. The most painful realization for me was that we had no possible means to correct those lies.

A few months later, I had an opportunity to share this article with my mentor and friend, Rabbi David Rosen, who is regarded as one of the most respected and savvy interfaith activists in the world.

Rabbi Rosen was succinct. "Ruth, this is obviously a newspaper that represents a significant faction of people in Egypt who are opposed to the peace treaty with Israel and who do not like Jews. Did you know that before you agreed to be interviewed? Did you inquire about the newspaper ahead of time?"

"No," I replied, feeling sheepish and embarrassed. "We were so taken by the young journalist, by his apparent enthusiasm for our mission, and by his ability to connect with us, we never imagined such an article could be published. It was a total disconnect."

"Next time you'll ask," he assured me sympathetically, which led me to wonder if he had also been "stung" once upon a time by the same bee.

Mustapha's final prophetic words to us before he left echoed in my head. "I can't promise what I write will be published as I wrote it."

The world media have an extraordinary platform for either promoting or demoting peace. As we witnessed during the eighteen unforgettable days of the 2011 Egyptian popular revolution, journalists for the State TV and government newspapers were forced to report inaccurate news from Mubarak and his council, false reports which later they recanted and for which they apologized.

Considering the overload of information flooding us daily, sometimes it is a mission impossible to distinguish truth from propaganda. Nevertheless, it is a responsibility we must not take lightly for, in many instances, the pen is still mightier than the sword.

And, as we now know, following the Egyptian Revolution and the "Arab Spring," the Internet is even mightier than the pen.

Visit to the Al-Azhar Mosque in Cairo.

Our 2000 Festival of Freedom delegation offers gifts of peace to the late Muhammad Sayyed Tantawi, Sheikh of the Al-Azhar Mosque.

More presentations with Egyptian officials following a press conference.

The Al-Azhar Sheikh composes a prayer to add to our 13-foot prayer shawl.

Emphasizing importance of Muslim participation in the Festival of Freedom project.

Front page article in Al Osboa, an Egyptian daily newspaper; behind it page 3 of the same article about our pilgrimage.

Close up detail of page 3.

The late Muhammad Sayyed Tantawi holding our peace offering. Behind him the Al-Azhar Mosque is depicted with a jagged crack running the length of the tower.

2000 – Fourth Festival of Freedom

Festival of Freedom participants display "prayer shawl for peace" near Giza Pyramids, Egypt, 2000.

Chatting with Israeli Arab Ibrahim Abu el-Hawa, a Jerusalem peacemaker, his Bedouin guest, and 2000 Seder Leader Rabbi Marcia Prager.

(Left) Izzeldin Bukhari, son of Sheikh Asis Bukhari, receives a peace T-shirt from Aaron Kessler, the son of Rabbi Marcia Prager.

(Below) Seder Participants dancing at the 2000 Universal Freedom Seder.

Be Careful What You Wish For

2000 Festival of Freedom Leader Rabbi Marcia Prager and I are singing. Displayed behind us is the original prayer shawl inscribed with more than 100 prayers for peace from 1993, 1994, 1995, and 2000.

A young Muslim child, sitting with his mother and brother, samples a matzah.

(L. to r.) Seder leader Rabbi Marcia Prager, Ruth, and the late Sheikh Aziz Bukhari (z'l) discussing the fine points of the Interfaith Seder.

An opportunity for serious Muslim/Jewish Dialogue at the Universal Freedom Seder.

Be Careful What You Wish For

Making new friends at the 2000 Universal Freedom Seder.

(Credit: 2000 Festival of Freedom Photos by Adam Kotel)

War is never won... Only peace can be won and winning peace means not only avoiding armed conflict but finding ways of eradicating the causes of individual and collective violence: injustice and oppression, ignorance and poverty, intolerance and discrimination.

~Federico Mayor

CHAPTER 13

The Bumpy Road from Terror to Reconciliation

If I hadn't totally lost my innocence after I returned from Egypt and discovered that my interfaith peace group and I had been purposefully maligned—on no less than the front page of a Cairo newspaper—I think I lost my last vestige of innocence on September 11, 2001.

I suspect I was not alone.

"Where were you when you heard the news?" became the inquiry *de jour.*

I was sleeping when the devastating event occurred. A close Israeli friend, Avital, called me on the phone in the early morning of September 11 to tell me to turn on the TV. It was urgent, she said. A plane had hit the World Trade Center in New York City. "It might be an attack against the U.S.," she suggested in a trembling voice.

Still not quite awake, I turned on the TV and watched—together with millions of people around the world—as the TV stations replayed over and over again the same footage of the airplane plowing into the World Trade Center. We all watched, transfixed, in what I later realized must have been a collective state of terror. Then, in what seemed to be a Sci-Fi flick gone berserk, a second plane sliced into the second tower.

On the ground pandemonium reigned. People who were lucky enough to escape the Twin Towers were fleeing from the burning buildings, along with police, firefighters, and innocent bystanders who had been caught in the radius of the disaster. They all pawed at the air, some crying, some mute, all blinded by a gray blizzard of pulverized metal from the colossal incineration of twenty-first century technology.

People on the top floors who knew they were doomed, had leaped from the fiery inferno, and were now being caught on camera as their bodies fell silently toward the ground. There was an eerie, mesmerizing quality to their descent. How could death look so lyrical and brutal at the same moment?

The streets were now coated in layers of particles, a somber gray snow punctuated by horribly twisted metal sculptures. Those fleeing kept sneaking a look behind them, like Lot's wife in her last terror-filled glance, as she turned to look back at the burning cities of Sodom and Gomorrah. It was her last glance before she became a pillar of salt.

I can still recall the eerie scene in my head, the jagged flash of orange as the plane exploded upon impact, and the billowing gray smoke forming into a giant poison mushroom cloud. Documentary footage of Nagasaki and Hiroshima from Alain Renais' film *Hiroshima Mon Amour* flashed before my eyes.

Was it an atomic bomb? Was this the beginning of the "End of Times?"

No, it wasn't an atomic bomb or a hydrogen bomb. But the aftermath of the 9/11 attacks would have consequences just as profound, for America and for the world.

In the months that followed, we Americans remained in a state of shock and grief mourning the more than three thousand innocents who had been obliterated by a single, monumental act of terrorism. We were now preoccupied with rearranging our world view. We watched the endless stream of family and friends of those who had been lost in the disaster returning to the rubble daily, hoping somehow their loved ones would be found and resuscitated from the "Valley of the Dead." We viewed the rows and rows of photos of the missing, plastered on the concrete walls, a grim reminder of the enormity of loss. We heard stories of survival, of heroism, of despair and grief, and the cracked and humbled voices of clergy who assembled for a mass mourning ceremony, not able to explain any better than the rest of us why this had happened.

The sheer power and madness of the deed kept our TV anchors and pundits scrambling for new and original adjectives to describe the aftermath we were experiencing. The 1941 Pearl Harbor attack would come up frequently as the commentators attempted to find a modern equivalent to describe the country's shock resulting from the 2001 attack.

The onslaught of information that emerged was both chaotic and inconclusive. If we had been living at the peak of the information age just before 9/11, now we were drowning in an information surfeit that left us exhausted and not necessarily wiser.

A confusing maelstrom of news and urgent updates surrounded us, whirling and swirling, expanding and contracting. We were bombarded with jagged and unsatisfactory bits and pieces of information, information we simultaneously craved and dreaded. We became obsessed with the latest news and TV reports, as our emotional turmoil increased and psychological stress became pervasive. Young and old, we tried to make sense out of our new reality. Parents could not explain the events to their children, nor even to themselves.

And just who was our enemy this time? Who were our attackers? Who were the countries or individuals who financed and organized the attack? What did they want to achieve? Had the American government received prior warning it ignored? Why had President Bush not responded immediately when he heard the news? Was Saudi Arabia, our primary oil supplier and supposed ally, interested in crippling their biggest customer? Why did Bin Laden's family leave America in such haste? Was the act of terrorism actually orchestrated by the American government so that we could have an excuse to create a war in Iraq?

Like the phoenix, conspiracy theories rose and died and then rose again. I couldn't help thinking of President Kennedy's assassination. Even today we still don't know who was really responsible, and what really happened. And will we ever?

Little by little the information began to assemble itself into a jigsaw puzzle that ultimately the majority of Americans would accept. We were told that Muslim radicals primarily from Saudi Arabia, proclaiming to be "warriors for Allah," wanted to bring us to our knees. We were told we were being punished for who we were in the world, and the master villain and brains behind the attack was said to be Osama Bin Laden, the wealthy outcast son of one of Saudi Arabia's most prominent families.

In previous years we had been brainwashed to think of every airline terrorist as a Muslim extremist. That idea was reaffirmed by each new action film in the theatre that recreated those highjackings, and supported by each new TV series that uncovered a terrorist cell of Middle Eastern fanatics chanting in Arabic "Allah is Great" just before they pressed the detonator. Many believed we now had a name for our enemy: Islam. It was only a short leap from that conclusion to labeling as villains the entire Muslim population, about one and a half billion people.

For some Americans having a single identifiable enemy responsible for the tragedy of 9/11 was the perfect, tidy solution. By blaming everything on Islam and the crazed followers of radical theology, they were satisfied. Further discovery and analysis were unnecessary. For many people who had never met a Muslim or knew nothing about the Holy Kor'an or the tenants of the Islamic religion, it was an easy leap to condemn all of Islam.

But for those of us who had been working together with Muslims in the interfaith community, and for those of us who had Muslim friends, it became a time of great personal discomfort, because the deeds of the Islamic extremists on 9/11 did not match our own experience with Muslims, and we could not find a way to sway the tide of public opinion. We discovered we were definitely in the minority when we tried to defend Islam itself or our Muslim friends.

For the Muslim population in America, it became a time of high anxiety. Many Muslim women were told by their husbands to remove their headscarves so as not to call attention to themselves in public. People who had been lifelong adherents of Islam suddenly went mum, and wouldn't speak about their traditions or practices in the places they worked. (And for some, it is still true today. As I recently learned from a friend of mine from India, she has yet to reveal to her long-time co-workers that she is Muslim.)

After 9/11 the air swarmed with fear and loathing. Across the country, anybody who wore a turban became suspect and racial profiling became the norm, especially in airports. In Oregon, a Sikh was killed in a gasoline station because someone thought he was Muslim and, hence, "deserved to be killed in retribution for the Twin Towers tragedy," his attacker claimed.

More months passed, and our president now had a name for our enemy, the "Axis of Evil." Terror alerts blared from televisions. People strained to find out if today was an "orange" day or just a "yellow" day, while sipping coffee and eating their "breakfast of champions" cereal. Would the world ever be the same again? We all doubted it.

Within that suffocating climate of fear and bewilderment, I made a determination to complete the film project I had been working on for years. I had over one hundred hours of footage on the diverse and creative practices Jews and non-Jews alike had developed to celebrate the holiday of Passover. It was the interfaith aspect of those celebrations that amazed me and fascinated me the most. I couldn't help but think of the many Muslims I had encountered at Passover Seders over the years, Muslims who were keenly interested in the Exodus story themselves.

I found myself thinking in particular about Sheikh Abdul Aziz Bukhari, one of the kindest and gentlest individuals I had ever met. A descendent of the Naqshabandian Sufi order, Sheikh Bukhari lived with his family in the old city of Jerusalem, on the Via Dolorosa, opposite the nuns of the Ecci Homo Monastery, who were all close friends of his. A frequent world traveler for peace with his Orthodox Jewish soul brother, Eliyahu McLean, Sheikh Bukhari had welcomed our 2000 Festival of Freedom group to his home in what turned out to be one of the most memorable group experiences we shared.

Although he treated us as if we were special and unique, the truth is we were only one of multiple interfaith groups from all over the world who experienced Sheikh Bukhari's warm hospitality and his message, both of which never varied. He reminded me of our common forefather, Abraham, ever eager to speak about Allah's fervent desire for us to love one another, to be forgiving and to live in peace. No matter how dire the Middle East conflict became and even during the most violent periods of the intifadas, Sheikh Bukhari was an island of peace and calm, always advocating forgiveness and reconciliation.

I remember him vividly in his flowing robes and colorful turban when he participated in the 2000 Universal Freedom Seder in Jerusalem. Rabbi Marcia had asked him to represent one of the four worlds delineated in Jewish mystical teaching called *Atzilut*, the realm of pure potential. Rabbi Marcia and I agreed afterwards that Sheikh Bukhari didn't really have to do anything or say anything to represent pure potential. He personified *Atzilut*, and when we were with him we could imagine peace. (Unfortunately, he died prematurely and suddenly in 2010, a great loss for the peacemaking community around the world. Fortunately, his children are continuing in his footsteps to promote peace.)

In the spring of 2003 it came as no surprise to my family and friends when I told them I was hiring a cinematographer to film an unusual event that was about to take place at the Islamic Center of Southern California—an event connected to Passover.

The head of the center at that time, Dr. Mahmoud Abdel-Basset, had placed an ad in the newspaper inviting the community at large to come to the mosque and celebrate the Muslim holiday of *Ashura*. The Muslim communities around the country, post 9/11, were realizing how important it was for them to become "transparent" to their non-Muslim neighbors and to dispel the current stereotypes that existed about Muslims in America. What better way than to invite strangers to come and witness Muslim religious practices, to share a meal, and to get to know one another?

What I didn't know, until I interviewed Dr. Abdel Basset, was the holiday of *Ashura* actually commemorated two events. The first was the anniversary of the bloody "Battle of Karbola," in which the Sunnis and Shi'a were pitted against one another and, as a consequence, Ali, of the Shi'a sect, the grandson of Prophet Mohammed, was martyred with his entire family. This created a painful rift in the history of Islam between the Sunnis and the Shi'a, a rift which has persisted until today.

The second reason for the celebration was new to me. I learned that *Ashura* is the day the Prophet Mohammed chose to celebrate the Jews' Exodus from Egypt. According to Dr. Abdel-Basset's explanation, in the seventh century when the Prophet of Islam saw the Jews of Medina in Saudi Arabia celebrating Passover, he inquired what they were doing. He was told it was to commemorate the Jews' liberation from slavery under the leadership of Moses.

Prophet Mohammed was supposed to have commented to the Jews of Medina, "I myself am even closer to Moses than you, and I will celebrate this day with you." What an amazing discovery for me (the self-appointed "Queen of Passover Documentation") to learn my Muslim brothers and sisters had an historic connection to the Jewish holiday of Passover!

As I was filming in the mosque, I recognized some Jewish friends of mine who were participating. One of them, Jean Katz, later commented to me. "We know so little about our Muslim neighbors who are living out their lives next to us. We need to remember that, like us, they want their children to grow and thrive."

Albert and Arlette Cohen, a Jewish couple originally from Egypt, also showed up, a first-time visit for them at the Islamic Center. They were amazed to learn of the connection between *Ashura* and Passover. "They are even celebrating Passover in our honor," observed Albert Cohen, "so how did we get so far apart, and how can we bring things back together?" he lamented.

Accompanying Albert and Arlette was Dr. Nur Amersi, a representative from the Ismaili Muslim Community, followers of H.R.H. the Aga Kahn. Little did I know my chance meeting with Nur that night was an auspicious beginning to what would develop into a close, deep friendship that has lasted for almost a decade. Over the course of the years, as our friendship blossomed, Nur and I made a solemn commitment that we would never let world events come between us.

The spokesperson for the Islamic Center, Dr. Maher Hathout, surprised the Jews in the audience that night when he said, "Although I am an Egyptian, I identify with Moses and not with Pharaoh." He also pointed out that Moses' name is mentioned more times in the Kor'an than any other prophet—another surprising discovery for Jews who have never taken the time to study the Kor'an.

During the course of the evening I was delighted to learn of an upcoming "Seder of Reconciliation," to be held between Muslims and Jews, hosted at Kol Tikvah Synagogue in Woodland Hills, California. This will definitely be the very last Seder I will film, I promised myself with a smile, knowing full well it was a promise I would probably never keep—and I haven't!

I felt compelled to film the Seder at Kol Tikvah (which literally means "voice of hope"). The reconciliation theme summed up everything I had yearned to say about the ability of Passover to bring people together for personal transformation and healing—especially in a time of great discord and distrust between Muslims and Jews.

Some one hundred and fifty Muslims and Jews, along with several Christian guests, gathered together at Kol Tikvah Synagogue in April of 2003. Before filming the Seder, I had an opportunity to interview the co-organizers, Rabbi Steven Jacobs and Dr. Nazir Khaja, a medical doctor and producer of videos for a Muslim Cable TV station.

Rabbi Jacobs, spiritual leader of Kol Tikvah and outspoken activist—sometimes considered a maverick by his co-religionists for going out on a limb to promote controversial political causes—was in high spirits. He was savoring in advance the opportunities for Muslim-Jewish fellowship and dialogue that evening. "We are brothers, we are truly brothers," Rabbi Jacobs affirmed, placing his arm firmly around Dr. Khaja, "and tonight is but one step on our long road together, on a path of healing and reconciliation."

"We should see this Seder as a model," Dr. Khaja emphasized, "so people all around the world, in the Muslim countries and in Israel, could begin to see the possibilities for dialogue and personal liberation. After all," he pointed out, "the communities most enslaved around the world at this moment are our Muslim communities."

The tables were laden with *matzah* and the other traditional culinary symbols of Passover: a shank bone (representing the Pascal lamb), parsley, hard boiled eggs, bitter herbs, and a mixture of dates, apples, and nuts called *charoseth*. Rabbi Jacobs explained to the participants that *matzah* represents both "the bread of affliction and the bread of liberation." He also reassured the Muslims who were present that four cups of grape juice would be substituted for the ritual four cups of wine, out of respect for the Muslim injunction against the drinking of alcohol.

At the conclusion of the Seder, Father Ed Bacon, pastor of the All Saints Church of Pasadena, was asked to speak. "Tonight I had a revelation," he said, his face beaming with contentment as he looked around the room at the participants. "This is a first—and years from now people will remember this evening and say, I was there at a first. Tonight is the way to advance God's agenda for peace, individually and as a body, by coming together as a community." And then he added, "Let us pray."

Behind him, as he spoke, Rabbi Jacobs and Dr. Khaja embraced one another. That brotherly embrace was wordless recognition of what they had co-created. I admired their courage in ignoring the country's toxic atmosphere of mistrust and stereotype, and their creativity in organizing a symbolic dinner of reconciliation between Ishmael and Isaac, the estranged sons of Abraham.

The message of the Seder so impressed Reverend Bacon, the next weekend—on Easter Sunday—he preached a sermon about the Seder and what he had witnessed. And, as a result, the following year Reverend Bacon and his congregation decided they wanted to be organizers, not guests, so the three communities co-sponsored a Seder of Reconciliation for

Muslims, Jews, and Christians.

The expansion of the initial interfaith Seder into a cooperative undertaking sponsored by the three communities is perhaps the most vivid and concrete example of how concentric circles are formed when a single pebble is thrown into a river.

Miracles, like pebbles, come in all sizes.

The Bumpy Road from Terror to Reconciliation

Arlette and Albert Cohen, Egyptian Jews, visit the Islamic Center for the first time.

Prayer time at the Islamic Center.

Yusef Jordan, a young teenage Muslim, describes the matzah as the symbol of liberation for the ancient Israelites.

Women socializing at the Seder.

Muslim mother and daughter listening to a lecture about Moses at the Islamic Center.

Rabbi Steven Jacobs (l.) and Dr. Nazir Khaja (r.), co-organizers of the 2003 Muslim-Jewish Seder of Reconciliation.

Dr. Mahmoud Abdel Baset, director of the Islamic Center of Southern California, shares details about the Muslim holiday of Ashura and its connection to Passover.

Dr. Maher Hathout, spokesman for the Islamic Center, praises Moses, the prophet most frequently mentioned in the Kor'an.

Rabbi Steven Jacobs (l.) greets Reverend Ed Bacon (r.) at the follow-up Seder one year later in 2004.

Rev. Dr. George Regas, Rector Emeritus of the All Saints Church of Pasadena.

The first peace, which is the most important, is that which comes within the souls of people when they realize their relationship, their oneness with the universe and all its powers, and when they realize that at the center of the universe dwells the Great Spirit, and that this center is really everywhere, it is within each of us.

~*Black Elk*

CHAPTER 14
God and Allah Need to Talk

A billboard changed my life.

I was visiting an area of Hollywood I had never visited before. It was in April of 2003. My girlfriend, Brittney Browne, had invited me to see her perform in a new Hollywood play. On my way home, as I crossed the intersection of Hollywood and Sunset Boulevards, I spied a giant billboard proclaiming:

GOD AND ALLAH NEED TO TALK

At first I laughed out loud, but then I became agitated. I pulled my car over to the side of the road and turned off the motor. What could that mean? Don't the people who commissioned the billboard know God and Allah are the same, but simply different ways of addressing the Creator? Is it because of our collective trauma following 9/11 that we have become so alienated? What has happened to us? Have we not only divided ourselves but God as well? Or, is God schizophrenic? Does the God part talk to the Allah part?

These were disturbing questions. I sat for ten minutes in silence, my mind racing. Finally I restarted my car and drove home.

For three days and three nights I thought about that billboard. I decided the billboard was God's clarion call to me to make a film, with those six words as the title—a concise, provocative way of indicating that our society was in deep trouble. Perhaps as a filmmaker I could shed some light on our troubled national psyche and hopefully even provide a possibility for healing.

On the fourth day I loaded my camera and tripod in my car and drove back to the intersection to film the billboard. But the sign had disappeared. In its place was an empty space for advertising, and a contact number. Had I really seen that billboard or just imagined it?

Still in my car, I called the phone number on the billboard, and asked for the name of the person who had put up the God and Allah sign. The woman who answered was suspicious at first. "Who wants to know?" she demanded.

In a time of suspicion and fear, perhaps her question was not out of line. I told her I wanted to make a film using that same title, and I wanted to get permission from the person who had authored it. She was placated by my response, and gave me the telephone number of Rush Riddle.

I called Rush and discovered he worked not far from where I lived, at the Department of Power and Water. We made an appointment to meet. Fortunately, Rush had still photos of the billboard, and he agreed to let me integrate them into my film. He was tickled at the idea that I would make a film based on a billboard he thought up, but he did not realize he was a divine messenger, "my angel." And I did not realize the words on his billboard would launch a new chapter and direction in my life.

My godly messenger broke all physical stereotypes I might have entertained. Rush was an aging hippie in his fifties, with long, gray hair tied in a ponytail. He wore faded light-blue jeans and a matching jeans shirt. He told me he was single and lived in a co-op near the University of Southern California campus.

His expressive eyes behind his rimless glasses sparkled as I explained how his billboard had stopped me dead in my tracks. He wasn't exactly sure why he had put it up, he admitted, but he felt he needed to give expression to what had happening in our country since 9/11, and what he viewed as a serious lack of communication among us. Clearly, we were unable to reach across the great religious divide.

I told him that until I saw his billboard, I didn't realize I needed to make a film to mend my broken heart. "When we not only divide ourselves, but divide God as well, then we are in deep trouble," I lamented. He nodded in understanding.

"What would your film be about?" he asked.

"I have absolutely no idea," I answered honestly, "but I am sure God wants me to make a film using the title of your billboard."

Rush was gracious in letting me borrow the only photographs he had of the original billboard. I brought them home, filmed them, and sent them back to him with a note of thanks.

What next? I asked myself. I was as yet unclear about the nature of the film.

I heard a still, small but very clear voice reply inside my head: You already filmed the material you need—the celebration of the Muslim holiday of *Ashura* at the Islamic Center of Southern California, and the Muslim/Jewish Passover *Seder of Reconciliation* held in Woodland Hills. That footage would constitute the flesh of the film, I understood, but the sinew I would have to provide myself.

From that moment on, the entire process of making the film appeared miraculous. It proved to be one of the easiest projects I had ever undertaken, with one door opening after another, in easy succession, with virtually little effort on my part.

As most documentary filmmakers will acknowledge, one has to have a great deal of patience, resilience, and stamina in order to complete an independent film project. I had already been working on my Passover film for over ten years, and still had not been able to gather the funds to complete it. An earlier film I made took four years, because I had to raise the money to make it three times, looking for new investors after each setback. The shortest amount of time I had ever spent on making a documentary was eighteen months. But now everything fell into place almost immediately.

The message was clear: When God wants something to happen, the entire universe will conspire to make it so.

The key footage had been shot and needed to be edited. I called my previous documentary editor, Irit Raz, whose work I greatly admired from the days when we first worked together fifteen years before. She had since become a much sought-after feature film editor. The weekly salary she commanded was beyond my meager budget. But in an extraordinary stroke of serendipity (which in retrospect I know was not luck but divine providence), she found herself in-between films. She was experienced working on an Avid editing machine, but now she wanted to learn to use Final Cut Pro on a Mac computer. She agreed to take on my project for a fraction of her regular salary with one proviso: that we complete it in three weeks, when her next assignment would begin. Her assistant, Peter Gallagher, could help her master the technical side of Final Cut Pro, she said, if I committed to the time line.

Three weeks? I had never before attempted to complete a film in such a short amount of time, but I was emboldened by the series of serendipitous events that had transpired before I contacted her. Three weeks? Why not?

When I outlined the story behind the film, Irit said to me. "You have to do the narration; because you are the connective tissue for these events. This is also about your discovery of the billboard and how you see the situation in our country right now. You are the glue, and you have a lot of passion about this, so it's up to you to tell the story behind the story.

"You have two days at most to write and film the narration," she said pointedly, "and another day to find and film the news articles you want to include as archive footage. In the meantime I'll begin assembling the footage you have already shot." Irit was a no-nonsense kind of person.

The clock was ticking, but as I was clearly on God's time, I knew the impossible could be made possible. I was in miracle territory, I sensed, so there was nothing to worry about. I took up the challenge.

The first day I tracked down a newspaper archive, and found the headlines I needed from 9/11 and its aftermath. I filmed the newspapers, hand-held, while they were spread out on the floor of my van, and then drove over to Irit's studio in record time. I spent one day writing the narration, and then began looking for a cinematographer to film me. In the meantime, Irit and Peter were plowing ahead, assembling the first rough edit for me to review.

I couldn't find a cinematographer who was available to film me, so I called my friends, Marty and Rosita, and asked whether I could use their garden as a backdrop for filming my narration, hoping secretly Marty would film me.

A health-writer, journalist, and photographer, Marty told me he was facing an urgent deadline for a book, and couldn't help me. I did the next best thing I could think of. I decided to film myself.

I set up my camera on my tripod in their garden, and turned the viewfinder to face myself, so I could see if I was properly framed. I memorized each line of narration ahead of time and then jumped up to press the red button to begin filming. Then I sat down again and repositioned myself in my chair and recited the next line of narration. Then I jumped up, put the camera on pause, reversed the tape on playback, and reviewed what I had just recorded on the view finder. (I felt a bit like the "Little Tramp" working the assembly line in a Charlie Chaplin movie.)

Film, jump up, pause, reverse, review, sit down…Film, jump up, pause, reverse, review, sit down. And so on.

This went on for about an hour until I was finally able to complete the filming of the narration except for one shot I couldn't possibly achieve myself, unless I had been a contortionist. I had reached an aesthetic decision that, after my last line of narration, the camera would tilt up, past my face and past the branches of the lemon tree in the background, reaching towards the sky. There was no possible way I could achieve that myself, while sitting in the chair.

I went into the house and appealed to Rosita to come out to the garden and help me for the last shot. A talented artist who had created a powerful series of paintings of the Costa Rican rain forest, Rosita was not, however, experienced in using a video camera. But she was game to try. On the fourth take, she tilted the camera just right. I checked the footage on the viewfinder, hugged her, and then rushed back to the editing studio to Irit who was waiting eagerly for the narration.

One last element was needed. Music. By then we only had two days left before Irit would have to begin her next assignment. Irit mentioned that she knew a very talented Palestinian musician and composer, who lived in Los Angeles, and she thought his evocative music would be perfect for the film, if he agreed to let me use it.

I called Nabil Azam and he agreed to come and view the rough edit. He loved the film and said I could use music from the CD Irit had mentioned, entitled *The Fertile Crescent*, which he had composed and played on his violin.

Actually, Nabil and I were not strangers. I had met him many years before when he had been invited to play his violin on the eve of my Jewish community's *Yom Kippur* (Day of Atonement) service. He began his performance with the opening prayer, the *Kol Nidre*, a prayer which is heard in virtually every synagogue around the world on the eve of our most solemn holiday, when we are exhorted to scrupulously examine our sins and our behavior of the previous year.

In the midst of the haunting Kol Nidre melody, I suddenly heard the evocative Muslim call to prayer. It startled me. Had I heard correctly? I opened my eyes to look at Nabil. I realized that Nabil was purposely interweaving the two melodies together. I was so moved I went up to him afterwards to pay my respects. He noticed I had tears in my eyes, and he took my hands in his when I told him how I had recognized the incorporation of the *muezzin* call to prayer within the Kol Nidre melody. I explained how deeply it affected me and many others who were there in the congregation. "We have been agonizing over the seemingly intractable Muslim/Jewish conflict raging in the Holy Land, and suddenly your music was able to accomplish something that has eluded us for decades," I told him. "Not one melody replacing the other, but the two blended together in a harmony elevating them both."

"Thank you, thank you," he repeated, and bowed his head deeply.

So here I was with the same Nabil, many years later, and he was eager and willing to provide the perfect music for *God and Allah Need to Talk*. We agreed on a mutually acceptable fee for the musical rights for the film, quite minimal because of my small bank account, but acceptable because of Nabil's large heart.

The final piece was in place. Irit and Peter and I completed the project within a three-week period. A miracle with nary a minefield in sight.

I felt ready to show the film to the Los Angeles interfaith community. I rented the Laemmle Fairfax theatre for Sunday, September 13, 2003, my birthday, and two days after the second year anniversary of September 11. Nur Amersi, a member of the Ismaili Muslim community who had become a close friend, and my girlfriend, Julie Heifetz, agreed to help me organize the event. They were my ground angels.

With no budget for advertising, we were all amazed at the overwhelming response when word about the screening got out. Rabbi Alan Frehling, who headed the Human Relations Department of Los Angeles, screened the film and said he would wholeheartedly endorse it. Emails were flying back and forth in cyberspace. The phone began ringing off the hook. I received an email from someone in Egypt who had heard about the film from a friend in Tel Aviv, who had written to people in LA, telling them to go to the screening. It soon became clear that all of the four hundred and fifty seats would be filled.

More than thirty religious communities from LA County and beyond sent representatives to the event. The LA Tourist Bureau somehow heard about the event and spontaneously offered a much-needed donation—more evidence of angels at work. Nur's Ismaili community showed up in full force. Adults and youth alike served as volunteers to sell tickets and help usher.

Keynote speakers from the Christian, Muslim, and Jewish community addressed the audience at the premiere, as well as LA County Sheriff Lee Baca and Congresswoman Diane Watson.

Musicians and dancers from Iran, Jordan, Ethiopia, the US, and Israel performed, as well as a troupe of Ismaili teenage dancers. Yuval Ron, an Israeli musician/composer, and two percussionists showed up at the Laemmle Theatre, eager to take part in the event. Even though Yuval was in the middle of a rehearsal—his new concerto was scheduled to debut that same night at a performance of the LA Jewish Philharmonic—in an astonishing show of solidarity he took a break to join us in making a statement about interfaith harmony.

In truth, it was not an event; it was a happening. We were sold out and had to turn away two hundred and fifty people who showed up but couldn't get a seat. As I looked around the packed auditorium, I couldn't help but laugh. "Who ever heard of an interfaith event selling out?" I asked incredulously. A huge ripple of laughter and appreciation echoed around the auditorium.

"What could it all mean?" I asked the audience earnestly. "The truth is," I answered my own question, "the truth is that in our time of fear and confusion we all want to know: where do we go from here?"

I shared the fact that several Muslims had called me on the phone prior to the screening, their voices full of consternation. "The title of your film is very provocative, especially after 9/11," they complained. "If you are going to screen a film showing God and Allah is not one and the same, we don't want to come."

"Don't worry," I reassured them, "I promise my film will show that God and Allah are the same."

As the film concluded, I received a standing ovation. I was caught off guard by the audience's response because, during the screening, like any conscientious filmmaker, I had been concentrating on the blemishes of the film. It had been completed in such haste, with such a low budget, I hadn't had time or money to make color-corrections and there were some outstanding sound problems I hadn't fixed (which I finally did two years later). But at the moment, none of that mattered. The audience rose spontaneously to their feet to acknowledge the message of my film, which demonstrated how interfaith dialogue, community outreach, and even dinner conversation could be channeled to dissolve fear and suspicion and, ultimately, create a path towards true reconciliation.

The final words of the film, white letters on a stark black background, posed the key question of our times:

God/Allah is always talking to us, but are we talking to one another?

Afterwards, in the entrance and foyer of the theatre, in a definitive answer to that lingering question, the audience continued to dialogue, network, sample ethnic treats, make new friends, and sign up for follow-up interfaith activities.

Syed Zafer Abbas, the editor of the *Urdu Times*, came up to me and kissed my hand. "Thank you for showing Muslims as people," he said sincerely. Other individuals surrounded me and offered their thanks for bringing so many different communities together after 9/11, something we all badly needed, they acknowledged gratefully.

The air was teeming with good will and enthusiasm. No one wanted to go home. Eventually the theatre manager had to ask us to leave, although he did so with a gracious smile. People were arriving for the next feature and we had to clear out.

The next year I hired Renée De Palma, another accomplished editor, to make the final corrections. I also added seven crucial minutes of another interfaith Seder to the film to illustrate how the Christian community had become co-organizers with the Muslim and Jewish communities.

After that, *God and Allah Need to Talk* took on a life of its own. I was invited to show the film in Barcelona at the Parliament of the World's Religions Conference, at mosques, churches, synagogues, and universities across America, at the Bangladeshi Embassy in Washington, DC, in Toronto, Canada, and in Monterrey, Mexico, at the Forum's Worldwide Interreligious Encounter.

The concentric circles of interfaith influence were spreading to distant shores.

The surprise of the film is that its message is even more relevant today than when I first made it. People are no longer content to nurse their confusion and fear. Today the interfaith net has spread wide and deep and people are ready to sign-up and volunteer for interreligious activities in larger numbers than anyone could have imagined.

And so, whether God/Allah speaks to us in a still, small voice or in a larger-than-life-size billboard, the important thing to remember is God is hoping we will speak to one another.

Just as we have prayers for God, God has prayers for us.

The billboard sign that changed my life, located on the corner of Sunset and Hollywood Boulevards.

With my premiere co-organizers, Julie Heifetz (l.) and Dr. Nur Amersi (r.).

September 2003 World Premiere of *God and Allah Need to Talk*, held at the Fairfax Laemmle Theatre in Los Angeles.

Addressing the standing-room-only audience at the premiere, I asked incredulously, "Who ever heard of an interfaith event selling out?"

Los Angeles County Sheriff Lee Baca, a well-known supporter of interfaith engagement, speaks at the premiere of my film.

California Congresswoman Diane Watson (second from left) with friends at the premiere.

Volunteers from the Los Angeles Ismaili Muslim community selling tickets.

After-screening meet and greet.

God/Allah is always talking to us, but are we talking to one another?
Endorsed by the Human Relatios Commission, City of Los Angeles

L.A. Premiere of
GOD AND ALLAH NEED TO TALK
A Film for Healing and Reconciliation
Bby Ruth Broyde-Sherone
Aat Laemmle Fairfax Theatre, L.A.

Ruth Broyde-Sharone
Producer/Director/Organizer

L.A. Happenings

"You must set no bonds to your love, just as your heavenly Father sets none for Him". Matthew 5:44-48

You must see this film! To obtain a copy of the film, call (310)837-2294 Or email: RABSHARONE@AOL.COM

Pictorial Report by **Syed Zafar Abbas**

A billboerd at the corner of Sunset and Hollywood inspired the provocative title of a documentary that premiered at the Fairfax Laemamie Theatre, leading off a citywide interfaith event and artistic program of local and international artists, speeches by some renowned interfaith scholars like Jack Miles, Xandra Kayden and Amir Hussain.This colorful, memorable and soul-stirring event was also attended by the Los - Angeles County Sheriff Lee Baca, Ecumenical and Interreligious Officer of Archdioses of L.A. Rt. Rev. Alexi Smith and the President of Copaa Mr.Ahmed - Ali who extended their greetings andheartfelt appreciation to the event organizer, producer and director Ruth Broyde-Sharone. Individuals dedicated to the interfaith dialogue and outreach were recognized & honoured at the event, and interfaith organizations enhanced this opporunity to network and offer the unaffiliated audience members to sign up for future interfaith activities.

Producer/director of the film, and organizer of the event, Ruth Broyde-Sharonr, literally stopped her car when she saw the original billboard "God and Allah talking would be like God talking to himself", Broyde commented during her introductory speech, "but after 9/11 it perfectly sums up how frustrated and fagmented we feel. We even view God as having multiple personalities."Broyde -Sharone , who has been an interfaith activist for more than a decade, said she saw the film as a vehicle for healing and reconciliation. The separation between God and Allah in the film's title underscores how in our minds we have created a separation between the non-Muslim and Muslim communities, when in truth God and Allah are one. "He is always talking to us" she maintains, "but are we talking to one another?" She believes the film demonstrates and encourages " a new consciousness and a new conscientiousness"about transcending stereotypes that religious communities and individuals hold about each other.

The 18 minute documentary, endorsed by the Human Relations Cimmission of the City of L.A., points out the new approach of the Islamic Center of Souther California to welcome individuals of other faiths to celebrate Muslim holidays with them in their Center's mosque. The film also documents a Muslim-Jewish- "Seder of Reconciliation" held during a Passover at Temple Kol Tikvah in Woodland Hills. The brainchild of Rabbi Steven Jacobs and Dr. Nazir Khaja, director of the Islamic Information Services, this Seder brought some 150 participants, primarily jews and Muslims, alongwith some Christian guests, to symbolically reunite Hazrat Ishaq(pbuh) and Hazrat Ismail(pbuh)the estranged sons of Hazrat Ibrahim (pbuh).The intelligent decision of Rabbi Jacobs and Dr. Khaja, of incarporating the universal message of freedom of the Passover Seder, with it's retelling of the Exodus story, provided an immensely inspirative and meaningful environment for interfaith discouse.

The program was embellished by stunningly artisti performance of Mitra Rahbar, a singer/entertainer from Iran, Alula Tzadik, a Beit Israel musician from Ethopia, Nabil Azzam, a Palestinian violinist, musician and composer Stephen Longfellow Fiske, singer Stefani-Valadez, Yuval Ron trio w/Jamie Papish and teenage ethnic dancers.

Urdu Times devotes two full pages to God & Allah premiere.

Taking the Show on the Road:

Monterrey, Mexico.

Green Bay, Wisconsin.

Winston-Salem, North Carolina.

Minefields & Miracles

San Jose, Costa Rica.

Guadalajara, Mexico.

Toronto, Canada

Courage is the price that life exacts for granting peace.
~Amelia Earhart

CHAPTER 15
Willing to Be the Stranger

During the Passover Seder, we say: "Let everyone who is hungry come and eat. Remember to welcome the stranger because you were once strangers in the land of Egypt…"

One of the great lessons I learned on my interfaith journey was actually a variation on the commandment enjoining us to "welcome the stranger."

In most cases, it is not that difficult to welcome a stranger into your own home, into your own environment, where you are comfortable and where you have long-standing alliances, including family and friends. Our forefather, Abraham, was the master host, keeping all flaps of his tent open, north, south, east, and west, day and night, to welcome any strangers passing by. But when I began to enter communities where I had no sense of belonging, where I could easily experience myself as an "outsider," I discovered it is not always easy to "be the stranger."

The path of my film, *God and Allah Need to Talk*, and the independent life it seemed to be leading, now took me into situations in which I often trembled in advance. My support of Israel was unwavering, even though I often found myself criticizing Israel's actions and policies towards the Palestinians. I knew with profound conviction I would not be willing to give up—under any condition—Israel's right to exist, regardless of how compassionate I might be towards establishing a separate state for the Palestinians and for bettering their lives. Israel's existence was non-negotiable for me.

In spite of my political views, could I still have something useful and inspiring to say to a Muslim group, knowing that most of them would not approve of my politics? Would I be comfortable to be the only Jew in support of Israel in a mosque that supported Palestinians and decried Israel's position in the Middle East? I froze at that thought. Would it be possible for me to create a field of unity when I spoke, that could somehow transcend our divergent views and enable them to feel I was a friend?

The work of establishing rapport and trust, and ultimately creating a foundation for friendship that could withstand personal and world politics—this became my immediate challenge, and I have to admit I was not always comfortable in meeting this challenge.

When I am exhorting audiences to the next level of interfaith engagement, I often say I practice and promote "Interfaith Pilates." Invariably I get a great laugh when I use that phrase. I then go on to explain the term I coined. "It is an exercise program for advanced interfaith activities utilizing the same principles as when we do advanced physical exercise."

I then dissect my metaphor. "Pilates, the popular program invented to help people stretch from their core can also apply to interreligious work because, in interfaith engagement, we also have to stretch from our core—not from our extremities."

Next I pose the following question: "How do we know if we have actually exercised properly and gotten the most benefit from our exercise? We know if we don't feel a pinch of discomfort, we actually have not done the exercise properly. It is precisely the discomfort that tells us that we are fulfilling our mission. If we don't sweat, if we don't feel the strain on our muscles, if we don't notice an increased heart rate and a flush on our faces, we haven't really done the work.

"So, what I am encouraging each of you to do in the 'interfaith gym' is to consciously and willingly leave your comfort zone, to stretch in a way that leaves you wondering if you'll make it to the end of the exercise. That, my friends, is 'Interfaith Pilates,' and it has to be undertaken just as seriously as any exercise program you do at the gym.

"I don't want you to go home just feeling warm and fuzzy," I tell my audience. "If I've only managed to achieve that, then I haven't done my work. Now let's lock the doors, and nobody leaves until you've taken on an exercise for yourself that moves you out of your comfort zone." They all laugh. They know I'm not serious, not entirely serious, that is.

I never lock the door, of course, but I do encourage them, as part of my final "call to action," to make a verbal commitment to the person sitting beside them, either a friend or someone they've just met.

"Before you leave this hall, please write down or share one small, profound act you are willing to commit to. And remember," I warn them, "the bar gets higher, and the workout gets more intense as you continue. But that's when the rewards are the greatest as well!"

As I look back over my more than twenty years of interfaith activism, I realize my willingness to invite a stranger into my home was the fun and easy part. But leaving my comfort zone, and taking on the "Pilates Interfaith Stretch" meant I had to be *willing to be the stranger*. That was definitely not an easy task, but I have well-developed interfaith muscles to show for it!

I attended my first Muslim convention in 2005, in Long Beach. I knew my longtime friend, Jack Miles, a Christian, would be a keynoter that evening, and I was confident I would probably see him and also my Sufi friend, John Ishvaradas. However, I also knew I would be one of perhaps only a handful of Jewish individuals in a crowd of several thousand Muslims.

A Christian friend of mine, who didn't know any Muslims personally, was incredulous at my plans. "Aren't you terrified to go there?"

"I'm not afraid," I assured her, "but I'm feeling edgy, because I don't know how they will view me. That's always the hard part, until you are accepted—but that was also true in high school and college, wasn't it?" I reminded her. "You remember how it felt when everyone was invited to a party, and we weren't?" Not belonging, being an outsider—none of those issues were new for me, but not being accepted still troubles me even now as an adult.

A Jewish friend, Cheryl, drove me to the Long Beach convention center, but said she would be leaving early, which meant I would have to find a ride home on my own. I did find a ride, through my Sufi friend, and through Jack Miles. It was with Omar Huda, a Muslim-American originally from Bangladesh, who not only agreed to take me home, but on the way confided in me about a delicate family situation in Bangladesh that was troubling him and his siblings.

When he drove up to my house, we sat and conversed for another forty-five minutes before saying good night. I made several suggestions to Omar about how I thought he might be able to resolve his family dilemma, and he was grateful. A few months later, after he returned from Bangladesh, he called to thank me and to let me know my advice had worked. He also called to invite me to meet his wife and two daughters.

Thus our friendship began, talking about family troubles and family dynamics, not about religious differences. Our friendship continued to flourish at the same time I was discovering that our political views concerning the Israeli/Palestinian conflict were miles apart. Omar had pursued studies in "Abrahamic Religions" for four years at UCLA and began to attend many interfaith events with me. His stand on Israel, as he described it, "is no different from Jews on the left such as Noam Chomsky, Amy Goodman, Amira Haas, Marcy Winograd, and Richard Joseph Goldstone (author of the controversial *Goldstone Report*)."

However, I experienced Omar's criticism of Israel as being too strident, too one-sided, and too far left for my comfort. I acknowledged my principal concern was for Israel's security and Israel's ability to survive the hostility of her neighbors and the UN, and, at the same time, I also supported a two-state solution and Palestinian self-determination.

At times our conversations were extremely thorny and challenging. Sometimes I smarted at Omar's ideas and comments about Israel, and experienced them as not only objectionable but cruel. I told him so. I did not hide my feelings.

"Why do you care so much about Israel?" Omar demanded to know on one occasion when we were discussing the Middle East situation. "For heaven's sake, you're an American Jew!"

I responded with equal vigor. "Omar, considering the history of the Jewish people, I do not want to live in a world in which Israel could no longer exist."

When we would argue, our voices would get louder, and I would feel my ire rising. I even entertained the idea of ending our friendship several times. And yet, I could not, because there was something about what we had created together, his family and me—the human connection—that transcended even politics and religion.

We couldn't help but notice that—politics aside—we truly liked each other on a personal level. His wife and daughters always wanted me to come to family gatherings and, ultimately, our political differences, as sharp and pointy as they might get in our emails, on the phone, and in person, could not dampen our enthusiasm to keep our friendship alive and well.

When their younger daughter, Amberine, a talented scholar and musician, received a citywide scholarship and was invited to the Mayor's office to be honored, the Huda family asked me to come and be a witness. When their elder daughter, Karishma, was formally engaged to her fiancé, Shehriyar, I was invited to their home to be part of an intimate family gathering, and I was privileged to give the couple a blessing in Hebrew.

At the wedding, I was reminded by Zarin, Omar's wife, how much they treasured my friendship. The truth was we had indeed transcended our countries of origin and our religious traditions to become friends in the unified field Rumi so beautifully describes.

"Somewhere beyond the idea of right and wrong, there is a field: I'll meet you there."

Soon my connections to Muslims grew to be communal as well as personal. I was asked by Syed Zafar Abbas, my Pakistani journalist friend, and his co-organizer, Imran Raz, to help them organize a peace march for the Los Angeles Shi'a community during their *Ashura Celebration*. I did not hesitate for a moment. On their behalf, I contacted LA Sheriff Lee Baca, who often appears at public functions that support interfaith engagement, and asked him to address the group. Then I called the Mayor's office and arranged to have a proclamation sent to them, honoring their peace march. I also helped them write a press release about the event. Finally, and most importantly, I agreed to speak to the fifteen hundred Muslims who were going to gather in downtown LA. I was there as a representative of the LA Jewish community, as an interfaith activist and, as Zafar described me when he introduced me, "a friend of the Muslim community."

His description of me was significant since I was the first woman and first Jew to be asked to address their rally.

All of the marchers were wearing black as a sign of mourning for their martyred saint, Hussein ibn Ali, and his family, who were murdered on October 10, 680 A.D. Muslims in many parts of the world gather annually on the holiday of Ashura to honor and memorialize Hussein—the grandson of the Prophet Mohammed and the son of the fourth Caliph Ali—for his courageous fight against corruption and injustice. After Hussein and his family were killed, the subsequent rift between the spiritual leadership of the Household of the Prophet and the temporal power of the later Caliphs became the "longest running revolution in history," a Muslim friend once explained to me.

I remember my heart was pounding when I reached the lectern.

I had donned a headscarf out of respect, and I looked around at the huge crowd of men, women, and children, mostly seated on the ground. *Salaam Aleikum*, I began with the traditional Arab salutation (Peace be upon you).

They responded with the refrain *Walikum As Salaam* (Peace be upon you). Then the audience showered me with a very warm and extended welcome in Urdu, the principal language spoken in Pakistan.

"You have taken your grief and sorrow and perhaps even your anger," I told them, "and transformed them into something noble and inspiring, by organizing a peace march, and emphasizing what we can do together as a community. I honor you for that."

I then acknowledged the presence of my interfaith colleagues who were on the dais with me, Rabbi Steven Jacobs, Nirinjan Singh Khalsa of the LA Sikh Community, and Reverend Rich Bolin, who were all scheduled to speak.

"After all these years and months and days and hours of interfaith activism, my colleagues and I often get up in the morning, look at ourselves in the mirror, and ask ourselves in all honesty: Are we making a difference?"

At that moment, one of the men in the crowd of fifteen hundred shouted out loudly, in response to my question. "You are making a difference! You are!" Many of the others cheered in unison.

His response was manna for me.

As I concluded my speech, I told the audience, "There are people here today who are asking themselves: what can we do to make a difference? When the peace rally is over, please see me if you want to join an interfaith dialogue group. I will help you find one in your neighborhood, or I will help you start one of your own. And if you work with youth, and you want to teach them about interfaith principles and help them meet other young people from other religions, please see me afterwards and I'll find a way to help you."

It worked. Several people approached me after my talk including a woman who wanted to know where to find a women's dialogue group, a man who agreed to start his own interfaith group, and a young Muslim youth leader who participated in a city wide interfaith event my local interfaith group organized several months later. The youth leader came to our day-long event called "the Challenge of Respect," featuring twenty-seven workshops, and he brought with him five Muslim youngsters who were ready to experience "Interfaith Pilates."

The ultimate proof, as they say, is in the pudding, or in this case, in the letter I received from my friend Omar.

I had given Omar a book about Rabindranath Tagore, knowing full well Tagore was his favorite poet and all-around hero. A Bengali renaissance poet from British Raj Bengal, India, who excelled in philosophy, art, music, poetry, and humanity, Tagore was the first non-European recipient of a Nobel Prize in Literature in 1913.

The letter of thanks I received from Omar was a testimonial not only to our friendship, but to the rich reward I reaped because I was willing to be a stranger.

He has graciously given me permission to include it in this book.

Dear Ruth:

Gitanjali—'Songs of offering'—is a book I should have given you—a friend found and bound in the context of our respective religious affinity. Instead, by some divine ploy (that we rarely comprehend), you picked it up and gifted it to me!

As I opened the cellophane wrapped book today, I wondered what that "ploy" might have been. Then it hit me. We met some years ago at the Annual MPAC (Muslim Public Affairs Council) Dinner—a gathering of American Muslims to establish their rights in America. But YOU were there on "my turf"!! Our friendship grew and deepened—to the extent that my wife and daughters embraced you as one of "us"! Again, you have been there on "my turf."

But our friendship has remained within the restraints of our "presumed" identities—you a Jew and I a Muslim…

We would have continued in that state had it not been for yet another mysterious entry! I almost fell when you invited me to a convention of Rabindranath Tagore in January. Excitedly I shared with you how it was Tagore who brought me into faith as I read him in my POW cell in 1971 in Pakistan.

I could not attend the Tagore convention with you because I was heading to London to meet our first grandchild. But you attended—and even remembered to get me the book of Tagore's compilation that earned him the Nobel Prize in 1913.

Agnostic until I read Tagore, the songs and poems listed in this book—(translated by the poet himself)—were the ones that changed my thoughts, and heart forever! I of course read (and poured over the "songs") in Bengali, the language he wrote them in. I never read the English translations—why should I? I had tasted the real music—his "offerings" to the Creator. How did they impact me? The cover of the book has a note by one Paul Nash thus: "I find my confused thoughts and feelings expressed so clearly and so beautifully that I have sometimes laughed for joy, sometimes tears come … I would read Gitanjali as I would read the Bible, for comfort and for strength."

For me, much more—the God I worship I find most deeply in Tagore's bows of surrender -penned in the book you gave me. Ruth, this time you have indeed come to the innermost part of "my turf." Thank you.

Love, Omar

With Karishma and Shehriyar at their wedding in LA.

With Omar Huda and his daughter, Karishma, at her baby shower.

Bonding with Zain, Omar's grandson, in London.

I was honored to address more than 1,500 participants at a Muslim Peace Rally in Downtown LA, 2007.

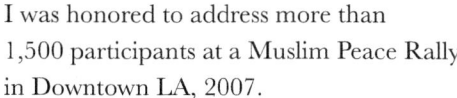

Speakers at the Lomita Mosque in South Bay, California, 2006. (L. to r.) Dr. Muzammil Siddiqi, Kalan Brunick, and me; behind us is the mosque's interfaith event organizer, Dr. Yahyaa Jordan.

With (l.) Ayisha R. Jeffries from the African American Islamic Institute, and (r.) Nogi Imoukhuede, Women Rights Watch, Nigeria at the WISE Conference for Muslim Women, held in New York City in 2006.

The structure of world peace cannot be the work of one man or one party or one nation. It must be a peace which rests on the cooperative effort of the whole world.

~Franklin Delano Roosevelt

CHAPTER 16
A Taste of Interfaith Paradise

What would the world look like if we lived together in peace?

What would it taste like? What would it smell like? What would it sound like? What would it feel like to the touch?

Is there anything that we have already experienced in our own life that could give us a hint of how the world would look and feel, taste and smell, if we could live together in peace?

I had a chance to satisfy all my senses in June of 2004, when I attended the largest interfaith global conference in the world, convened by the Council for a Parliament of the World's Religions. I hadn't known about the work of the Parliament until a friend of mine sent me an email suggesting I submit my film *God and Allah Need to Talk* as a potential program I could present in Barcelona.

Chicago, 1893

After researching the Parliament online, I discovered that the very first Parliament held in September of 1893, took place in my hometown, Chicago, on the shores of Lake Michigan. It was held in conjunction with the Columbian Exposition of the World's Fair which lasted for about six months, from spring into the early fall of 1893.

The Parliament event marked the first time religious leaders of the East were invited to join with their counterparts in the West for interfaith exchange. Great excitement was generated in the city and at the fair when religious dignitaries descended on Chicago from all around the world. From accounts subsequently published, it was lauded as a singular, unforgettable event, one that opened the doors to new possibilities for international exchange and, more specifically, for the religions of the East and West to engage. The opening day of the conference was September 11, 1893. When I mention that fact to audiences, most people gasp. They recognize the strange irony of that September 11 date—what it meant then and what it means today.

One of the leading figures of the first Parliament was Paul Carus, an American scholar and editor originally from Germany, who had corresponded with and published the works of leaders in the fields of mathematics, philosophy, world religions, and related disciplines. He was invited to present a paper called "Science: A Religious Revelation" which affirmed the connection between science and religion. When he wrote about the event, he could barely contain his enthusiasm:

> *The Parliament of Religions is undoubtedly the most noteworthy event of modern times. What are the World's Fair and its magnificent splendor in comparison with it?...It is evident that from its date we shall have to begin a new era in the evolution of man's religious life...Whether or not the Parliament of Religions be repeated, whether or not its work be continued, the fact remains that this congress at Chicago will exert a lasting influence upon the religious intelligence of mankind. It has stirred the spirits, stimulated mental growth, and given direction to man's further evolution. It is by no means an agnostic movement, for it is carried on the wings of a religious faith and positive certainty.*

Following the Parliament, Carus directed his energies towards building awareness and understanding of Eastern philosophies and religions in the United States. He gathered massive information about the various Buddhist traditions and a year later wrote *The Gospel of Buddha* to help Christians understand Buddhist philosophy.

Not only was the 1893 Parliament a landmark for the East-West religious encounter, but it also forged the way for women's rights, a significant fact not always emphasized in the historical account. New York-born Augusta Jane Chapin, also a Parliament organizer, was known as a champion of women's rights. The second woman to be ordained as a Universalist minister in America, she was the only woman to present a session at the Parliament, and she was the first woman ever to receive an honorary Doctor of Divinity degree, which was presented to her at the Chicago World's Fair.

In her opening address, she said:

> *My memory runs easily back to the time when, in all the modern world, there was not one well equipped college or university open to women students, and when, in all*

A Taste of Interfaith Paradise

> *the modern world, no woman had been ordained, or even acknowledged, as a preacher outside the denomination of Friends.*

In short, interfaith engagement and women's rights were inextricably intertwined in 1893, a trend that continues even more powerfully today.

Rev. John Henry Barrows, one of the main organizers, wrote a glowing description of the opening ceremony:

> *More than four thousand people had gathered in the Hall of Columbus, when at ten o'clock a dozen of representatives from different faiths marched into the hall hand in hand. At the same time, the Columbian Liberty bell in the Court of Honor tolled ten times, honoring the ten great world religions—Confucianism, Taoism, Shintoism, Hinduism, Buddhism, Jainism, Zoroastrianism, Judaism, Christianity, and Islam.*

One of the stars of the conference turned out to be Swami Vivekananda, 32, a member of the Ramakrishna Order in India, who was urged by his disciples to participate.

He made a great splash upon his arrival, with his striking appearance, dress, and manner of speech. The story goes that Vivekananda crossed the ocean and, via Vancouver, landed in Chicago more than a month before the Parliament was officially scheduled to open. Upon arriving he was informed no one would be admitted as a delegate without the proper references and the deadline for applying for official papers had expired. This unexpected development, "almost broke the Swami's spirit," as described in *The Life of Swami Vivekananda*, written by his Eastern and Western disciples,

> *To have come all the way from India for nothing. It was too much! He also discovered that he should have come as a representative of some recognized organization. He wondered why he had been so foolish as to have listened to his ingenuous and rhapsodical followers in Madras, who were ignorant of the formalities involved in becoming a delegate ... They thought Vivekananda had only to appear, and he would be given his chance.*

But even if he were to wait and attend as a spectator and not a delegate, the Swami realized he did not have enough money to cover his expenses. The book account says he had no idea of the value of money and "was cheated right and left wherever he went."

Fortunately, he recalled meeting Miss Kate Sanborn on the train from Vancouver. Miss Sanborn had extended an invitation to him to visit her in Boston, which he was told was the "Athens of America" and, most important for his situation, much less expensive than Chicago.

He took a train to Boston and was well received by Miss Sanborn, a lecturer and author of note, who also introduced him to her cousin, Professor John Henry Wright, a professor of Greek History at Harvard. Although Swami Vivekananda had given up all hope of speaking at the Parliament of Religions, Professor Wright was so deeply impressed with the Swami he insisted he represent Hinduism at that important gathering, saying, "This is the only way you can be introduced to the nation at large."

When the Swami demurred, explaining he had no credentials, Professor Wright exclaimed, "To ask you, Swami, for credentials is like asking the sun to state its right to shine."

The professor assured the Swami he would arrange for his credentials and see to it he had a place as a delegate. The professor kept his word, arranged for letters of introduction, and even gave the Swami train fare to Chicago.

His adventures continued. After spending three weeks on the East Coast, after having delivered numerous lectures and having mingled with the intelligentsia and Transcendentalists of Boston, Swami Vivekananda, newly recognized for his brilliant mind and radiant personality, returned to Chicago where no one knew him. In fact, in Chicago many found his dress and manner suspicious. At the Chicago train station, he discovered he had lost the address of the person who was supposed to host him. He was in the area where many Germans lived and no one could understand him. "Night was coming on. He was lost and knew not what to do," his disciples wrote. "At length, he lay down in a huge empty box in the railway yards."

How ironic that after sleeping in an empty box, "two days later he was to shake America with his address at the Parliament," the narrative continues. "But now, so destiny decided, he had to sleep like some outcast—unknown, unaided, and despised—or perhaps, more truly, like some *sannayasi* (sage) in his own land, sleeping where the evening found him."

The next day, the Swami arose early, put on his colorful turban, and followed the scent of fresh water to Lake Shore Drive, "the most fashionable residential avenue in the city, where millionaires and merchant-princes dwelt. He was extremely hungry and, like the true *sannayasi* that he was, commenced begging from house to house, asking for food and for directions to the offices of the Parliament Committee."

As luck—or destiny—would have it, one of the women who answered the door to the begging Swami, realized he must be one of the delegates to the Parliament. Mrs. George W. Hale fed him and made sure he was well cared for before she took him to the site of the Parliament.

His speech to the Parliament was described in vivid detail:

> *His face glowed like fire. He eyes surveyed in a sweep the huge assembly before him. The whole audience grew intent, and then he addressed his audience as "Sisters and Brothers of America." And with that, before he had uttered another word, the whole Parliament was caught up in a great wave of enthusiasm. Hundreds rose to their feet with shouts*

of applause. The Parliament had gone mad; everyone was cheering, cheering, cheering! The Swami was bewildered. For full two minutes he attempted to speak, but the wild enthusiasm of the audience prevented it.

When silence was restored, the account continues, he quoted two evocative passages from Hindu scriptures:

As the different streams having their sources in different places all mingle their water in the sea, so, O Lord, the different paths which men take, through different tendencies, various though they may appear, crooked or straight, all lead to Thee.

Swami Vivekananda's words at that first Parliament have been saved, savored, and memorized by many, because in retrospect his words appear to have been prophetic as well as historic.

Here are the concluding lines of Vivekananda's address:

Sectarianism, bigotry, and its horrible descendant, fanaticism, have long possessed this beautiful Earth. They have filled the earth with violence, drenched it often with human blood, destroyed civilization, and sent whole nations to despair. Had it not been for these horrible demons, human society would be far more advanced than it is now. But their time is come; and I fervently hope that the bell that tolled this morning in honor of this convention may be the death-knell of all fanaticism, of all persecutions with the sword or with the pen, and of all uncharitable feelings between persons wending their way to the same goal.

And then something inexplicable happened. Nothing. After that seemingly momentous first Parliament gathering in 1893, nothing happened for another one hundred years. One could ask, "How is that possible?" After four thousand people turned out for the electrifying closing ceremony, one would have thought there would have been sufficient momentum to sustain a worldwide interfaith movement. We do not know exactly why no future events were planned, but what we do know is one hundred years later, people from the Vedanta society in Chicago decided it was time to celebrate the centenary anniversary of that historic event.

Chicago, 1993

The second Parliament of the World's Religions was held in Chicago in 1993. As the organizers later remarked, "people seemed to come out of the woodwork." Seven thousand people arrived from every part of the world, representing every religion. The energy and financing necessary to create the 1993 gathering convinced the organizers they would need another five or six years to repeat it.

Dr Hans Küng, a well-known Swiss Theologian, wrote the first draft of *Towards a Global Ethic: An Initial Declaration*, which was signed by religious and spiritual leaders from around the world at the 1993 Parliament. Kung's emphasis on the connection between peace and interreligious dialogue has become one of the most recognized quotes in the interfaith community worldwide.

> *There will be no peace among the nations without peace among the religions. There will be no peace among the religions without dialogue among the religions.*

Cape Town, 1999

The second modern Parliament was held in Cape Town in 1999. Nelson Mandela, South Africa's president, released from prison in 1990 after twenty-eight years of incarceration, was a featured keynote speaker. Also in attendance was His Holiness, the 14th Dalai Lama. Some eight thousand people attended.

The Executive Director of the Parliament, Reverend Dirk Ficca, remembers that conference as a heady time and an inspiring gathering. In assessing the overall success of the conference, he also realized that, in the future, more work would have to be done on the front end to make sure the work of the Parliament could contribute to lasting positive developments in the host country after the Parliament was over.

Barcelona, 2004

Those lessons were incorporated into the next major Parliament, held in Barcelona in 2004. The city of Barcelona had decided to organize a major cultural, economical, and religious Forum that would run for three weeks. The Parliament was one segment of the Universal Forum of Cultures, and proved to be enormously successful and popular. This time the influence of the conference continued to reverberate in Barcelona and other cities across Spain even after the conference concluded.

To my delight, I was informed I was one of three hundred fifty individuals, chosen from among fifteen hundred potential candidates, to present a program in Barcelona. I would be able to screen *God & Allah Need to Talk* and present an interactive interfaith program similar to the ones I had taken to many university campuses in the United States, but this time, I would have an opportunity to address a world forum.

My excitement at the prospect of going to the Barcelona Parliament was contagious. Three friends decided to join me: Thomas Hedberg and Rebecca Tobias, interfaith colleagues of mine, and Stefani Valdez, an extremely talented musician and singer who had agreed to perform for my workshop.

We all instinctively understood the importance of the Parliament's work in the world, and we began to brainstorm to figure out how to finance the trip. We decided to take advantage of our frequent flyer miles, and to apply for "home stay" offered by the Parliament. Rebecca and I were invited to stay with an extremely hospitable Spanish widow; Stefani stayed with a local musician friend of hers; and Thomas found lodging in a Catholic monastery.

We arrived in Barcelona to discover we would be sharing our Parliament experience with more than nine thousand people from eighty-five countries. People from around the world continued to arrive daily in their colorful native dress, representing every religion I had heard of—and some religions I had never heard of—speaking a symphony of languages. A feeling of euphoria took over.

This is what Paradise would look like and taste like, I decided: people of good will on a pilgrimage of discovery, to greet and meet one another with respect, curiosity, and an openness to observe and share religious practices, to discuss our differences without making excuses for having differences, and to confront the most urgent problems of the globe with the understanding that these were collective problems that deserved collective solutions.

The menu of daily activities of spiritual practices, seminars, workshops, lectures, panel discussions, and plenaries was so appetizing, I often found myself torn between five offerings. Sometimes I had such a hard time deciding, I went nowhere, and then lamented about the workshops I missed. I found myself wishing the conference would never end. Once you've tasted Paradise, why would you want to leave?

It wasn't all perfection. Challenging issues were discussed in panels and seminars, with many scholars, clergy and laypeople reflecting on the cause of violence in religion, on the brewing ecological crisis, on national debt, the worldwide refugee problem, and many other issues of the day.

A special two-day seminar had been created to discuss innovative peace practices being implemented by courageous Israeli and Palestinian peace workers in Jerusalem, as they confronted what seemed to be an intractable political issue. Sufi sheikhs, rabbis, imams, male and female peacebuilders all, many of whom I knew and held in great esteem, were invited to hold heart-to-heart talks about their struggle to transform their world-at-war. People from around the world, not personally involved in the struggle, but yearning to help find an equitable solution for the Holy Land, sat in the room with the Middle Eastern peacemakers, hour after hour. It was obvious they were contemplating deeply how they themselves could help to broker peace. By the end of the seminar they had a clearer idea about the conflict, but unfortunately they were no closer to coming up with a solution.

Jane Goodall, a heroine of the environmental movement, spoke to a standing-room-only audience, and passionately reviewed and dissected the future of our ecological challenges. No one wanted her to leave the room when her talk was over. Reconciling with the Indigenous populations of the world was another topic she underscored, but it was clear the Indigenous populations of the world were not there to take an active part in the discussion. (Full representation of Indigenous groups would have to wait until the next Parliament in Melbourne held five years later.)

In one of the daily plenary sessions, Ammaji, known as "the hugging mother," was invited to give the keynote speech. Suddenly in the middle of her talk, the simultaneous translation to Spanish, Catalan, and English failed. The teleprompter froze, but no one seemed to mind. I realized that her talk in her native Malayalam was not what people were responding to. It was her presence and her compassion which poured out into the audience like a stream of fragrant flowers, needing no translation. That night Ammaji continued to give her world-famous hugs. Many spent the entire night pressing tightly against one another, waiting to reach her transformative embrace.

The climax of the Barcelona Parliament was the musical concert held outside of the famous Gaudi-designed church, La Familia Sagrada, which featured artistic performances and religious observances from all over the world. It was an audio-visual feast that even now, seven years later, is still hard to describe. The variety and beauty of the evening's events, which lasted for three hours, included Native American invocations, operatic arias from Italy, Taiko drummers from Japan, whirling dervishes from Turkey, Hindu monks from India, dancers from China, and a finale orchestrated by a contemporary religious rock group from Israel that brought over six thousand people to their feet. Long into the night the exhilarated crowd continued to applaud and marvel as they were absorbed into the glorious crescendo of music, religious devotion, dancing, and interfaith celebration in the streets of Barcelona.

A cornucopia of transcendent and profound experiences enveloped us daily. However, one aspect of the Barcelona Parliament proved to be the most visceral and tactile experience of all, an experience that was shared and described in detail by almost everyone I interviewed who attended the Barcelona Parliament.

The Sikh community of Birmingham, England, headed by Bhai Sahib Mohinder Singh, decided they wanted to demonstrate one of their most sacred religious principles: hospitality and feeding people. They rented a large area, the size of an airplane hanger,

A Taste of Interfaith Paradise

walking distance from the Parliament venue, laid out red carpeting, set up a kitchen, and a Sikh place to worship, and erected two large circus tents to house their "langar." (*Langar* is the term used in the Sikh religion for free food, served in a *Gurdwara*, a place of worship.)

For six days, twice a day, the Sikhs served savory vegetarian meals for four to five thousand people at the Barcelona Parliament. A story about the Sikhs soon began to circulate that captivated all of us, and pointed to the exponential power of generosity.

At the very start of the conference the Sikh participants from Birmingham had located a local vegetable store near the Forum and, for the first three days, they bought out the entire stock of produce. The owner was gratified to sell all of his merchandise, but he was puzzled about the huge quantities they were buying all at once. On the fourth day when the Sikhs arrived to make their purchases, they were told by the merchant they could no longer purchase anything. Stunned, they asked him to explain.

"Because from now on till the end of the conference," he is reported to have replied, "I am giving you all of my vegetables. I will not accept any more money from you. I have learned how you are feeding thousands of people daily as a gift, so this will be my gift to you."

We told and retold the story as we arrived daily to be fed. We came in large, unwieldy, talkative and hungry groups. They calmed us down by asking us to remove our shoes, wash our hands, and cover our hair with white handkerchiefs. We were then invited to sit cross-legged on the ruby-colored carpet as, one after another, shift after shift, the Sikh volunteers brought out huge containers of delicious, vegetarian food, enough to feed everyone who had come or might come.

At one of these dinners I sat next to my friend and mentor, Rabbi David Rosen from Jerusalem. A vegetarian for most of his adult life, Rabbi David was savoring the vegetarian fare with great enthusiasm. We both looked around in amazement at the landscape of humanity. "So this is what heaven could be like," I fantasized out loud. Rabbi David smiled broadly and replied, "Vegetarian heaven, for sure."

When I returned home to Los Angeles, I attempted to convey to my friends "the breadth and depth and height" of my Barcelona experience. I longed to share the interfaith discoveries I had made, the musical harmonies I had heard, the new ideas I had encountered, the friendships I had developed, the culinary delicacies I had sampled. My words always seemed inadequate until I understood there was only one way to sum it all up: I had witnessed the miracle of Interfaith Paradise.

Minefields & Miracles

1893 Chicago Parliament of the World's Religions

(photos courtesy of the Parliament of the World's Religions: www.parliamentofreligions.org)

Overlooking the site of the Columbian Exposition.

Group photo of the delegates to the first Parliament.

Cover of the 1893 Parliament Program.

Swami Vivekananda, the "star" of the 1893 Parliament.

Paul Carus, scholar and organizer of the first Parliament.

Chapin Augusta Jane Chapin, Parliament organizer and the only woman presenter.

A Taste of Interfaith Paradise

1893 Chicago Parliament Participants
(Photos courtesy of the Parliament of the World's Religions)

1893 Chicago Parliament Participants
(Photos courtesy of the Parliament of the World's Religions)

A Taste of Interfaith Paradise

1993 Chicago Parliament Participants
(Photos courtesy of the Parliament of the World's Religions)

Dr. Hans Küng, presented his first draft of *Towards a Global Ethic* at the 1993 Chicago Parliament.

Minefields & Miracles

1999 Cape Town, South Africa Parliament Participants
(Photos courtesy of the Parliament of the World's Religions)

A Taste of Interfaith Paradise

2004 Barcelona, Spain Parliament

(Photos courtesy of the Parliament of the World's Religions)

Buddhists create a mandala out of colored sand particles.

Sikhs serving Parliament participants.

Keynoters at the 2004 Barcelona Parliament.

Ammaji, "the Hugging Mother," addresses participants.

Keynoter Raimon Pannikar, the great 20th century scholar and expert in inter-religious dialogue.

Jane Goodall addressing the future of global ecological challenges.

Rabbi David Rosen greets a Muslim colleague.

2004 Barcelona, Spain Parliament

(Photos courtesy of the Parliament of the World's Religions)

Presenting "God & Allah" Workshop.

Music Festival outside of Gaudi's famous church known as "La Familia Sagrada."

Whirling dervish from Turkey.

Buddhists chanting.

Traditional Indian dancer and Taiko drummers.

*It isn't enough to talk about peace. One must believe in it.
And it isn't enough to believe in it. One must work at it.*

~Eleanor Roosevelt

CHAPTER 17
Think Globally, Act Locally

After Barcelona I was reinvigorated. I had experienced a "high" from sampling the global possibilities for increasing interfaith engagement. It became clear, however, that my local involvement would become more critical. Even though I was still traveling extensively, presenting my *God and Allah* program in different venues across the country, I also became more involved with local interfaith groups. Think globally, act locally, I decided, was a perfect motto for interfaith consciousness-raising.

I joined two existing groups in Los Angeles, both in my neighborhood. One, in existence for about a year, was a group specifically dedicated to dialogue between Muslim and Jewish women. I'll share more about that later.

I also helped to form a third group, primarily composed of Parliament alumni from the Los Angeles region. Imbued with the spirit of our global experience in Barcelona and from earlier Parliaments, it seemed almost inevitable we would gather together to relive our "taste of Paradise." In the process our enthusiasm attracted many more people who aspired to be part of the Parliament community.

Like the elders in all religious communities, we told our stories in great detail to our "uninitiated" tribe members, reliving the narrative of our experiences in Barcelona, going over each aspect of the adventure with relish. We regaled our audiences with details of the Sikh hospitality and their non-ending buckets of lovingly-prepared vegetarian food. We described the dazzling array of seminars and panel discussions and quoted the exciting keynote speakers and diverse religious dignitaries. We enumerated details of the chanting sessions, meditations, and religious services, the lunchtime film screenings and musical performances and, of course, the joy of making new friends from distant and exotic lands.

We also had a reservoir of stories recalling the beauty of the city of Barcelona, especially the charm of Gaudi's park with its intricate, colorful ceramic benches and stone sculptures. I recall vividly their carved profiles jutting out in stark relief against the cool, shadowed arbors where we walked, often in silence. We also recalled the passionate flamenco guitarists dotting the landscape like native fauna and flora. Ah, the memories...

Of course, as expected in any good campfire story, there needed to be an element of danger begging to be recounted. Several of our group had been robbed in Barcelona, and we all knew at least three to four other people who attended the conference from other parts of the world whose belongings had been literally spirited away under their own eyes. Thomas would describe in detail how he had been pick-pocketed in the subway by a cunning thief who actually stole his money and credit cards from the knee pocket of his cargo pants. It was a "one-two operation," he would elaborate, relishing the details as only one who has been robbed can do. "One person jostled me," Thomas recounted, "to draw my attention away just as I was exiting the train, while the second person then helped himself to my money. By the time I realized what had happened," Thomas admitted, "the doors of the train had closed and they were gone and so was my money!"

Our stories were told and retold, until it became clear it was time to create new, positive stories in our own city, stories for the next generation of interfaith activists. We began to draw a wider net and soon we had a steady group of fifteen. We recognized that we shared a keen desire to participate in the energy centers of the interfaith world, and Los Angeles was certainly one of them.

It was fascinating to research the makeup of our Parliament group because of what it implies about emerging interfaith communities in the U.S. and around the world as well, I suspect.

A few of us in our local Parliament group, Jeff, Richard, John, Jasmine, and I, are still intimately connected to our birth religions. Richard, raised Christian, is a minister of the African Methodist Episcopal (AME) Church. Jasmine is a third generation Christian Scientist. Jeff, who was ordained as a minister in the United Church of Christ in 1968, is still a Pastor forty-three years later. (He was introduced to Hinduism through his wife, Sharon. Although Sharon was originally ordained as a minister in the same UCC church, her spiritual quest "led her Eastward," as Jeff describes it, when she joined a local Hindu spiritual community. Her guru, Sri Vijayeswari Devi, lives in India.)

Joseph, a professor of philosophy and religion and a noted Gandhi scholar, was raised Catholic in India, a primarily Hindu country. He sees himself, like his mentor Raimon Panikkar, as a Hindu-Buddhist-Catholic and, as he puts it, he considers "denominational affiliation in our pluralistic age to be fluid." A long-time Parliament aficionado who attended the Barcelona Parliament in 2004 and the Melbourne Parliament of 2009, Joseph has also served on the Parliament's Board of Trustees.

Noor-Malika was raised Christian in the Midwest. She embraced Islam and also Sufi practice thirty years ago. Formerly married to a Buddhist, they had two children, one who now practices Taoism, and the other who follows Native American customs. "As you can see," she says with a Cheshire cat smile and twinkling eyes, "we are an interfaith family to the core."

Sura, a teacher and leader in our local Hare Krishna community, was born to a Jewish family, studied in an Orthodox synagogue, and later took up Hindu practice in 1973. He is the founder of the Temple Bhajan Band, a Hare Krishna group that plays sacred music in many venues around the country. He is considered an expert by his community in both teaching and reading the Vedic texts in the original Sanskrit. "Of course, you're an expert," I like to tease him, "because after learning ancient Hebrew and memorizing biblical texts, what's the big deal to learn Sanskrit?" Sura assures me he has never lost his ability to tell great Jewish jokes.

SimranKaur was raised in a non-religious environment by a non-practicing French Jewish mother whose father died in Auschwitz during World War II, and a non-religious German Father whose parents were Protestant. Raised free of any religious background or traditions, SimranKaur says her parents taught her "to love and respect all human beings." When she encountered the Sikh community and realized how deeply she resonated with their teachings, she formally adopted the Sikh way of life.

Our resident Swami, Shiva, a monk and long-time devotee of the spiritual path, was born into a Christian family. "I found fulfillment and a home in the local Vedanta Society when I was twenty-five years old, fifty-six years ago."

Laura, born in American Samoa, was raised and is active in the Church of Jesus Christ of Latter-Day Saints (Mormon). She still maintains strong ties to the spiritual practices of her Indigenous culture and her Pacific Island people.

Thomas served as a missionary and a Catholic priest for over twenty-five years, but at a later time in his life, he chose to leave his position as a clergyman. He became a psychologist, spiritual director and family therapist, and then co-founded the Center for Sacred Psychology with Betsy Caprio, who later became his wife.

I recall a humorous situation involving Thomas that occurred at one of our interfaith functions. A woman whom he had just met asked him what religion he practiced. Thomas, enjoying the opportunity to be a renegade, offered this in response, "I'm a Christian-Jewish-Muslim-Sufi-Hindu-Buddhist-Agnostic by practice and choice."

"That must be very confusing," the woman said to him with a pained look on her face. Thomas, not missing a beat, replied with an enormous grin, "Oh, I'm sorry you're confused. Let me explain it to you…"

Clearly, almost everyone in our group has had experience with multiple religious traditions before becoming interfaith activists. Shayna, raised as a Jew, became an interfaith minister several years ago and her husband, Eli, a musician and composer, was raised as a nondenominational Christian, but left Christianity when he was fifteen, and then converted to Judaism thirty-four years ago.

Which brings us to the "C" word: Conversion. A potential minefield, to be sure.

I find the issue of conversion is one that surfaces often when discussing interfaith activity with people who are not involved in the interreligious movement. Originally, the word interfaith was used to describe a marriage between two people of different faiths. Later, like the evolving meaning of the word "ecumenical"—which was initially a description of intra-faith activity among Christians—interfaith became a word to describe the dialogue and face-to-face experience among people of diverse religions.

While visiting a church in Los Angeles one day, I was introduced to a young Jewish man whose last name was Cohen. He told me he had accepted Jesus as his Savior. I could tell he was hoping I would consider following his example at the end of his testimonial or perhaps by the end of the Church service. Faced with an open invitation to convert, I didn't panic. It wasn't the first time a Christian had lobbied for my Jewish soul, and it definitely would not be the last.

Now, after more than twenty years in the trenches, I can honestly say I have never encountered individuals devoted to the interfaith movement who proselytize. What I notice is that all of us are primarily interested in learning about other religions and, in the process, we often discover where we are weak in verbalizing the tenets and practices of our own religion. We discover we may even need a refresher course for ourselves!

British born Reverend Marcus Braybrooke, Director of the World Congress of Faiths (WCF) and a prolific author, is considered by many to be one of the most knowledgeable and influential men in the interfaith movement. In his book *Pilgrimage of Hope*, he outlines the major challenges of interfaith dialogue:

> *There are various levels of dialogue and it is a process of growth. An initial requirement is an openness to and acceptance of the other. It takes time to build trust and to deepen relationships. This is why some continuity in a dialogue group is helpful and why patience and time are necessary – all of which are particularly difficult to ensure at an international level. Too easily, we find ourselves imposing our presuppositions on the conversation. Christians, for example, often assume that Muslims really adopt a critical attitude to the Qur'an similar to that common amongst Christians in their reading of the Bible. We have to learn to enter another world that may seem alien and which has different presuppositions. We have to allow our deepest convictions to be questioned...*

When asked about the same subject, Reverend Dirk Ficca, a Presbyterian minister and the Executive Director of the Parliament of the World's Religions for the last 12 years, shared his personal observation.

"In all of the years I have been doing this work, in all of the interfaith activities we have convened and sponsored, I have never heard of anyone converting to another religion because of their involvement with the Parliament. On the contrary," Dirk emphasized, "I have found that people who are genuinely committed to an interfaith path tend to delve more profoundly into their own spiritual tradition, to educate themselves more thoroughly about their own religious principles and practices, and to make themselves more accountable for accurately representing their religion to the world."

For anyone reading this book who might be worried that people in the interfaith community will try to convert you, please be reassured it is not so. That is not on our agenda. On the contrary, we appreciate the variety and beauty of the many religious practices we have encountered on our journeys.

However, I believe keeping an open mind is absolutely essential for some of the minefields you might encounter as you learn about your new friends' religions, which brings me to the story of the prayer shawl, and what might have turned into an interfaith explosion. . .

Thomas, the former Catholic priest whom I had asked to help facilitate my interfaith presentation in Barcelona, was also one of the core group formed in Los Angeles to support the Parliament. Although Thomas often acknowledged being raised in an anti-Semitic environment, he would describe how he was transformed in his connection to Judaism primarily through his mentor, Dr. Arthur Lerner, a Jewish clinical psychologist. Thomas became enamored of Jewish wisdom and teachings, specifically through the writings of Maimonides, Martin Buber, and Elie Wiesel. He also acknowledged being profoundly affected by the writings of Anne Frank. After I got to know him, Thomas developed an endearing habit of saying goodbye to me on the phone in Yiddish. *Zei Gezunt*, (be well and healthy) he would always sign off.

Thomas would often tell me he considered me the group's "rabbi." I accepted that as a true compliment because he knew I took my Judaism seriously, and that I had even considered becoming a rabbi. He also knew studying Torah was one of my chief pleasures.

At one of our group's weekend retreats, unbeknownst to me, Thomas in his role as our interfaith chaplain had arranged a surprise for me. On our first communal night, after I had lit and blessed the Sabbath candles, he stood up as the group's representative and held out an elegant white, black, and gold striped bag.

"Ruth, you are our co-chair and our honorary rabbi," he announced, "and I would like to give you this prayer shawl as a token of our esteem and gratitude to you and in recognition for what you bring to our group from the Jewish tradition."

He then ceremoniously unzipped the bag and produced a beautiful *tallit*, a prayer shawl with fringes many Jews use to wrap around themselves when they pray. Thomas then took the *tallit* and reverentially wrapped it around me. The entire group applauded.

I felt profoundly touched by the gesture. I hugged the *tallit* around my head and shoulders, and thanked Thomas and the entire group. I told them I would be proud to wear it at my synagogue the following Saturday for the Sabbath service.

Then I folded the *tallit* neatly and replaced it in the bag. I noticed it had a decorative Menorah (a seven-branch candelabra) and a Star of David embroidered in gold. I zipped it up, and put it in my tote bag, looking forward to the moment I would envelop myself in it, knowing it was a symbol of gratitude and respect from my interfaith colleagues.

On Saturday I brought my new *tallit* to the synagogue. I said the Hebrew prayer ("Thank you, God, for giving us the commandment to wrap ourselves with this fringed shawl"), kissed the *tallit*, and placed it around my shoulders. I was admiring the gold stripes in the pattern and feeling the warmth of the fabric and my colleagues when I suddenly noticed there was some writing on the corners of the shawl.

The first corner had a quote in English from Malachi, Chapter 4: verse 2:

> *But to you who fear my name, the Sun of Righteousness shall arise with healing in*
> *His wings.*

I did not recognize the quote. I then looked at the second corner of the left hand side and found a quote from the New Testament, from Matthew, Chapter 14:36:

> *And they desired of Him that they might only touch the hem of His garment, and as*
> *many as touched it were made well.*

I was beginning to feel very uneasy. I reached out to examine the other two corners, dangling from my shoulders on the right side. The first corner had a quote from Isaiah, Chapter 53:5:

He was wounded for our transgressions; He was bruised by our iniquities. The chastisement for our peace was upon Him, and by His stripes we are healed.

The fourth corner was a direct quote from Second Corinthians, Chapter 5:21:

For He made Him who knew no sin to be sin for us that we might become the Righteousness of God in Him.

This was definitely not a Jewish prayer shawl.

I removed the *tallit* in shock. I held it in my hands and once again noticed the Menorahs and Stars of David. I looked at the Hebrew inscription embroidered on the edge that rests against the neck when the *tallit* is placed on the shoulders. My mouth dropped open as I finally got the full message of the ritual shawl I had donned. The Hebrew sentence I encountered was not the traditional Hebrew prayer we Jews say just before we wrap ourselves in the *tallit*. Because I read Hebrew, I was able to understand the meaning immediately. It said: "Blessed are you, our God and King of the Universe who fulfilled the voice of the Torah in the person of Jesus the Messiah who envelops all of us with his righteousness."

My hands trembled as I realized Thomas had brought me a prayer shawl from the Jews for Jesus community. I looked closely at the bag used for carrying the shawl. I saw for the first time that, in addition to the golden Menorahs and Stars of David, there was also the symbol of a fish, a symbol associated with Christianity. I hadn't noticed it before. I folded up the *tallit* gingerly, my heart racing, and placed it in the bag, trying to make sense of what had just happened. I could not pay attention to the rest of the service because I was contemplating the consequences of my incursion into the world of interfaith sharing.

Many rabbis warn Jews about the dangers of entering into another house of worship, lest they be deceived by "strange practices." I knew without a doubt who I was, a committed, practicing Jew, who also viewed interfaith exchange as a vital and necessary activity to bring peace to the world. But I felt deceived and betrayed. I believed I was donning a garment that belonged to my ritual world, when in fact it was a "borrowed" symbol from my faith which was then converted into a symbol for Jews who accepted Jesus.

As much as I treasured Thomas' gesture in giving me the gift, I knew I would never wear it again. And I also realized that Thomas had no idea of the significance of the Hebrew writing inscribed onto the prayer shawl. I believed beyond a shadow of a doubt he had given it to me in total innocence.

When the service concluded I approached my rabbi and showed him the *tallit*. I explained I had received it from an interfaith colleague.

Rabbi Mordecai Finley, a worldly and wise man, read the Hebrew inscription about Jesus, threw back his head and emitted such a deep belly laugh that it startled me and some of the people standing near us.

"You wanted interfaith, Ruth. You got yourself interfaith!"

We laughed together. It was a humorous moment, and yet I was still trying to overcome my dismay.

Later, during my Torah study class, I shared with my friends what had happened during the service when I discovered what was written on the *tallit*. Several of my friends were convinced I had been given the *tallit* in a deliberate attempt to convert me. Since many Jews have experienced the zeal of Christians hoping to "save our souls" for two thousand years, it was natural for my friends to come to that conclusion. But because I knew Thomas well, and knew he would never attempt to convert me, I defended him to my friends. "I know his heart," I assured them. "He values the fact that I am Jewish and steeped in my tradition."

I could tell the doubters were not convinced, but my next major challenge was to determine how to tell Thomas about his gift and how to explain why I could no longer wear the *tallit*. I agonized over what I would say to him, not wanting to offend him, but realizing something had to be said.

At our next interfaith group meeting, I asked Thomas to step outside for a private conversation. I pulled out the *tallit* in question, unfolded it and read him the quotes on each of the four corners. His eyes grew wide like saucers. Then I read aloud the translation of the Hebrew prayer embroidered on it. When I mentioned the words "Jesus the Messiah," he gasped.

"Oh my God!" he exclaimed. "I didn't know! I had no idea…"

"Thomas, my dear friend, where did you get this *tallit*?"

"At a fair during a Roman Catholic convention," he answered, "but I had no idea what was written on it, or that it came from Jews for Jesus. Please believe me. In fact, I bought it from a Jewish vendor: He also sold me a *shofar* (the Ram's horn Jews blow during their High Holiday services).

"Of course I believe you," I reassured him. "Actually I showed the *tallit* to my rabbi. It was very sobering when I realized our ancient religious symbol had been adopted and adapted."

Thomas apologized again and then I said to him, "Dear Thomas, dear friend of mine, I need you to know I am not going to be able to wear this *tallit* ever, but neither am I going to return it to you, because it is still a symbol of your affection and regard for me, and a reminder to me that interfaith engagement is full of minefields, even when good will and generosity are the motivating factors."

Thomas smiled in relief. Though the information had caused him great discomfort, he appreciated my reaction, because I did not blame him for the error. I had explained the *faux pas* and he accepted his responsibility for not examining the garment more carefully before giving it to me. The quotes on the four corners might have been suspicious, but I knew there was no way he could have understood the Hebrew phrase about "the Messiah" written on the shawl.

When I took out the stored *tallit* to re-examine the quotes and write this chapter in my book, I once again relived my initial shock and my chagrin. But I also remembered my rabbi's laughter and his comment.

"You wanted interfaith, Ruth—you got interfaith!"

I am no less of a Jew for keeping the *tallit*, which I will never wear, but I believe I am wiser than I might have been, and I would like to end this chapter with a word of caution to those who have already embarked on an interfaith journey.

Trust me. No GPS has yet been designed to help us avoid the minefields.

A corner of the tallit I received from my interfaith group, inscribed with a quote from the Gospel of Matthew in the New Testament.

Our local interfaith Group, the *Southern California Committee for a Parliament of the World's Religions* (SCCPWR), on a weekend retreat.

SCCPWR Executive Committee with LA County Sheriff Lee Baca, an advisor. (L to r.) Noor Malika Chishsti, Renée De Palma, Joseph Prabhu, Sheriff Baca, Ruth and Doris Davis.

Think Globally, Act Locally

Presenting SCCPWR award to delegation from the Soka Gakkai International (SGI) Buddhist center in Santa Monica for their outstanding contribution to interfaith engagement.

Offering blessings at the opening ceremony of "Making a Difference," organized by SCCPWR and hosted by the SGI Buddhist Center, April 2009.

Welcoming new Archbishop Jose Gomez to LA. are (l. to r.) Father Alexei Smith, the Catholic Interfaith Liaison in LA, Archbishop Gomez, SCCPWR Co-Chair Ruth.

(L. to r.) Israeli musician/composer Yuval Ron, Ruth, Iranian Muslim singer Mamak Khadem, and Alex Patico, Sec'y of the Orthodox Peace Fellowship.

(L. to r,) Ruth, Sande Hart, founder of S.A.R.A.H., Ambassador Mussie Hailu, URI Global Trustee from Ethiopia, and Margie Cole, of the URI North American Leadership Council, at the 2011 NAIN Scottsdale, Arizona Interfaith Conference.

We look forward to the time when the Power of Love will replace the Love of Power. Then will our world know the blessings of peace.

~William Gladstone

CHAPTER 18
Nineteen Persians and Me

The original plan was to travel to Turkey bringing together people of diverse religious and ethnic backgrounds from countries around the world to honor the poet Rumi. We planned to visit his historical homeland in the fall of 2007, and pay tribute to him on his birthday, in Konya, Turkey, where he was buried seven hundred and thirty-two years earlier. Along with our clothes we would pack our favorite Rumi poems and for ten days, as we toured Turkey, we would indulge ourselves in a poetry love fest, reciting the inspiring, lyrical verses of the "Universal Poet of Love."

Born in the thirteenth century in Persia to a prominent, erudite, and highly respected Muslim family, Rumi became a legend in his own time. As Kabir Helminski says about Rumi in his *Pocket Rumi Reader*, "There is no doubt that he is one of the great literary figures of all time. Within Islamic cultures, especially from the Balkans, through Turkey, Iran, to Pakistan and India, he is deeply loved."

Who could have predicted that eight centuries later Rumi would become a universal muse and the best selling poet in America?

I thought at least thirty-five people would sign up, but when the dust of expectation settled, twenty people were on the final passenger list. Aside from me, there were no other native-born Americans—just nineteen Persians and me.

The group—all but one from Los Angeles—included physicians, real estate brokers, businessmen, a jeweler, hospital and university personnel, several retirees, a radio/TV talk show host who also headed an Iranian cable station…and me.

Minefields & Miracles

Like many Americans, I had been introduced to Rumi, or *Mowlana Jalaluddin*, as the Persians refer to him, through the translated works of Coleman Barks. That changed when I was invited to screen my documentary, *God and Allah Need to Talk*, at the Iranian Muslim-American Cultural Center (IMAN) in Los Angeles. Following my program I also had an opportunity to hear Rumi's poems in Farsi, the original language in which they were first uttered. I didn't understand the words, but I resonated to the melody, the beauty of the rhyme, and the cadence of each verse. That was it. I was hooked.

> *O pure people who wander the world,*
> *Amazed at the idols you see,*
> *What you are searching for out there*
> *If you look within, you yourself are it.*

Several months later some friends and I organized a Rumi-inspired interfaith event in a local church in Los Angeles, which attracted more than one hundred fifty people from around the city. In America, the "universal poet of love," had become a veritable tuning fork for multicultural outreach. Even people who don't particularly care for poetry or spiritual disciplines like to quote Rumi. Soon he would become a household word, I mused.

My Persian friend Kiumars convinced me it would be a natural extension of my interfaith work to organize a trip to Turkey to honor Rumi. A devoted Rumi fan himself, Kiumars helped to organize the trip and served as my "culture coach" for several months before and during our adventure. He knew I had already organized four interfaith trips to Egypt and Israel, so a comment he made caught me off guard. "You may have organized trips like these before," he said, smiling enigmatically, "but you haven't traveled with Persians. This will be a unique experience for you," he predicted. "Americans don't know our culture."

He was right. Most Americans are ignorant when it comes to world history. America's brief and expurgated version of world history generally starts from the cavemen, leaps to Medieval times, with a brief stop for the Renaissance, the French Revolution, our War of Independence from the British, the Civil War, and then on to World War I and World War II. The Persian Empire and the Ottoman Empire are small blips on our American radar screen. But for me all that was about to change.

After twenty-four hours of traveling non-stop from Los Angeles, with a short stopover in New York City, we arrived in Istanbul in the early afternoon on a Friday. A fascinating, colorful city with a multi-layered history, Istanbul was once home to the Byzantine Empire, which lasted a thousand years or so. It then became the seat of the Ottoman sultans in an unbroken succession that lasted for five hundred years.

As travel-weary as we all were, once we were on the bus to our hotel, suddenly the group perked up. Our tour guide, Yeshim, a lovely, intelligent Turkish woman in her late twenties, with hazel almond eyes and a charming accent, had uttered the magic words: "Shopping at the Grand Bazaar!"

The largest covered shopping mall in the world, the Grand Bazaar literally vibrates with shopping frenzy. With over four thousand stores, the Grand Bazaar is a maze of passageways and detours, each one leading to a crowded cache of handmade rugs, exquisite gold jewelry, leather goods, and the ubiquitous tourist souvenirs. Cobalt blue ceramic eyeballs stare at you everywhere, from wall hangings to bracelets to key chains, promising to ward off evil— and even casual malevolence.

As we were parking, I found this fitting verse in my pocket Rumi book.

> *In this world you have become affluent and well dressed,*
> *But when you come out of this world, how will you be?*
> *Learn a trade that will earn you forgiveness*
> *There's also traffic and trade*
> *Beside those earnings, this world is just play.*

Our first night in Istanbul found us cruising on the romantic Bosphorus River, waxing ecstatic over the dinner fare: a rainbow of imaginative, colorful salads laced with artichoke hearts, chickpeas, fresh bell peppers, avocado and radish, followed by fragrant rice and pasta dishes, spicy chicken, and hearty meat kabobs, one of Turkey's culinary specialties. The city lights winked and illuminated our way. Our host was Ibrahim Anli, a resourceful Turkish graduate student specializing in conflict-resolution. After speaking with Turkish-American friends in Los Angeles and our Chicago travel agent, he had managed on very short notice to create an enchanting candlelit-dinner. We socialized over dinner and desert, sampling baklava smothered in honey and other Turkish delicacies made of pistachio and hazelnuts.

Ibrahim, a Muslim, shared how he, too, had been inspired by the possibility of uniting people through Rumi's poetry. In fact, when he was in the States, he held the job of outreach coordinator for the Rumi Forum for Interfaith Dialogue in Washington, DC. Kindred spirits can be found everywhere. That night I found one cruising down the Bosphorus River.

For the next three days we toured Istanbul, with Yeshim guiding us through a host of impressive historical sites. We visited the Blue Mosque, the only mosque in the world to boast six minarets, named for the brilliant blue mosaic tiles lining its vaulted and domed ceilings. It is still used for daily worship, so after we had removed our shoes, we were ushered in through a side gate, where we could marvel and meditate simultaneously.

We also toured Topkapi Palace, which stands on the site of the great Acropolis of Byzantium. Isolated from the rest of the city behind huge defensive walls stretching from the Golden Horn to the Sea of Marmara, once upon a time the palace had served as the administrative heart and seat of government of the Ottoman Empire. The opulence of the palace, the painted ceilings, the two-ton crystal chandeliers, endless kilometers of winding staircase, and the silk upholstery reminded me of the Czars' palaces I had visited in St. Petersburg, Russia. As an American, that was my only frame of reference for "opulence," but my Persian friends were having a different experience. They understood genuine opulence for it was an equally appropriate word to describe their own royal past.

What became clear, early on our trip, was that my Persian companions had an edge on being able to appreciate the importance of the sites we visited. They were profoundly aware of themselves as being descendants of what was once considered the greatest empire of all times, the Persian Empire, reaching its zenith in 490 BC. Mosques with Persian names and designs can be seen even today in Tajikistan and Uzbekestan, illustrating just how far east Persian culture extended as a result of their political conquests. Persian art and architecture were universally admired and their influence reached a climax during the reign of the Safavid dynasty, from 1502-1736.

World history became a constant companion on our bus. I learned that the idea of organizing people from various religious communities for dialogue, even beyond the Abrahamic religions, is not at all new. A prime example was in Mogul, India, under the leadership of Akbar the Great, who ruled in the second half of the sixteenth century. At the end of his reign in 1605, the Mogul Empire covered most of northern and central India and was one of the most powerful empires of its age.

Akbar's persona fascinated me. A Sunni Muslim, Akbar was a man known for chivalry, valor, and statesmanship—and his interest in the arts. He was at first known to be intolerant towards Hindus and other religions, but subsequently he changed his attitude—historians believe—because he initiated marriage alliances with Hindu princesses. An epic Indian movie (released in 2008), entitled *Jodhaa-Akbar*, depicts how Akbar's deep love for a particular Hindu princess, Jodhaa Bai, prompted his change of heart. It seems that love hastened his transformation from an intolerant person into an interfaith activist, something to take note of in our interfaith endeavors!

While some Rajput women who entered Akbar's harem converted to Islam, they were generally provided full religious freedom. Their families, who remained Hindu, formed a significant part of the nobility and served to articulate the opinions of the majority of the common populace in the imperial court, according to the New World Encyclopedia. The practical result of Akbar's actions was that numerous Hindu landlords, courtiers, and military generals formed part of his administration, and he was known for hiring people on merit regardless of creed—an ancient form of "equal opportunity employment."

Also to his credit, Akbar launched a series of religious debates between Muslim scholars and Jains, Sikhs, Hindus, Jews, and Portuguese Roman Catholic Jesuits, even including atheists in the mix. He is especially remembered for treating religious leaders of all faiths with great consideration and reverence.

While the Mogul Empire reigned in India, the Ottoman Empire that lasted from 1299-1922, changed not only the geography of the world, but also Persia's monopoly on the land and the language. Even in the modern republic of Turkey, remnants of the once great Persian empire abound. The elaborate calligraphy and mosaic tile signs we frequently spotted were not written in Turkish, but in Arabic and Farsi. Our well-educated Turkish-born tour guide could not read them, but our Persian entourage could. They even admitted they felt nostalgia for Iran while they were visiting Turkey. Most of them had begun new lives in America as refugees after the Shah was ousted and, since they cannot return to Iran today for political reasons, modern Turkey has remained the culture closest to their own. My Persian companions reveled in the similarities.

Our Turkish tour bus had morphed into a Persian cultural oasis. Sohrab, a radio talk-show host and filmmaker, had brought a recording of a radio interview he conducted with Dr. Mohammad Pakravan, a leading expert on Rumi's life. For several hours over a two-day period, the group listened in fascination to the details of Rumi's life and his connection to the mysterious dervish, Shams, who became Rumi's mentor, teacher and inspiration. Shams influenced Rumi to leave his family for months at a time in order to study with him, and their intense and intimate relationship became the subject of many of Rumi's poems. After his tutelage with Shams, and as an indication of his induction into a new spiritual realm, Rumi began to whirl ecstatically and, in a state of trance, gave voice to his poetry in a continuous ribbon of verse and rhyme. Others would record his words as he spun them out, poem after poem, in frenzied succession. As scholars would later explain, it is through this turning movement, body posturing, mental focus, and sound, the dervish achieves ecstasy and unites with God.

> *Daylight, full of small dancing particles*
> *and the one great turning, our souls*
> *are dancing with you, without feet, they dance.*
> *Can you see them when I whisper in your ear?*

Rumi was amazingly prolific during his ecstatic dances. His works include a massive collection of lyrical poems (*ghazels* and *rubiyat*) as well as the six-volume *Mathnawi*, a collection of rhymed couplets incorporating stories, humor, and spiritual teachings.

During our long rides together, when Yeshim wasn't introducing us to the landscape and history passing outside our windows, I encouraged the group to use the bus microphone to share Rumi's poetry, in Farsi or in English.

I decided to recite a portion from "The Apprenticeship" in Yeshim's honor.

> *If anyone goes traveling without a guide,*
> *every two days' journey*
> *becomes a journey of a hundred years...*

Yeshim smiled broadly in appreciation of my offering.

Simin, a Rumiphile to the core, was the first to approach the microphone when I asked for volunteers to follow my recitation. She read with great passion and the group applauded her enthusiastically. Her husband, Jamshid, was the next to come forward. He sat near me and began to chant a Rumi poem in a plaintive melody that engulfed the entire bus. I was deeply moved and then I noticed out of the corner of my eye that our tour guide was crying. Later Yeshim confided to me that even though she didn't understand Farsi, there was something about the quality of Jamshid's voice and his connection to the poetry that touched her soul. Yeshim admitted she wasn't very familiar with Rumi's poetry, even though she had learned a lot about his life and adventures, to satisfy the curiosity of the eager tourists who came to learn about their poet-hero.

I told her we were planning to have a special ritual celebration honoring Rumi on his birthday, on our last day in Turkey. We would hold the ceremony while visiting his tomb in Konya. I invited her to recite one of Rumi's poems in Turkish. She agreed and said she would prepare something, adding "I've never been with a group like this before. This is a first for me."

I interpreted that as a compliment, although at times she seemed to be overwhelmed by the group's constant negotiation to change departure times, destinations, and even hotels. My friend and culture coach Kiumars had foreseen this possibility before we left Los Angeles. "Let me put it to you this way," he elaborated. "In America, you negotiate and then you agree. We Persians first agree, and then we negotiate." We both laughed at his analysis, I out of innocence, and he out of experience.

Our tour of Istanbul continued, constantly reflecting the intersection of Muslim, Christian, and Jewish histories. We marveled at the absolute symmetry of the grand Sultan

Ahmet Mosque, and then continued to the Underground Cisterns and the "Sunken Palace" (Yerebatan Sarayt), constructed in the fourth century during the reign of Constantine. One of my favorite historical sites was the mosaic-filled Haga Sophia Church (Church of the Holy Wisdom), which now serves as a museum and is considered one of the world's greatest architectural marvels.

Also on my mind was Turkey's admirable rescue of thousands of Jews expelled by Queen Isabella of Spain during the Inquisition. In a gesture of extreme hospitality that still inspires amazement by those familiar with the history of Jewish persecution, Sultan Beyazit II sent ships out to welcome the Jews who were fleeing for their lives. Expelled for refusing to convert to Christianity in Spain, those fortunate Jews were given safe haven and granted religious freedom in Turkey for almost five centuries, until Israel was established, and then most of them moved to Israel. I thought about the Sultan's generous welcome while we were visiting the Jewish Museum and Neve Shalom Synagogue, both under very heavy security as a result of a terrorist bombing in 2003. The realities of our contemporary world were never far away.

On our last evening in Istanbul we were divided up into three groups, and chauffeured to the homes of three Turkish Muslim families for dinner. Our tour guide had arranged for a personal foray into Turkish family life, calling it "Turkish Delight"—which indeed it was. Our small group, made up of Dalia, Farideh, Sohrab and myself, found ourselves in the aesthetic, colorful home of an upper middle-class family. The husband, Yakup, was a manufacturer of shirts, a successful businessman, and a man well versed in the Kor'an. His wife, Hanife, in headscarf and modest dress, stayed in the background most of the evening, even though we encouraged her to join us.

Their twin nine year-old daughters, Humeyra and Sumeyra, were more adventurous and came to sit with us in the living room. I asked for a globe and showed the girls where America was, our home across the ocean. They smiled and seemed genuinely interested in everything about us, and they agreed to join us at the dining room table while we enjoyed our only home-cooked meal in Turkey: creamy mushroom soup, tomato-cucumber salad, baked chicken, fried potatoes, and saffron-flavored rice.

Sohrab requested permission to film the family interacting with our group, explaining that he was making a film about Rumi and our trip to Turkey. He told them that he, also a Muslim, deeply appreciated their willingness to open up their home to us.

We lingered in their home, even after dessert, not wanting to dispel the warm feeling of hospitality and camaraderie that had developed. I discussed similarities between Judaism and

Islam with our host, with the help of our translators, two young Turkish men who had studied in America. We all agreed we had more in common than what separated us. I gave the wife an extra-long hug when we tearfully said farewell.

We left Istanbul the next morning and flew to Izmir and then, by bus, continued to Ephesus, the best-preserved classical city on the Mediterranean. It is also considered the cradle of Christianity, with its spectacular ruins from the period of Saint Paul. Some say it is the best place in the world to get the feeling for what life was like in Roman times. The Virgin Mary is believed to have spent her later days nearby.

From Ephesus we drove to Pamukkale, "The Sacred City," in south central Turkey. The orange sun was brazen, filling almost the entire sky as it retreated behind a purple and lavender horizon. Barefoot, we walked in awe and silence across the white "Cotton Castle" of Pamukkale, splashing in the pools of water with their lime cascades that once upon a time had been a Roman spa.

The next morning, after more Rumi on the bus, we made our way to Cappadocia, a natural wonder of the world caused by mighty volcanoes of the Central Anatolian Plateau that over millions of years erupted and spewed their contents across the land. Miraculous cave towns and gorges were later carved from the new formations, carvings that defy the imagination until you can see them for yourself. Yeshim directed us to the caves that were accessible by foot or by ladder and, once inside, she pointed out the still visible frescoes created by the monks and Christian devotees who had fled to Cappadocia to escape their oppressors. Religious persecution seemed to be as old as history itself.

I was marveling how easily we crossed religious and historical borders on our trip as we moved from site to site, city to city, era to era. We listened with curiosity and respect as we learned about each site and its special significance to Muslims, Christians, and Jews. Why can't we treat people with the same respect and open curiosity we show our historical sites? The living deserve as much respect as the dead—even more respect, I would say—but what makes that understanding so elusive?

> *We are puppets in the hands of God*
> *The power is His, we are all beggars*
> *Why are we always trying to outdo each other*
> *When we have all come from the same home?*

Our trip was fast drawing to a close as we headed for Konya and our birthday celebration for Rumi. Unlike the other modest hotels in the interior of Turkey, we were surprised by the creature comforts and sublime styling of the ultra-modern Rixos Hotel, owned by Russians.

It was a fortuitous place for us to land because that night they were honoring Rumi and Mrs. Esin Chalabi, the poet's blood relative, twenty-two generations later.

We were overjoyed by the rare privilege of meeting one of Rumi's descendants. A handsome, blonde woman with enormous personal presence, Mrs. Chalabi listened to our testimonials about Rumi, and the reason for our pilgrimage to Turkey. She touched her hand to her heart in a gesture of gratitude.

I also had the opportunity to view an extraordinary exhibit of whirling dervish paintings and to meet the artist, Turkish-born Gulcin Anil, who had arrived that night for the Rumi event. Her Sufi dancers, painted in incandescent colors, seemed to leap off the canvas and spin around the room. I learned from her that once she began painting the dervish series, she herself entered into a trance state, and for eight months she continued painting daily until she had produced ninety-nine paintings, the same number as the names of God in Islam. She told me that people who had bought her paintings later reported having profound mystical occurrences. One woman, she said, claimed that her nightmares abruptly stopped when she hung the dervish painting in her home and could view it from her bedroom.

Konya was obviously the best place to learn about dervishes. Our travel agent arranged for us to see a special demonstration of "Sema," the whirling dervish ritual dance practiced by Sufis in Turkey and many parts of the world.

We watched as three fresh-faced young acolytes, in their early twenties or perhaps even younger, first bowed in respect to their teacher, and then took up their positions to begin their spinning. Their white skirts twirled up and around their bodies as they pivoted around, their left foot used as a fulcrum, the right foot acting as a wheel. The left foot, I learned, is never lifted up from the ground and the knee is never bent. As they spun faster and faster, their arms gracefully moved into a sideways "S" position. Their arms were extended, right palm facing upwards, towards heaven, their left palm facing down, as a physical manifestation of their belief that "we flow into the heavens and pour into the earth; we take from God and give to man," as they explained to us.

The musicians played unobtrusively in the background, mostly with their eyes closed. Like the dancers, they were local people who had volunteered to demonstrate their religious practice. We were told not to applaud, because it was a religious ceremony, not a performance.

Our group was very quiet on our ride back to the hotel. I imagined that, like myself, they were thinking about the dervish dances and the exotic rituals which have continued uninterrupted for more than seven centuries. The rules for joining monastic life are very strict, we would later learn, as strict as in the time of Rumi. Only the most dedicated make it through the trial period. If they make an error during their one thousand and one trial days, for example, they are required to begin their training all over again, and the days they have already invested do not count.

> *One went to the door of the Beloved and*
> *knocked. A voice asked, 'Who is there?'*
> *He answered, 'It is I.'*
> *The voice said, 'There is no room for me and Thee.'*
> *The door was shut.*
> *After a year of solitude and deprivation he returned and knocked.*
> *A voice from within asked, 'Who is there?'*
> *The man said, 'It is Thee.'*
> *The door was opened for him.*

Rumi's poetry suggests that when we view ourselves as no different from "the other" and part of "the Beloved," then the door to Paradise will be opened.

The next morning we drove to downtown Konya to visit Rumi's tomb. I wondered what it might have been like to be part of his funeral procession. I remembered reading that on Sunday, December 17, 1273, when Rumi died, all the people of Konya stopped their work and the people of the surrounding villages came down to Konya, pouring into the streets—Muslims Christians, Jews, and Hindus alike.

But we were not mourning Rumi that day. On the contrary, we were celebrating his birthday, to mark the end of our tour. We must have been a striking group, all twenty of us dressed in white. When we completed the tour of the museum and the interior quarters of the huge tomb where Rumi was buried with his family, Yeshim directed us outside to a small corner garden. We lit the candles I had brought from Los Angeles, just for this occasion, and we joined hands in a circle, first to pay our respects to Rumi and then to sing the traditional American birthday song. I noticed, out of the corner of my eye, a small man in a gray suit hovering near us, but I soon forgot his presence as we began to take turns, one at a time, reciting Rumi's poetry in Farsi, English, and Turkish. Yeshim didn't disappoint us!

When we had finished our poems and rituals, suddenly a young boy approached us juggling a tray laden with small glasses of Turkish tea. "Compliments of the museum director," he told us, grinning broadly.

We looked around to see who was responsible for our refreshments. I realized the man in the gray suit was the museum director. No doubt Dr. Erdogan Erol's curiosity had been aroused by our candle-lighting and poetry recitation. Now he was smiling and waving at us. We motioned for him to join us and then, during what could only be described as "a peak moment" of our trip, we learned that he spoke fluent Farsi. "How could I be the director of the Mawlana Museum and not know Farsi, if I truly wanted to know Rumi?" Dr. Erol asked rhetorically. My Persian friends were beaming. Dr. Erol had paid the ultimate compliment to Persian culture by learning their language, history, and traditions, a valuable lesson for border crossers traveling to parts unknown.

We hastened to buy a copy of his book on Rumi so that he could inscribe a personal note for each one of us. Then we climbed on the bus for our last stop in Konya, the home of a Turkish cardiologist, Dr. Huseyin Ozdil, who had invited all twenty of us for refreshments and conversation. We crowded on to his patio where he and his wife had laid out platters piled high with "Turkish pizza." Other Turkish treats included small spicy vegetable and grain balls and flavorful cherry juice, the "national" soft drink of Turkey. The ubiquitous American soft drinks were also plentiful.

We related highlights of our adventures in Turkey, and the doctor and his young wife, Bahar, surprised us by bringing out a huge birthday cake, to help us celebrate Rumi American-style. We put only one candle on the cake, to signify our unity with our hosts and with one another. Then we joined hands in a circle to sing "Happy Birthday" to Rumi, to bless the family, and thank them for their hospitality. They in turn showered us with souvenirs and a fond farewell.

Since Rumi was born in what is now called Afghanistan, grew up, lived and taught in Persia, and died in Turkey, all three countries claim him. The truth is, however, that he can be claimed by all of us the world over. And isn't it a miracle, after all, at a time when Muslim extremists are feared around the globe and when there is so much suspicion about the religion of Islam, that the most beloved poet of our times is a Muslim mystic who, even after death, has the ability to unite us?

> *I am not an entity in this world or the next,*
> *did not descend from Adam and Eve or any*
> *origin story.*
> *My place is the placeless, a trace of the traceless…*
> *Neither body nor soul*
> *I belong to the Beloved.*

Touring Turkey on the bus.

With our tour guide, Yeshim.
(Credit: Sohrab Akhavan)

Our group in Turkey.

My "culture coach" Kiumars posing with the ubiquitous blue ceramic eyeballs.

Visiting the spice market of Istanbul.
(Credit: Sohrab Akhavan)

In front of the "Celsus Library" In Ephesus.
(Credit: Sohrab Akhavan)

Examining the globe with twins Humeyra and Sumeyra at their home in Istanbul.
(Credit: Sohrab Akhavan)

Inside the Rumi museum, a shrine to the "Poet of Love."

Reciting Rumi poetry in the garden outside the Rumi Museum. (Credit: Sohrab Akhavan)

Mrs. Esin Chalabi, Rumi's blood relative, twenty-two generations later.

Celebrating Rumi's birthday with a local Konya family.
(Credit: Sohrab Akhavan)

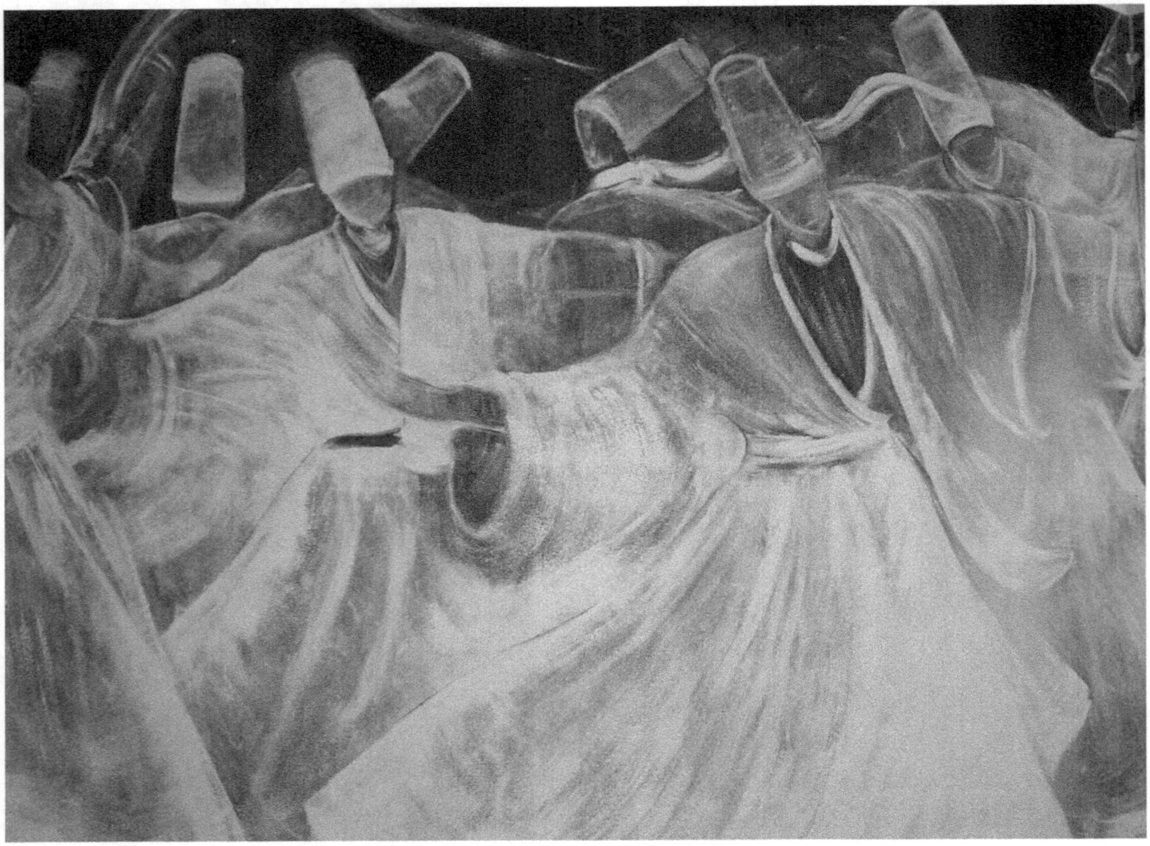

One of 99 Dervish paintings in a series by Turkish Artist Gulcin Anil, (with artist's permission).

Allah guides those who seek His approval. He guides them to the paths of peace, leads them out of darkness into the light by His leave, and guides them in a straight path.

~Kor'an (5:16)

CHAPTER 19
The Summer of My Spider Bite

Individuals who have been inspired to follow a sacred path, when pressed, can usually pinpoint a particular, precise moment or event in their lives when they knew their decision to pursue that path received "heavenly" approval.

Many events in my life had encouraged me to pursue my path in peacemaking. In 2000 I received a gold medal for my contribution to Cultural Education at a ceremony held in Victoria Hall, in Geneva, Switzerland, organized by the *Fete d'Excellence*. I was in the company of people I greatly admired, other laureates from around the world and the organization's founder, Wilda Spalding.

Wilda, a prodigiously talented and indomitable "force of nature," spent twenty years at the UN in Geneva, championing the rights of the Indigenous people of the world and speaking out on behalf of the handicapped. She also organized annual intergenerational delegations as well as youth summits, eager for young people from around the world to become familiar with the internal workings of the UN. She encouraged the delegates of all ages to feel a sense of ownership and, as she put it, "to recognize that although the UN is an organization of nations, at its core the *Universal Declaration of Human Rights* belongs to each individual."

In the nineties Wilda initiated a series of exciting round table discussions and symposia with adults and youth at the UN. I was invited to address the themes of racism, freedom of the press, and the power of the media to influence world events. It was admittedly a heady experience to have an opportunity to speak at a global forum and to share my ideas, my films, and my views about the importance of interfaith engagement. It was also an opportunity to underscore the urgent need to create a world media that cares more about peace than it does about violence.

In April 2009, during their annual Baisakhi Celebration, the Sikh community of Southern California honored me for my commitment "to creating worldwide spiritual understanding through interfaith dialogue." Two years later, at a gala event celebrating the one hundredth anniversary of International Women's Day, I received a Sparkie Catalyst Award for being a "bridge builder" among people and religious communities. My sister awardees included the well-known spiritual leader/writer Marianne Williamson and Rev. Doris W. Davis, an interfaith minister who chose to walk across America during a six month period in 2011, to emphasize women's rights and women's full participation in partnership with men.

The night of the Sparkie Awards I was also afforded an opportunity to honor three intrepid female interfaith colleagues of my own choosing. I selected Rev. Dr. Gwynne Guibord, an Episcopalian priest and founder of the Guibord Center—Religion Inside Out; Yoland Trevino, a Mayan Indigenous leader who serves as the Global Chair for the United Religions Initiative, and Dr. Mehnaz Afridi, recently appointed as an Assistant Professor of Islam and also as the Director of the Holocaust, Genocide and Interfaith Center for Manhattan College, a Catholic institution in New York. I was thrilled to be in such good company.

Those were very rewarding public moments in my life, which contained an acknowledgement that my desire—or perhaps obsession—to pursue interfaith engagement was appreciated by others. We all need encouragement and positive feedback at some point in our lives to let us know we are on the right track.

Nevertheless, if I had to pick one particular time in my life when I felt I was initiated by Spirit it would be the summer of 2006. In fact, I received two initiations that summer, one from my beloved Rebbe, Rabbi Zalman Schachter-Shalomi, and one from a spider.

I shall begin with my Rabbi Zalman story.

Reb Zalman—as he is affectionately known by his community and by many other people in the world—first appeared in my life in 1992. Reb Zalman was a founder and visionary of the Jewish Renewal movement in the United States, along with the late Rabbi Shlomo Carlebach. They revitalized Jewish practice and brought joy to Jews around the world, helping them reclaim their faith and their Judaism from the ashes of the Holocaust. Though originally from an orthodox background, Reb Zalman became an important teacher for Jews of all denominations. He taught us to love Judaism with modern eyes, to creatively expand Jewish practice, and to be compassionate and forgiving toward a world historically not kind to Jews.

When I met Reb Zalman, I instinctively knew he would play an important role in my life. That became more obvious to me after he led our 1994 Festival of Freedom Seder in Jerusalem. Although he lives in Boulder, Colorado and I have not had many opportunities to study with him in person, he continues to be a source of inspiration for me.

Aside from his profound influence on the Jewish Renewal community, I was also keenly aware of the role he had been playing for many years in interfaith circles, nationally and internationally. He has intimate knowledge of the Kor'an and ability to speak Arabic, close connections to H.H. the Dalai Lama, and deep appreciation for the beauty in all of the great religions of the world.

One of my favorite Reb Zalman interfaith stories—there are many and they are all good—is when he was visiting with some Zen monks. The head monk confessed to Reb Zalman that he had an urgent problem he didn't quite know how to resolve.

"What is your problem?" Reb Zalman asked, wondering how he could possibly help.

"Well, you see, Reb Zalman, I have ten students in the monastery and seven of them are Jewish. What should I tell them?"

"Ah, indeed," Reb Zalman replied. He reflected for a moment and then said, "Tell them to come home and study Judaism with a Zen consciousness!"

Reb Zalman understands how learning about another culture's spiritual practices and traditions can often enhance a Jew's appreciation of his own heritage. He has never been afraid to incorporate regional and even pop cultural traditions into Jewish liturgy—in fact he encourages it. He would often sing Jewish prayers to "Row, Row, Row Your Boat," "Amazing Grace," or even an Austrian marching song, if it happened to have the right syncopation.

In the summer of 2006, Eliyahu McLean, an Orthodox Jew and a Jerusalem peacemaker who has devoted his adult life to promoting peaceful co-existence in the Holy Land, informed me he had an important announcement for me from Reb Zalman. Eliyahu had been ordained by Reb Zalman a few years earlier as the first *Rodeph Shalom* (Pursuer of Peace) and, in subsequent discussions, they agreed it was time to appoint a woman, a *Rodephet Shalom*, in the lineage of Reb Zalman. They decided that woman would be me.

I was deeply moved by the announcement.

Eliyahu was instructed to hold a provisional ceremony for me in the summer, when he and I would be co-teaching a peacebuilding class in Woodstock, New York, at the Elat Chayyim Jewish Retreat Center. Eliyahu also told me Reb Zalman planned to bestow the "Pursuer of Peace" title on me personally at a later date, when he could perform his own ceremony for me.

Before I left for the retreat in New York, knowing I would be away from my home for several weeks, I went out to my garden to curb my over-enthusiastic grapevine. I became aware of an important horticultural and philosophical discovery through the process of tending my grapevine and observing its growth pattern. It dawned on me why we use the expression "I heard it through the grapevine." The grapevine grows in all directions simultaneously. It also grows very rapidly. When not tamed or pruned, it can go wild, thrusting its vines hungrily in all directions and tenaciously grabbing onto anything that will give it holding power, including telephone and cable lines, other trees and, in my case, a patio chair. When given an opportunity, it can even suffocate the garden hose supplying it with water.

In thinking about the danger of rumors run rampant, the wisdom one derives from observing the growth of a grapevine was not lost on me. You can never know how far a rumor will spread. Stereotypes about groups of people and other cultures can also spread unchecked.

I was afraid I wouldn't even be able to get back into my garden if I left my grapevine unattended. And it was while I was pruning the grapevine a spider bit me, in the middle of my "third eye," dead center on my forehead.

I didn't know it at the time; in fact I didn't discover it until the following morning just before I was about to leave for the airport. I looked at myself in the mirror and saw a huge bump on my forehead. Nonplussed, I decided it was an insect bite. I cleansed it with a cotton swab doused in alcohol, finished packing, and continued on my trip to New York, unaware of the possible ramifications of that bite for my life. Once in New York, I noticed the wound was getting larger and redder, like an angry eye. Treating it with homeopathic remedies didn't help so, finally, I decided to go to the emergency room of the Roosevelt Hospital.

Yes, it was definitely a spider bite, the medical staff confirmed, and "badly infected." They warned me it was dangerous, perhaps life threatening. "You need to take an antibiotic urgently, and you should come back the next day unless it improves," they emphasized.

I left the hospital and a strange phenomenon began to occur almost immediately. The infected area began to morph and change, as did the responses of strangers who noticed it.

At one point it was so red, a young man on the subway asked me if I was Hindu because he thought it was a bindi, the red dot Hindu women apply to their third eye as a religious practice. I ended up having quite an interesting conversation with the young man, a Hindu from India, working in the financial sector of Manhattan. When he heard about my interfaith work, he said he also wanted to get involved. He gave me his email address to inform him about any interfaith programs I might be organizing in New York City. (I later sent him information about an interfaith community in Manhattan and today we are still in touch.)

Next I tried to calm down the redness of my spider bite by applying clay to my wound, an old trick I had learned from a healer. Supposedly the clay would extract the redness and dry up the wound. The day I applied the clay I met someone who, upon seeing my forehead, exclaimed: "Oh, dear, it's Ash Wednesday. I didn't realize we were already at that time of year."

I laughed and told her it was actually a wound covered by clay. She moved a bit closer to me and confessed she wasn't as good a Catholic as she used to be.

Gradually the wound calmed down, but I was still left with a big bump. A young Muslim man I met the next day, Usman Mustafa, asked me if I was Muslim, speculating the bump was from putting my head to the floor in prayer five times a day. I thought he was trying to be facetious, but he was serious. "No," I assured him. "I am Jewish and the bump is from a spider bite."

When the wound was almost healed, I noticed there was a strange scar that looked remarkably like the Hebrew word, *Chai*, (life), written at an angle. Since I am Jewish, naturally I would be inclined to see Hebrew letters in the symbol. A group of young men and women, who lived on the grounds of Elat Chayyim, noticed my wound and told me there was a healer, a Native American Shaman, in residence. They urged me to visit him.

He was a man in his forties, with long hair and chiseled features. He examined my forehead, and nodded appreciatively. Then he fixed his gaze on me, and looked deeply into my eyes. "You realize you have been initiated by a spider, don't you? It is a spiritual initiation because it is in your third eye," he said definitively. "Yes, it's definitely an arrowhead!"

I told him I was grateful for confirmation of what I had surmised on my own, but I hadn't recognized the "arrowhead." I thanked him for his interpretation.

Eliyahu organized a temporary ordination for me at the end of the week, when we were concluding our class, Peacebuilding 101. He asked the entire class to surround me, and lay hands on my shoulders as they offered me a blessing upon my becoming a *Rodephet Shalom*. Eliyahu then produced an official ordination form, signed by Reb Zalman, and he read it out loud. I was deeply moved.

This is to certify that

Whereas the Rev. Ruth Broyde Sharone, R.S. has over the last decades devoted herself to peacemaking and has served as ecumenical bridge between the children of Abraham in the Holy Land and in the Diaspora and she has been received by Jews, Christians, and Muslims as a peacemaker, I, Rabbi Zalman Schachter Shalomi, MA and DHL, Rebbe and Rabbinic Chair for Aleph, Jewish Renewal, Past Holder of the Chair of World Wisdom at Naropa University, and Professor Emeritus of Religion at Temple

> *University, do hereby affirm, ordain, and commission said candidate to serve in the sacred capacities of "Rodephet Shalom," Authentic representative of our people in Ecumenical Dialogue.*

I knew Reb Zalman's personal blessing would come in a few months, but when I returned home a week later, I was greeted by another form of heavenly confirmation of my life's mission.

My son picked me up at the airport and we drove home. With my suitcases in tow, we were following the curve of the path and approaching our front door when we both suddenly stopped in our tracks. We were awestruck. An extraordinary spider web, larger than we had ever seen, seemed to be welcoming us in a magnificent iridescent arch over the entrance to our home."

"Wow!" Alexander said. "I've never seen anything like that before." Neither had I.

Next morning, as I was about to go out to check the undisciplined grapevine in the garden where I had been bitten, I stopped abruptly in my tracks once again. There, stretching across my back door was another perfect spider web, glistening in the sun. I called my son to witness it, because I needed a witness. Two huge intricate spider webs had magically appeared, one at the entrance to our house and one at the side door to the garden, within twenty-four hours of my return home.

Alexander stared in open-mouthed amazement. "Mom, you're the Spider Woman now!"

Elish, a good friend who had lived with the Hopi Indians for several years, was extremely excited to hear about my spider adventure. She immediately located a book explaining the symbolism of the spider in Native American culture. According to Hopi belief, she read to me, the spider was supposed to have spun the world into existence.

For me, the spider web symbolically represented what we in the peace movement were eager to achieve: to create a web of connective tissue that would be continuously spun by conscientious weavers of peace, in all parts of the world.

I have never killed a spider since that summer. I now recognize them as kindred spirits, or my totem animal, if you will. And if I hadn't already received enough confirmation from the universe that I was on the right path, and indeed a sacred path, a few months later I received one more sign in the ancient and sacred language of my people.

I was in Los Angeles, at a post-ordination celebration for my good friend, Tmimah, whose Rabbinic ordination I had attended in Boulder, Colorado, the same week I finally received Reb Zalman's personal blessing as a *Rodephet Shalom*. It was a memorable week for both of us, and we were enjoying the afterglow of both celebrations.

The Summer of My Spider Bite

I noticed a deck of cards on the table, in a box which said "Kabbalah," the word used to describe Jewish Mysticism.

"They're like Tarot cards," Tmimah explained, "but they only have Hebrew letters on them." She indicated there were two complete sets of the Hebrew letters. Since there are twenty-two letters in the Hebrew alphabet, that made a total of forty-four cards.

"You shuffle them and lay out four cards on the table, and see what they spell. Try it," she urged.

I excitedly took out the cards and began to shuffle them. Then I cut the deck in half, took the upper four cards, and laid them out on the table. The letters from right to left were *Resh, Shin, Tof,* and then *Aleph* (Hebrew is read from right to left).

"*Reshet Aleph*," I belted out excitedly. "That's the name of the very first and most important television station in Jerusalem, where I worked as a documentary film director when I lived in Israel. The word *reshet* itself means net or web of communication. I felt goose bumps on my body. Feeling playful and a bit mischievous, I decided I would shuffle and then lay out the cards just one more time. Carefully I put the four cards back in the deck, inserting each one in a different section. I then spent ten minutes reshuffling, splitting, reshuffling, and dividing the deck, all the while hoping the cards would reveal a second symbolic message to me.

Slowly I laid out the four new cards, once more from right to left. To my utter amazement, the identical four cards came up in exactly the same order. *Reshet Aleph*, the primal net, the net for communication and dissemination of information.

Mathematically, what were the odds after such meticulous shuffling that the same four cards would miraculously appear in the exact same order as before? It was mind boggling.

There it was, all laid out in an inescapable metaphor, for me to interpret and to decipher. I had been asked to spin a web of interfaith connection around the world. My spider bite confirmed whoever looked into my third eye saw a reflection of himself/herself.

We are all mirrors to one another. What is most deeply reflected in each of us is the gift of humanity we have been granted, the humanity that binds us and reminds us that we are all sacred children of the universe.

And sometimes it takes a spider bite and an unruly grapevine to drive that lesson home.

(L. to r.) Dr. Mehnaz Afridi, Rev. Dr. Gwynne Guibord, Ruth, Rev. Doris Davis, Yoland Trevino, Dalit Argil at the first annual Sparkie Awards, 2011. (Credit: Myra Vides)

Interfaith awards given at the Sikh's annual Bisakhi Celebration in Los Angeles, 2009 (I am second from the right).

The Summer of My Spider Bite

Receiving a gold medal at the 2000 Fete d'Excellence in Geneva, presented by sculptor Tina Allen (z'l).

Wilda Spalding, tireless advocate for Indigenous rights at the UN in Geneva, and founder and director of Fete d'Excellence.

An infected spider bite in the middle of my "third eye."

Receiving blessings from my colleague, Eliyahu McLean, and students in our peacebuilding class.

Receiving the official title as a *Rodephet Shalom* (Pursuer of Peace) from my mentor, Rabbi Zalman Schachter-Shalomi, 2007.

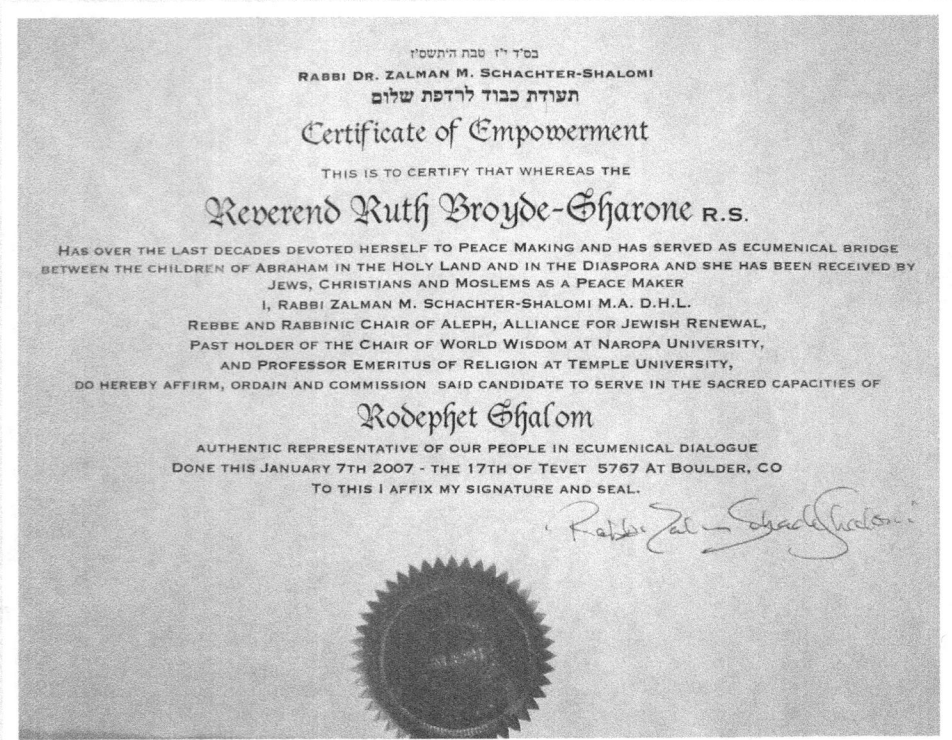

I like to believe that people in the long run are going to do more to promote peace than our governments. Indeed, I think that people want peace so much that one of these days governments had better get out of the way and let them have it.

~Dwight D. Eisenhower

CHAPTER 20

Citizen Diplomacy

"I'm just one person. What can I do?"

This is the refrain of most people who feel powerless as they sadly survey multiple conflicts happening around the world. Many point a finger at the powerful military-industrial complex and the new multinational corporations to prove the inability of a single individual to effect change.

We are all struggling to overcome our own personal impotence in the light of world events. Twentieth century history, however, tells a different story when we examine it more closely, because we have seen with our own eyes how one individual—such as Gandhi, Mother Teresa, Martin Luther King, Jr., Nelson Mandela—have transformed our world. Similarly, almost single-handedly, talk show host Oprah Winfrey transformed the world of TV and publishing. In their early days, before they were well known, all of them simply "did their thing," or as Joseph Campbell would say, "They followed their bliss."

When they started their journey none of them had access to the halls of power. But when they discovered what they cared about and what they could do best, they changed the world.

I heard a wonderful story recently about an elephant and a hummingbird. They were both aware of the fact that there was very little water left in their creek, where all the animals would gather daily to drink the nectar of life. There was a river, but it was a great distance away, and not all of the animals could reach it, so the only solution was to find a way to transfer water from the distant river to the creek.

The elephant, with his enormous trunk, and great capacity to hold water, began filling his trunk at the river. He would then shoot a powerful stream of water across the plain, and it would cascade jubilantly into the dry creek. He continued this activity for some time, feeling powerful and important, until he realized there was a tiny hummingbird nearby, totally absorbed in her own activity. With her beak she would take a tiny drop of water from the river and, at dizzying speed, her iridescent body moving like a phantom rainbow in the sky, she would fly from the river to the creek to deposit that drop of water, and then back again to perform the same task, over and over.

In amusement the elephant watched the hummingbird for several minutes. It seemed to him she was performing a completely useless task. What could she possibly achieve by bringing one drop of water at a time? Her life would long be over before she had transferred even a spoonful, he mused.

He watched her, fascinated, as she continued to whiz back and forth from river to creek, bringing one drop of water at a time. Then he began to fill his trunk with even greater quantities of water. He projected the water in a huge arc which created a magnificent sparkling spray, checking in his peripheral vision to see if the hummingbird was admiring his feat. She didn't seem to be paying any attention to him, but continued on her own rapid trajectory, river to creek, river to creek, river to creek, one drop at a time.

Finally, he couldn't help himself. He stopped what he was doing and he called out disdainfully to the hummingbird:

"Little hummingbird, how foolish you are! Do you not see how powerful my trunk is, how much water I can transfer in one giant stream? How do you think your tiny drops of water can make any difference in bringing this creek back to life? Your task is impossible and you are a dreamer."

The hummingbird flapped her tiny wings at a dizzying rate as she buzzed close to the elephant's ear.

"I am doing what I can and what I do best," she said. Then she whizzed off on her rounds. River to creek, river to creek, river to creek. One drop at a time.

For those of us who are not heads of government, nor powerful clergy with large congregations, nor CEO's of multi-national corporations, nor venture capitalists with endless resources, the tendency to feel powerless is great, at times overwhelming. But it doesn't have to be so, especially in the world of citizen diplomacy.

In the eighties a group of private US citizens, on their own initiative, took a trip to Russia during the Cold War to let everyday Russians know Americans did not hate Russians. They were curious why the US government was calling the Russians their enemies; they wanted to meet some ordinary Russians and see for themselves. While the heads of the two mega-governments were locked in a fierce battle of wills, everyday Russian citizens and everyday North American citizens unofficially met together. They dialogued together and formed friendships that lasted and outlasted the Cold War. They were citizen diplomats, with no portfolios or titles, just people who could imagine many possibilities for engagement other than war.

Another example of this type of citizen diplomacy is practiced by The Compassionate Listening Project, founded by Lea Green. They have taken many private citizens to visit Palestinians and Israelis, not to offer solutions and unsolicited advice to end the constant war between the two political entities, but just to listen deeply and fully to the residents on both sides of the border. Everyday people meeting with everyday people: citizen diplomats.

Interfaith engagement is perfectly suited to citizen diplomacy. Meeting with people of other faiths is just like meeting with people of another country. They both require great diplomacy. On the one hand, we should be knowledgeable about the faith or country we represent, our own customs and history, our rules and rituals. On the other hand, if we are to be successful and effective in our communication, we need to devote time and effort to learn about the other faith (country) as well, lest we offend. A generous portion of respect, in additional to natural curiosity, will go a long way in creating successful interfaith citizen diplomacy.

At any given moment, each of us has a chance to become a citizen diplomat. And once in a while fate may give us a chance to connect directly with an official diplomat and in the process create an opportunity to influence people of influence.

Bangladesh

My Bangladeshi friend, Omar Huda, called me one day and said, "Our Ambassador in Washington, DC is coming to LA, and we are having a reception for him in the Bangladeshi Consul General's house, and I'd like you to come and meet him. He is an old friend of mine," he added. "We were POW's together in Pakistan, so we got to know each other very well. He's a career diplomat, very intelligent and well-traveled, and I know you'll enjoy meeting him."

A few days later I made my way to the residence of the Bangladeshi Consul General in Los Angeles. Omar was waiting for me inside. I paid my respects to the Consul General, his wife, and several of the other guests whom I had met on other occasions at interfaith gatherings. Then Omar led me to the back garden where I met Ambassador Shamsher M. Chowdhury for the first time.

A tall, broad-shouldered man elegantly dressed in a dark blue suit, robin blue shirt, and a yellow tie, the Ambassador was immediately friendly and accessible. Omar must have told him something about me, because straight away he launched into a discussion about interfaith engagement, wanting to know more about my film, *God and Allah Need to Talk*, and if I was planning to show it in Washington, DC.

We chatted about his diplomatic career and the time I had spent in Israel. He was very interested in the Middle East situation and had strong ideas about what would be needed to be an effective peace-broker for that troubled sliver of land. He was skeptical about President Bush's chances to achieve peace because he felt President Bush was too closely aligned with Israel, and the Arab nations wouldn't trust him. Then the Ambassador began to share details about his life and asked about mine as well, especially about my interfaith activities.

I suddenly saw an opening in the conversation and an opportunity. Dare I ask, I wondered?

I dared. I asked if he would like to host an interfaith event in his Embassy. His face lit up. "We could, we could do that," he said considering my proposal. "Just what would it involve?"

At that moment Omar came back to the garden and joined us. I turned to Omar and said, "The Ambassador is thinking of holding an interfaith event at the Embassy in DC." Omar burst into laughter and, shaking his head incredulously, said to me, "Ruth, I only left you out here for a few minutes and you've already got the Ambassador willing to host an interfaith event at the Embassy?"

I smiled warmly at Omar and then at the Ambassador. They exchanged glances.

"I think it's a great idea, "Omar said to his old friend. "I'll fly to Washington when you have the event."

The time was late, and other guests were waiting to meet with the Ambassador, so he gave me his cell phone number and suggested we meet once more before he was scheduled to leave LA the following day at noon.

We traded phone calls the next day, but never had a chance to meet or even speak personally. I left him a phone message, wishing him a safe trip home, and then I added: "This could be a very important event for Washington, and for Bangladesh. When an Ambassador hosts an event, it shows his commitment, and because I sense you are genuinely interested in expanding interfaith connections, I believe this could be a very important occasion to promote interfaith ties for the entire Washington community.

The Ambassador called me back a few days later and said, "Let me know when you're going to be in New York. I go to the UN often. We can meet nearby, have coffee, and discuss this further."

A few months later, in June, I traveled to New York City, with an infected spider bite in the middle of my third eye. I called the Ambassador and we made an appointment to have coffee near the UN.

When we met, he commented on my spider bite and told me to look after it.

"It looks angry," he said. I told him once he and I set the date for the interfaith event at the embassy, the bite would begin to heal, "if you're serious about it," I added with a smile.

He laughed and said appreciatively, "You're good." Then he picked up his cell phone, called his secretary, and set a time for me to come to his Embassy in Washington ten days later.

I left New York City to go to Elat *Chayyim*, the Jewish Renewal Retreat Center in Woodstock, New York, where Eliyahu McLean and I were co-teaching a course called "Peacebuilding 101." At the final session, I asked each of our students to formulate and announce "one small, profound act" they would commit to carrying out when they left the class and went home. I told them I, too, was willing to make a public statement.

"The bar gets higher each time you take on more responsibility for continuing this work," I explained to them. "So you are continuously challenging yourself, like in a Pilates class, to stretch much further from your core each time."

Each member of the class shared his/her plans with the group, and then I shared my plans. "I am on my way to Washington and, hopefully, I will be able to set a date for an interfaith event to be held at the Bangladeshi Embassy."

The Ambassador kept his word. We met, set a date, and chose a theme for the event, a Thanksgiving Interfaith Celebration that coming November. I would invite members of the interfaith community to come and participate, and he would invite members of the diplomatic community and from the U.S. government. The evening would begin with socializing and music and his welcoming the participants. I would show my *God and Allah* film, the Embassy would serve dinner, and then a government representative, perhaps even Karen Hughes, the Undersecretary of State for President Bush, would keynote. Finally, at the end of the evening, we would open up the event for discussion among the attendees.

I arrived three weeks before the event in Washington. The Ambassador generously offered me the Embassy conference room to serve as my office and headquarters to plan the event. My work was cut out for me. Washington, DC was not my city, but I was not daunted. Fortunately, an interfaith colleague in DC, Daniel Tutt, graciously came to my assistance, providing names and contact information of key interfaith leaders and the media. I began in earnest to contact representatives from every religious community, to invite them to attend, and also to make sure they would participate in an opening blessing ceremony before we ate. The Ambassador believed we would have representatives primarily from the Abrahamic communities, but I told him we were also inviting Hindus, Sikhs, Baha'is, Buddhists and Native Americans.

"Isn't that too many religions?" he asked. "Aren't just Jews, Christians, Muslims and Hindus enough?"

"No, I am confident you can raise the bar on what interfaith engagement means in the capital of our nation," I replied. "Trust me, this will be a memorable event, and you'll be glad we invited everyone."

I made a silent prayer after my declaration. I hoped I would not be wrong about my prediction. I had come this far because I believed God had wanted all of this to happen. I was just doing my part as His earthly instrument—admittedly with a lot of Jewish *chutzpah*, I acknowledged to myself.

In my subsequent phone calls to various religious groups in DC, I knew I had been right in wanting to include all the communities, not just the "usual suspects." When I called the Sikh community, I was told they often felt excluded because they were not usually invited to interfaith gatherings. Most of the time the gatherings favor the Abrahamic religions, they observed.

"That is why I am personally inviting you," I responded. "Your voice is also needed in the interfaith family."

The event was a huge success. I teamed a Jewish *klezmer* musician with a Bangladeshi Catholic bangra drummer to play the opening music. With only one short rehearsal the day before, the two musicians sounded like they had been touring on the road together for years. Their interfaith harmonies filled the room with good cheer. Lush canvases from a recent art exhibit were on display throughout the Embassy and provided great ambience. The room was awash with colorful costumes of saris and turbans, overflowing with people representing many cultures and nationalities: clergy, interfaith activists, diplomats, press people, and officials from the State Department—but mostly citizen diplomats.

Ambassador Chowdhury searched for me in the crowds to tell me there were seven other ambassadors in attendance that evening, many of them from the Middle East. "Maybe you can get them to hold an event like this, too," he said, with a broad smile and a wink. "Maybe I can," I said, playfully rubbing my hands together in anticipation of that possibility. "But, remember, you were the first!"

Karen Hughes, the Undersecretary of State, scheduled to keynote that evening, had to cancel her appearance at the last minute because she was traveling with President Bush to Jordan. She sent a note of apology. Instead of a keynoter, after dinner we opened the floor to discussion. We heard a plethora of comments and suggestions, as well as offers and commitments to further interfaith engagement in Washington, DC. The room overflowed with camaraderie and good will—confirmed through the wonderful feedback we received, verbally and in writing after the event.

Imran Sadiqqui, a producer/director from the Voice of America, was on the scene. While he was interviewing the Ambassador and me on camera, he asked how the event had originated. The Ambassador said without hesitation, "Ruth and I had a common vision we discovered when we met, and this evening is a result of that."

Morocco

My account of the Bangladeshi event might have ended here, but in the audience that night was Jamilla, the assistant to the Ambassador of Morocco. She came up to me afterwards and said enthusiastically, "This was so special. I had such a wonderful time. You must come tomorrow to the Embassy of Morocco to meet our Ambassador. He would love to do something like this."

The next day I arrived at the Moroccan Embassy, to meet His Excellency Aziz Mekouar. He told me he had hosted a Hanukkah celebration in his Embassy several times. I asked him if he would be willing to host an interfaith event for the entire DC community. He eagerly agreed, but we left the time frame open.

Two years later the event we had spoken of began to crystallize while I was working on the staff of the Parliament of the World's Religions. I met with the Moroccan Ambassador again in early 2009, just after President Obama's inauguration. I suggested to Ambassador Mekouar he might like to host an interfaith event connected to the Parliament's upcoming global conference in Melbourne, Australia. What an ideal opportunity to promote citizen diplomacy in Washington, DC! The Ambassador immediately agreed, and I began to set things in motion.

I was reminded of something Dr. Harold Saunders, the former US Assistant Secretary of State once observed: "There are some things only governments can do, such as negotiating binding agreements. But there are some things that only citizens outside government can do, such as changing human relationships."

I called my friend, Rabbi Marc Gopin, the Director for the School of Diplomacy and Conflict Resolution at George Mason University, and we met briefly over two cups of cocoa at a Georgetown cafe before I left DC. I suggested Marc be the organizer and contact person for the event in DC. I would introduce him to the Moroccan Ambassador, and they would take it from there. He agreed.

Within just a few weeks, a group of Washington interfaith activists whom I knew, along with university students, supervised by Marc, began planning together with the Ambassador. The timing was perfect because they were hoping to bring together the Muslim and Jewish communities of DC who were barely speaking to each other after the Gaza War.

As a result, two years after I first met the Ambassador of Morocco, he hosted an elegant interfaith dinner at his home. I flew back to Washington for the event. We each sat next to people we didn't know—a requirement of the evening. The pleasant hum of conversation got noisier as the evening progressed. I looked around delightedly. Representatives of the local interfaith community, professors, and university students—citizen diplomats—all were engaged in animated conversations with the Ambassador and members of his diplomatic staff. It was a perfect evening, with abundant and delicious Moroccan fare, and with guests who were deeply appreciative of an Ambassador's willingness to make his private home a site for potential miracles—just as the Bangladeshi Ambassador had done two years earlier.

Kenya

A third powerful example of citizen diplomacy took place during my trip to Kenya in April 2010. I had joined a women's delegation to attend a micro-finance conference in Nairobi. Marianne Williamson, well-known spiritual leader and best-selling author (*Return to Love, The Age of Miracles*) formed the delegation at the conclusion of "Sister Giant," a special weekend event for women she organized in Los Angeles. Her specific goal that weekend was to awaken and empower American women by first engaging their imaginations and then teaching them to become pro-active in ending hunger and poverty. "When American women get serious about a cause, they can move mountains like no other group of women in the world," Marianne assured the five hundred women in the audience.

She reminded us of how we run our own households. When a woman feels very strongly that she doesn't want a specific activity to take place in her home, her family knows she will not countenance any violation of her principles. "Not in my home!" the woman will declare with authority. Everyone in the family will comply because they know she is serious. "And you don't dare tangle with her!" Marianne emphasized with a knowing smile.

"Well, what if all of us American women got together and decided to end hunger in the world? We would simply make the announcement, 'not on our planet,' and the world would know we meant business. President Obama—or any American president in office—would feel obliged to support the annual foreign-aid appropriations to end hunger in the third world because he would be afraid to go counter to the will of the American women," Marianne said confidently.

Next she introduced us to Sam Daley-Harris, founder and executive director of Results, a non-profit organization dedicated to fighting poverty and ending hunger across the globe. Marianne announced that Sam had invited her to attend the Africa-Middle East Microcredit Summit, and that he was also extending an invitation to us. Marianne then announced excitedly she had decided to form a delegation of women from the Sister Giant weekend to make the journey to Kenya with her.

I rallied to the call, even though I was totally new to the fast-growing phenomenon called microfinance. It wasn't just curiosity. I felt I was being called there by destiny. Though I couldn't quite grasp the urgency I felt in being there—and my financial situation absolutely dictated against my going—within two days, using frequent flyer miles, I had booked my ticket on Virgin Airways. Next, I arranged to stay with my son's two friends, Jenny Wilson and Sam Cole, eliminating any hotel costs. Jenny and Sam were—luckily for me—living and teaching at a private school in Nairobi, where they had also established an organization to help neglected slum children who live in desperate conditions on the site of the largest garbage dump in the world.

I wasn't sure why I was going to Kenya, but I instinctively sensed God had a plan for me there.

The microfinance conference attracted fifteen hundred participants primarily from Africa and the Middle East. We Westerners were in the minority. Self-empowerment was the dominant theme discussed by a roster of distinguished keynote speakers such as Nobel Prize winner Muhammad Yunus, Queen Sophia of Spain, Princess Maxima of the Netherlands, and others.

The goal of the conference was to compare methodologies and share evolving organizational models from the last thirty years, which had been used to provide micro-loans to the poorest populations of the world, so the most marginalized and helpless would be able to lift themselves out of a vicious cycle of poverty and hunger. The solution to world poverty and hunger, everyone at the conference agreed, is not handouts, but an opportunity for self-empowerment. The idea was to extend small loans without any of the usual bank requirements of collateral or guarantors. The goal was to help families, in general, and women, in particular, to become self-sufficient and productive members of society.

Women who have benefitted from the micro-loans in countries like Bangladesh, India,

Pakistan, and many countries in Africa not only have the reputation of returning their loans on time and in full, but also have been known to lift their entire community economically and educationally. First they feed their children and themselves, and the very next thing they do is make sure their children go to school to receive an education. Some of the "micro-loan" children have already gone to universities, become doctors and lawyers and engineers, and have returned to serve in their own communities. The key for success in all of this has been self-empowerment, not charity. As Muhammad Yunus so succinctly and eloquently articulated, those children prove the point that "the world will be rich when there are no more poor."

After my brief but intense education in microfinance in Nairobi, I was ready to return to the States to find new ways of engaging in interfaith work. I wanted to weave the global web beyond my original plan. I was now ready to create bridges between communities that don't often dialogue. The spiritual community has traditionally viewed the religious communities with suspicion, because they see the religious groups as being too dogmatic and exclusive. The religious community, on the other hand, is often disdainful of the spiritual group. They use pejorative terms such as "New Age" or "woo-woo" as a way to put down and marginalize people who are not affiliated with what they would consider a bona fide traditional, mainline religion. And then, of course, there are the agnostics and atheists, as well as people often not deemed worthy of entering into the dialogue with believers. This, I decided, would have to change.

No one should be excluded from the dialogue.

At the end of my Kenya trip, I decided to stay an extra day after the rest of the delegation returned to the States. That turned out to be a momentous decision, because suddenly I found myself stranded in Nairobi. Almost all world air traffic came to an abrupt halt when Iceland's volcano re-awakened, spewing ash into the atmosphere. Air travel was considered dangerous and perhaps even deadly. Seven million travelers found themselves in limbo, I among them.

It was during this time that I met a fellow traveler, Alexander McLean, who helped load my suitcase onto the conveyor belt at the airport when we were originally scheduled to leave. We introduced ourselves and I thanked him for his chivalry. I also experienced an immediate affection for him because my own son is named Alexander, and they are close in age. In the ensuing conversation, I learned that Alexander, a young law student from Britain, half-Scottish, half-Jamaican, had founded the African Prisoners Project. It was created to serve the neglected and maltreated prisoners in African jails, to offer them legal representation, opportunities for education, and hospice care, he explained.

Citizen Diplomacy

Alexander, twenty-five when I met him in 2010, had first worked as a volunteer in hospitals in Uganda when he was eighteen years old, during his "gap" year. By the time he graduated from university, he had decided he would devote his life to helping the destitute. He already headed a staff of fourteen in Uganda and when I met him he was in the process of opening up a new office in Nairobi. He was also planning to develop a halfway house for ex-convicts, and a hospice for dying prisoners on a plot of land in Nakuru, donated to him by a generous white Kenyan, the son of a wealthy colonial family.

While we were stranded in Nairobi, unsure of our departure date, Alexander and I became friends. Impressed by his passion and his humanitarian mission, I arranged for Alexander to speak to the congregation of the Nairobi synagogue during the Friday night Sabbath service, although I was also a stranger in town. On our walk to the synagogue, I explained to Alexander the Jewish concept of *Tikkun Olam*, the responsibility Jews feel to repair the world and leave it a better place than the way we found it. "You yourself are involved in *Tikkun Olam*," I explained to Alexander, "through the important work you are doing for the disenfranchised prisoners throughout Africa."

Before the service began, I secured the Hebrew/English Bible for Alexander, and I explained that Jews all around the world would be reading the identical chapter that week. The week's Torah portion, *Tezaraa*, dealt with leprosy and behaviors that alienate us from society.

Alexander addressed the very same theme, describing how the prisoners he works with, the "lepers" of African society, are left to fend for themselves, without being offered any opportunity for rehabilitation or, at the minimum, a small measure of dignity before they leave this world. He related how they often die alone, unattended, in filthy overcrowded prisons across the continent. Some of them have been incarcerated for months or even years for the minor offense of stealing a mango, for selling alcoholic beverages, or for just being near the scene of a crime. And punishments meted out rarely fit the crimes. For example, one little girl he had met, four years of age, was incarcerated when the three-year old girl she was swimming with drowned. The four-year old was later charged with murder. The congregation shook their heads in disbelief, as did I. Where was the compassion of the judges who made these rulings? Where was justice?

In the days that followed, as we both waited anxiously to learn when we might return home, Alexander shared more details about himself and his family. He described how his Christian upbringing had informed his decision to volunteer in Uganda and then devote his life to serving the prisoners of Africa. When he found out about my interfaith activist background, he invited me to attend a Sunday church service at the All Saints Anglican

Church of Nairobi.

We attended the 11:30 A.M. service in a high-ceilinged stone cathedral. The cold gray of the stone walls was softened by the colorful stained-glass windows depicting the life of Jesus and his disciples. The majority of the worshipers were black, Kenyan-born. I was certainly the only Jew in attendance.

I had an epiphany at the church, as I was wondering about God's purpose for me in Kenya. Why had I been stranded these extra days? I have learned that, regardless of your religious orientation, you can have an epiphany in any place at any time. Mine had just transpired as the only Jew in an Episcopalian Church in Nairobi, not unlike the epiphany I had experienced at the Strait-Way Church in Watts in Los Angeles.

It occurred to me I was uniquely positioned to introduce Alexander to a variety of individuals I recently met while I was in Kenya, individuals who could aid him in his mission. My responsibility was only to make those connections, to weave the additional strands of the web, and thereby enhance his efforts so he could achieve his goals more quickly.

Prabhudas Pattni, national chairman of the Hindu Council of Kenya, said he would be happy to help Alexander.

Ajit S. Ghogal, a Sikh from Mombasa, a former civil engineer who ran an orphanage for children with AIDS, said he would gladly apply his engineering skills to help Alexander design the half-way house, hospice and gasoline station being planned for the ex-convicts.

Dr. David Silverstein, a leader of the Jewish community in Nairobi, who had established the cardiology department for the Nairobi hospital thirty years earlier, agreed to help Alexander recruit doctors to staff the hospice. Dr. Silverstein had served as the personal physician to the former President of Kenya, Daniel Arap Moi, and is considered a leader in the wider community in Kenya.

Bishop George Mechumo, the Episcopalian pastor I had met at the airport when air traffic was halted, also agreed to help Alexander.

On our fifth day in exile, the Virgin Atlantic agents called us at 5 AM and by 6 AM we were all packed tightly, but gratefully, into the shuttle heading for the Nairobi airport. I found myself laughing at the uncanny series of events of the last five days. A *chance* meeting with a young man who helped me with my luggage. A *chance* meeting in an airport waiting room with the Bishop and his wife. A *chance* exchange in the hallways of the hotel with the Sikh and his family. A *chance* meeting with a Jewish doctor who turned out to be the son of my mother's physician in Chicago. A *chance* meeting with a Hindu who was in the hospital when I arrived but whom I was able to meet in person when he was released because I had been stranded an extra five days…

I laughed because I realized I had just witnessed another miracle. The minefield created by the volcanic ash had rendered up a miracle. Alexander was now connected to a network of committed individuals who had agreed to help him: a Sikh, a Christian, a Hindu, and a Jew.

Was this all random?

"Nothing is accidental. It is only God's way of remaining anonymous," said Albert Einstein. That quote has become the leitmotif of my life.

And then it dawned on me. We have looked to God for modern-day miracles. We have prayed, beseeched, importuned, begged, and yearned for miracles. But what if, in this new era, we are being groomed to bring about miracles by our own thoughts, our own acts, and our own deeds?

What if God's ultimate plan is not micro-finance, but micro-miracles? Perhaps the greatest gift we have received is that we are created in God's image, God the Creator, God the Miracle-Maker, God the Kind and Merciful, Benevolent and Wise, full of Grace and Compassion. I am delighted with that thought. As Margaret Mead once said, "You only need four or five dedicated individuals to change the world." I am sure she must have been talking about citizen diplomats when she said that.

Table talk at the interfaith dinner held at the residence of the Moroccan Ambassador to the US.

2009 Pre-Parliament event at the Moroccan Embassy in DC, hosted by Ambassador Aziz Mekouar (fourth from left) in collaboration with students of George Mason University and their professor, Rabbi Marc Gopin (to the right of the Ambassador).

Participants at the 2006 interfaith event at the Bangladeshi embassy, (l. to r.) John Danner, Native American; Annuttama Dasa, Hindu; Bangladeshi Ambassador Shamsher Chowdhury; Ruth, and Imam Yahya Hendi, Muslim.

Citizen Diplomacy

Being interviewed with Ambassador Chowdhury for the Voice of America Radio.

With Professor Muhammad Yunus, the 2005 Nobel Peace Prize winner from Bangladesh.

Marianne Williamson and Professor Muhammad Yunus (center) surrounded by members of the Sister Giant delegation from Los Angeles at the 2010 Micro-Finance Conference in Nairobi, Kenya.

With Marianne Williamson, organizer of the Sister Giant Delegation to Kenya.

Sam Daley-Harris, (far left), founder and Executive Director of Results, facilitates a panel discussion at the Africa-Middle East Micro-credit Summit.

African participants at the Micro-Credit summit. On the far right is Ingrid Munro, originally from Sweden, who helped to found Jamii Bora, one of the most successful micro-loan associations in Africa.

Post-conference celebration.

Befriending a Kenyan giraffe.

Samson, a Masai warrior, offered me a cheetah's tooth as a gift, after I gave him a blessing.

Reading "The Princess and the Pea" with James, a young boy from the Dandora slum in Nairobi.

With Dr. David Silverstein, head of the Nairobi Hospital Cardiology department, and his wife Channa Commanday.

Standing with Jenny Cole, one of the co-founders of the special education/play program for the slum children of Dandora.

Episcopalian Bishop George Mechumo and his wife, Mary, my Nairobi airport friends.

Alexander McLean, founder of African Prisoners Project, speaks at the Nairobi synagogue about the deplorable prison conditions for inmates in Africa.

Take courage! God never forsakes His children who strive and work and pray! Let your hearts be filled with the strenuous desire that tranquility and harmony may encircle all this warring world. So will success crown your efforts, and with the universal brotherhood will come the Kingdom of God in peace and goodwill.

~Abdu'l Baha

CHAPTER 21

Green Bay Revisited: The Packers, Cheese, and Interfaith

In April of 2007 I was invited to be a keynote speaker in Green Bay, Wisconsin by the JOSHUA organization (Justice Organization Sharing Hope and United for Action). JOSHUA describes its mission as "an interfaith coalition of faith communities joined together to bridge differences and focus on common values to address community concerns."

I gladly accepted because I was curious to see what kind of an interfaith community existed in the town known primarily for its football team and cheese. The fringe benefit was that my sister, Leah, lives in Green Bay and we would have an opportunity to spend some time together.

I had been visiting my sister in her home for over thirty years. I thought I knew the make-up of the city well. The oldest incorporated city in Wisconsin, the "Green Bay" of Lake Michigan was "discovered" in 1634 by Catholic explorers who encountered the resident Native American Menominee and Ho-Chunk (Winnebago) tribes. Over the years, attracted by the fur and lumber trade opportunities and the rich farmland, French and Belgian Catholics arrived and built their own churches. Later German, Scandinavian and other groups, including part of the Oneida Nation, joined the original settlers, building their own churches of various denominations. A small group of Jews came early on, but by the end of the nineteenth century, the pogroms in Eastern Europe brought greater numbers to the Fox Valley and a synagogue was built in Green Bay in 1906 to accommodate Jewish observance.

My impression was that very few ethnic and racial minorities lived in Green Bay. In fact, one of my favorite facts about Green Bay was the name of the most popular restaurant in town, Stein's Chinese Restaurant. But I was in for a surprise.

The evening before I was to speak, my sister invited about 15 people for dinner. The guests included a Muslim couple from Bangladesh, a Muslim couple from India, some Jewish and Christian friends, and several of the local musicians of various faiths who would be performing at the event. Also present was the head of JOSHUA, Barbara Shiffer, known and respected in Green Bay for her dedication to the interfaith community and the one who had extended the invitation for me to speak

It was an evening of great ethnic food—my sister is an excellent cook—and delightful conversation. I learned that Sajita Shariff, one of the Muslim guests, had a black belt in Karate and was a teacher at the senior center. In talking to the Bangladeshi couple, Mohammad and Roksana Rashid, I had a new experience—playing "Muslim Geography" instead of "Jewish Geography" which is what Jewish people love to do when they first get together to discover what friends they have in common. I told the Rashids I had met and worked closely with the Bangladeshi Ambassador to the U.S. in Washington, and with the Muslim community in Los Angeles. They were pleasantly surprised to discover I was so well connected to the Muslim community and to Bangladeshi diplomats.

Roksana, a petite, vivacious and attractive woman, the mother of three sons, said she managed a motel they owned in Green Bay. Her husband Mohammad, a banker, and the head of the Muslim community in Appleton, Wisconsin, told me he would be introducing me as the keynote speaker at the event the following day.

As we were eating dinner, the conversation somehow drifted around to the differences between the stories that are found in the Jewish Bible and the Kor'an. I told Mohammad and Roksana that one of my first interfaith challenges occurred in 1991 when Delores, a black Christian minister, and I traveled to Egypt to set up our Festival of Freedom pilgrimage. Our Muslim travel guide was a very knowledgeable, university-educated woman, who specialized in Egyptology. Since Delores, the guide, and I spent most of the day together, we had opportunities to speak about many subjects. My antenna went up when she began to speak about the sacrifice of "Ishmael" by his father Abraham.

I interrupted her, to contradict her, violating one of the first rules of interfaith engagement. "You must be mistaken. You mean the sacrifice of Isaac."

"No," she insisted, "the sacrifice of Ishmael. It says so in the Kor'an. It says the firstborn son of Abraham. That was Ishmael."

I was prepared to debate the subject, but Delores turned to me and said, "Ruth, I would let this one go." And I did, but not easily.

Green Bay Revisited: The Packers, Cheese, and Interfaith

I was watching Mohammad and Roksana's face closely as I told them this story. They were intrigued, wondering where I was heading with my anecdote.

After being involved in ongoing interfaith engagement, and learning more about the Kor'an from my Muslim friends, I told them, "what I was able to understand many years later is that the core issue is not whether it was Isaac or Ishmael."

Mohammad looked at me intently. "What really matters," I continued, "is the message conveyed to us by the story. Are we ready to surrender everything we love the most, even our own child, if God asks us to? The lesson is about complete trust because, when God witnessed Abraham's faith, God made sure Abraham's son would not be sacrificed, and sent a ram instead." Mohammad was nodding, because the ram also appears in the Kor'an.

"Child sacrifice was very common in those days. God's clear message was: child sacrifice should be banned from that time on among the Hebrews. Therefore, does it really matter if it was Isaac or Ishmael?"

There was quiet at the table when I finished my explanation. The Christians present had not known that the "sacrifice" story in the Kor'an revolved around Ishmael, not Isaac. At first they were intrigued by the new information about one of their classic and best-known Old Testament stories. Then they were captivated by my declaration that "it didn't matter if it was Ishmael or Isaac; it's the message that counts."

The conversation got livelier after that and everyone chimed in and stayed longer than planned. It was close to 11 P.M. before the guests went home.

My sister was not at the table with us. She was in the other room with the other half of the guests, so she didn't know what had happened. She had noticed, however, that at some point in the evening it got very, very quiet at our table. "What was going on?"

"Oh, we were just comparing stories from the Bible and the Kor'an," I replied casually.

The next day when Mohammad took the podium to introduce me, he forgot to read my bio. Instead, he told the audience about our conversation the night before, and how he had considered late into the night what I said at dinner. "Ultimately it didn't matter whether it was Ishmael or Isaac; what counted was God's message." Later that day he told me he was embarrassed by his *faux pas* for not introducing me properly and he apologized profusely, but I laughed and assured him, "The intro didn't matter; it was your message that counted."

Almost six hundred people were in the auditorium of the Catholic Notre Dame High school that day, among them Lutherans, Catholics, Jews, two Muslim communities, Zen Buddhists, Presbyterians, Unitarians, Baha'is, and the local Hmong people.

Is this the Green Bay I knew? Is this the poster child for traditional Middle America?

Not any more, I told myself. This is the New America; and this is the New Green Bay: a multi-ethnic, multi-religious, multi-cultural city, like Los Angeles, or New York or Chicago..

I impulsively left the stage and went down into the audience. I looked around at all the eager, expectant faces and I asked them to raise their little finger, for an exercise in physics and metaphysics.

They were clearly puzzled, but they all complied and raised their little finger. "This is a physical law of the universe, and my sister's fiancé, Jim, who is a scientist, is here in the audience, so he can vouch for me that this is true," I said, searching for Jim in the crowd.

"When you raise your little finger, all the molecules in the rest of the world have to move to accommodate even that tiny movement of your finger, right Jim?"

"Yes, that's right," Jim called out in support.

"Well, Jim knows, and what I'm here to tell you today is that this same principle in physics is also a spiritual principle, so for every little movement you make, for every small act you perform, you have an opportunity to change the composition of the world."

The lights were dimmed and then I screened *God and Allah Need to Talk*. Afterwards, I invited the audience to turn in their seats and have conversation with no more than four to five people, to share what they were thinking while they were watching the film.

I stood and watched them for a while and then decided to join a few of the groups to "eavesdrop." They were deeply engaged in conversation and didn't pay attention to my arrival. I knew from past experience that was a good sign. Fifteen minutes later I brought them back as an audience to the final "call to action," and asked them, "What would you be ready to do to change the molecular composition of the world?"

They were silent.

"Let's brainstorm together," I suggested.

Immediately people began raising their hands to participate. "I'd like people who have never been to a mosque to visit our mosque," Mohammad said. A flurry of hands went up. Obviously, many people were eager to accept this special opportunity. Then one of the Buddhists stood and invited everyone to his community's holiday celebration the following weekend.

I called Roksana to join me at the front of the auditorium and asked if she would be willing to help form a local women's interfaith dialogue group. I knew I was putting her on the spot, but I was taking a calculated risk because the night before I had duly noted her ability to socialize easily and make friends. As I expected, she immediately agreed, and a flock of women's hands flew up. They were ready to sign up right there. And I am happy to report four years later the group is still active.

Green Bay Revisited: The Packers, Cheese, and Interfaith

There were other innovative and exciting suggestions. Inspired by having watched the Muslim/Jewish Seder in the film, one of the women in the audience stood and proposed that they hold an Interfaith Seder in the Atrium of the renovated Green Bay Packers stadium where meetings and events are held year-round.

"What a brilliant idea!" I exclaimed. "We can take a photograph of the Packers in their uniforms eating *matzah*. Truly a photo-op for interfaith athletics!"

The ideas just kept coming—an interfaith men's group, an interfaith music ensemble, an interfaith youth group, an interfaith movie group—but it was getting late and we still had tables laden with refreshments waiting for us in the foyer of the school. It is always important to socialize and share refreshments in any interfaith gathering and, besides, I knew people were waiting to register for follow-up activities. I closed out the event by asking all of the clergy in the audience to come forward and give a blessing for the food we were about to share. We ended by standing and singing, arm in arm, "Let There Be Peace on Earth, and Let It Begin with Me."

The follow-up sheets had been laid out on a long table in the school cafeteria. They included Women's Interfaith Dialogue, Men's Interfaith Dialogue, Youth Interfaith, Interfaith Music Ensemble, Mosque Tour, Synagogue Tour, Buddhist Temple Tour and Interfaith Seder. I watched in amazement as about half of five-hundred and fifty people present stood in line for up to half an hour to sign up for one or more of the activities.

This was not the Green Bay I used to know. Yes, the Green Bay Packers are stronger than ever, and Wisconsin cheese is still among the finest, but I have witnessed the miracle of the New Green Bay, and the miracle that is happening in small towns all over America and all over the world.

Interfaith is on the move!

Minefields & Miracles

Flyer for *God & Allah Need to Talk* event in Green Bay, Wisconsin.

Barbara Shiffer, head of JOSHUA, welcomes 600 participants.

Local musicians play a medley of songs.

Two Muslim girls offer an ethnic dance.

Green Bay Revisited: The Packers, Cheese, and Interfaith

Audience participation is welcomed and encouraged.

Standing with Roksana Rashid, a Muslim woman who agreed to head a new women's interfaith dialogue group in Green Bay.

Socializing with Imam Aziz and Mohammad Rashid after the event.

(L.to r.) Imam Salman Aziz, Mohammad Rashid, Dr. Alem Asres, Gayle Kagen, former Congressional Representative Dr. Steve Kagen, Ruth, Rev. Charles Mize, Rabbi Shaina Bacharach.

"The Golden Rule is of no use to you whatsoever unless you realize that it's your move."

~Dr. Frank Crane

CHAPTER 22

Beyond Theories, Where the Rubber Meets the Road

The joke would begin like this: It is a warm spring morning. A Jew, a Hindu, and a Buddhist are all standing in a kitchen facing one another.

Except it wasn't a joke. And the stakes were very high, because it was taking place in my kitchen, in my home.

As part of an ancient tradition that Jewish women have been observing for more than a thousand years, I was cleaning out my kitchen to get ready for Passover, the Festival of Freedom that commemorates the Israelites' exodus from Egypt.

Getting ready for Passover is not a simple process. We begin by getting rid of any food products that have been made with yeast, such as pasta, bread, cake, cereals, crackers, and the like. Then we empty out all the cabinets, all the drawers, and clear off all the shelves, still checking for stray breadcrumbs as we clean. We remove all dishes and cooking utensils, pack them away and replace them with a separate set of dishes and utensils that have been stored untouched for a year, to be taken out and used exclusively for the eight days of the Passover celebration. It can take days to achieve that level of cleanliness.

If I lived in the old city of Jerusalem, I could join thousands of religious Jews who make use of the 'koshering" stands that have been set up in the streets a week before the holiday begins. Groups of young men in their long black coats and black hats, their ritual fringes flapping at their waist, can be seen tending to the giant vats of boiling water on the Jerusalem street corners. It is a very colorful sight and a visual treat to observe them as they expertly dunk the dishes and pots into the huge vats, the vapor and mist from the scalding water rising around them like transparent cirrus clouds. This is a service they perform for families who don't have a separate set of dishes. The object is to purify the everyday dishes and pots to make them "kosher for Passover."

But I am not in old Jerusalem. I am in Culver City, California and I am in the process of making my kitchen "kosher for Passover." I will be storing all of my year-round dishes, pots and pans and silverware for eight days, and in their place I will put dishes, pots and pans and silverware that I only use on Passover.

When we first begin to study the traditions of Passover, we learn that this tradition is not just about changing dishes or surface cleanliness. It is about getting rid of what we call in Hebrew the *hometz*, the leavening, the yeasty part that makes our bread and our egos puff up. Passover has come to mean more than a spring-cleaning. For Jews this tradition of seeking out and then burning the leavening from the year before is also to lighten ourselves psychologically. We are just about to leave our metaphoric Egypt, the narrow place in our lives (in Hebrew the word for Egypt is *Mitzrayim*, which means narrowness). As the ancient Israelites discovered, there is no time for the bread to rise, and we must not tarry, because we are a people on the move, on the move to leave behind our shackles and our servitude, on the move to be free!

So, here I am, just one day before Passover, eager to clean out my kitchen with the help of Maria. It is too big a task for one person to accomplish in just one day, so I am grateful to have Maria at my side. A lovely, dependable woman who comes to help me clean my house from time to time, Maria is from Central America. She was born a Catholic, but now she is a member of the Hare Krishna community, and she no longer eats meat, and she also will not work in a place where meat is cooking.

Maria and I are in the entryway to the kitchen. I am frozen in disbelief as I hear Maria telling me she cannot help me clean the kitchen because she smells chicken cooking there. "What chicken are you talking about?" I ask, surprised by her comment since I am very familiar with her religious restrictions concerning meat. "I'm not cooking any chicken," I insist.

She points to the oven door. I open it and I see five plump drumsticks in a pan and, indeed, they are being cooked. Maria nods at my discovery and moves farther away from the stove. I am worried she may be on her way to the front door.

Patricia, a Buddhist friend, has been living in my home for several months in my son's vacant room, as a transitional place until she finds other accommodations.

At that moment she walks into the kitchen, and the plot thickens.

"Are you cooking this chicken, Patricia?" I ask. "And do you have to cook it now?"

Beyond Theories, Where the Rubber Meets the Road

Patricia is surprised by my query. "Well, I just took a break from an important Buddhist retreat," she explains. "I am on a special diet and I won't have any time to cook over the weekend or go shopping for food. I have to cook all of my food now and bring it with me back to the retreat. Is there a problem?"

"Maria can't stay and help me clean my kitchen for Passover if there's meat cooking in the kitchen," I explain to her. "It's against her religious principles. And I have to finish cleaning the kitchen today so I can transfer all my pots and pans elsewhere and replace them with my Passover dishes. It'll take most of the day and I need her help or I won't be able to complete the process in time for my holiday," I elaborate. "I have no one else available to help me. We have to get rid of the chicken now," I insist.

"But I have to finish cooking my chicken now," Patricia says with an urgent tone, "because I'm leaving for the retreat shortly, and I need to take the cooked food with me."

Well, there you have it. A Jew, a Hindu, and a Buddhist are all in a kitchen together, each with her separate religious traditions that ordinarily wouldn't create a conflict, but now there is an existential—as well as a religious—dilemma taking place in the kitchen.

Whose tradition gets to rule?

All three of us look at one another. No one says anything.

In my head, I'm trapped in my own monologue. After all, I say to myself, this is my kitchen, and it's my home, and shouldn't I have the final word about celebrating my tradition in my own home? This is where I live. I'm not in someone else's home where I have to respect their traditions. This is my home. But this is also Patricia's home now, where she lives, even though it's a temporary arrangement. She is entitled to keep her tradition as well. And we're not asking Maria to cook the chicken for her. Maria will just be in the same room where the chicken is cooking. But if Maria says she can't stay where meat is being cooked, then I have to respect that. And if she can't stay, then I can't get my kitchen ready in time for Passover, and if I tell Patricia that my religious practice is more important than her needs, what am I really saying?

Help!!!

As these frantic thoughts and counter-thoughts are careening through my mind, I look around at Patricia's and Maria's faces. I see that they are also going through their own mental permutations. Will Maria leave? Will Patricia stop cooking her food and then be angry with me? Should I forgo my sacred tradition in order to accommodate someone else's religious practice?

I am desperate to find a solution, but I realize something else is happening that is more important at that moment than the solution.

Trumpet fanfare! This is an interfaith conundrum of the first order, I tell myself.

This is where you have to go beyond theory. This is what all of your interfaith activity has been preparing you for, for the last twenty years. Here it is, Ruth. This is where the rubber meets the road. What will you do now?

I suddenly recall the words of Rabbi Mayer Shiller, an Orthodox rabbi whom I interviewed for my recent video *Listening with a Heart of Mercy*. He summarized my dilemma with his provocative question: "How can we be faithful to our own tradition and tribe while we are extending compassion and understanding to people of other faiths?" asks Rabbi Shiller and then hastens to admit, "That is the challenge."

I look into Maria's eyes, then into Patricia's eyes. What does it mean to see the reflection of someone else in your self?

What is the right thing to do? What is the decent thing to do? What is the respectful thing to do? Does one of us have to compromise to make it alright for the other two? Can someone in this situation compromise without feeling resentful? Will the decision we ultimately make change the nature of our relationships, our friendships? What did the poet Rumi really mean when he spoke about the field beyond ideas of wrongdoing and rightdoing?

What would God want us to do? Or Buddha? Or Krishna?

As I am writing these lines, I'm wondering if I should write the end of the story or let you, the reader, go through this scenario and come up with your own solution.

But even if I tell you what happened, I hope you will—just for a few moments—imagine yourself in my kitchen with us: a Jew, a Hindu, and a Buddhist, all trapped in an existential, philosophical minefield that could blow all of us up, or some of us, or one of us, or none of us…

This is when interfaith engagement becomes more than just a theory.

Here is what happened. After several moments of contemplating one another, which could have been measured in lifetimes because it seemed to be taking forever, I exclaimed. "I have an idea! Look! Here is a small toaster oven which I never use. I can take it out to the back yard, plug it in, and then Patricia can cook her chicken there and have it ready in time for her retreat. Maria won't be close enough to smell the meat, so she can stay and help me clean my kitchen for Passover."

And that's what we did.

A Jewish friend said to me later, "What would you have done if you hadn't had a toaster oven in your kitchen and there was no other place for Patricia to cook her chicken?"

Jews have a way of posing questions that cut so close to the bone. For Jews, the principal way of learning is through questions. The permutations and explanations of what the correct answers might be are recorded in the Talmud, the compendium of Jewish law derived from the Five Books of Moses. When you study the Talmud, you can clearly see how we love our questions.

In the upper right-hand corner of each page in the Talmud is the original biblical injunction under review. The rest of the page and the entire page on the left are both devoted to discussion and commentaries about that biblical text, written by rabbis who, throughout the centuries, have come up with varied and often conflicting interpretations of the same text. And they themselves pose more questions about the original question and then debate the implications of their own questions. It may be futile to look for a single, agreed-upon solution to the problem under discussion because all of the permutations and possibilities they are considering may only inspire further questions and further debate. If the rabbis can't agree on a single interpretation of Jewish law, you might ask, then how do you know what to do?

As Jews have discovered through centuries of study and deliberation, ultimately we are on our own. We can refer to the wisdom of our sages; we can select the best answer for ourselves at that moment; or we can remain in a quandary, hoping that some other insightful commentary will make its way to our moral doorstep and help us solve the conundrum.

What would you have done in my situation? Would you have insisted that Patricia remove the chicken from the oven? Would you have allowed Maria to "abandon ship," knowing that you wouldn't be ready for Passover? Would you have abandoned your own tradition out of deference to the two other women?

As for me, I am very glad I had a toaster oven in my kitchen. As my son pointed out, I averted the problem but I didn't solve it. I don't really know how—minus the toaster oven—I would resolve it now. For me it underscores just how important and challenging interfaith work can be as we struggle to bring peace to a world fraught with ongoing and persistent conflict, pockmarked by minefields, and dotted with only an occasional miracle to lift our spirits.

The miracles may be our friends, but the minefields are our teachers.

"You can't separate peace from freedom because no one can be at peace unless he has his freedom."

~Malcolm X

CHAPTER 23
A New Interfaith Era in Washington

On a cold, winter day in January 2009, I arrived in Washington, DC. Hundreds of thousands of people were all moving through the streets in perfect syncopation. I inhaled the energy and excitement from the crowds around me along with the frosty air. No one pushed or shoved. We all knew we would find the perfect spot for ourselves, and nothing could spoil our day. We were about to witness Barack Hussein Obama take his oath of office as the new President of the United States.

It had proved impossible to get a seat. The demand for tickets was enormous. For the majority of us, the only way to see the inauguration of our president was on a giant video screen. I remember how exhilarated I felt standing shoulder to shoulder with about one and a half million people on the Mall, the same Mall where in 1963 hundreds of thousands stood to hear Dr. Martin Luther King, Jr. as he spoke of a time when his four little children would "not be judged by the color of their skin, but by the content of their character."

I shivered from the cold and from the knowledge that I was living in the time of Dr. King's "fulfilled prophesy." Modern day miracles are often overlooked but this was, in my view, comparable to the fall of the Berlin Wall, the unexpected dissolution of the Soviet Union, and the beginning of a citizens' revolution in Iran, spearheaded by women.

A man with a white Christian mother and a black Muslim father was about to become President of the United States. Whether or not his election would end racism in America was yet to be determined, and, in retrospect, I realize that institutional racism is unfortunately still prevalent, but at that moment it felt like a profound shift had taken place in our country's history.

Minefields & Miracles

I ultimately found a place to position myself, near K and Sixteenth Streets. I had never participated in such a huge gathering before, although I had witnessed parades and marched in many a demonstration in my time. There was something both humbling and ennobling about being one individual among (what we would later learn) a million and a half people. Humbling, ennobling, and also comforting—emotions I hadn't expected to arise.

We began to introduce ourselves to one another almost immediately. To my left were an African-American man and his wife from Winston-Salem, North Carolina; in front of me a white woman from Utah; to my right two African-American couples, in their early forties; behind me a family with teenage children and a small baby. One of the women on my right, I discovered, was a principal of a Maryland high school. Soon we were discussing philosophy of education and the current challenges facing the schools in America.

The spectators in my particular section of the Mall had all arrived about 8:30 that morning. We positioned ourselves close enough to have an unobstructed view of one of the giant screens put in place by the fast-thinking inauguration planners. The planners knew in advance that the three hundred and sixty thousand tickets they had available for seating would not be sufficient, by any stretch of the imagination, but what they didn't quite know and couldn't quite calculate in advance was how many people would ultimately descend upon the nation's capital. And what would happen when they all arrived? Could the city and its metro system sustain that many visitors? That was part of the unknown, as we waited to see how many people would come and where they would all fit.

While we were waiting, we shared our personal stories. The people who were positioned closest to the stage, we were told, had arrived at six that morning, and the word was that many had spent the night sleeping on the ground in their sleeping bags, in the biting cold, so they could get the choicest places directly behind the seating area.

Although we had been warned that it might snow, to our collective delight, the morning was crisp and clear. People shivering from the cold were rubbing their arms and marching in place to keep warm. Many were using disposable heating packets that they slipped into their gloves or boots. Fortunately, I had bought myself a warm fleece vest and jacket a few days earlier in New York. I was also wearing a heavy turtleneck sweater, gloves, long underwear, tall winter boots, and a hat with an attached scarf that tied around my neck. The only exposed part of my body was my face. I had taken precautions, true, but I was not genuinely concerned about the weather. I was a Chicago girl; sharp wind and bitter cold were my childhood winter companions.

A New Interfaith Era in Washington

As we huddled close to one another in casual intimacy, we could see each other's breath rising in the sky. I watched how our separateness dissolved as we pressed together to keep warm. We were not strangers; we were comrades-in-history, watching the enormous hands of the distant clock on the tower of a building on edges of the mall. We did the countdown together for the inaugural blast off.

I noticed several tall, leafless trees nearby. Their bare winter branches were silhouetted against the morning gray-blue of the sky. Even the trees would bear witness that morning and, like us, they seemed poised in expectancy.

I examined the faces around me. The majority of the people present were African-American, and with good reason. This was one of the most significant moments in their lives as black Americans. The path to this moment officially began in 1870 when the Fifteenth Amendment was passed allowing black men to vote in America.

The Fifteenth Amendment had declared that "the right of citizens of the United States to vote shall not be denied or abridged by the United States or by any state on account of race, color, or previous condition of servitude." But there is theory and then there is practice. Although ratified on February 3, 1870, almost a century passed before suffrage for African-Americans was realized in American society. I remember reading how the segregationist diehards, primarily from the southern states, opposed the amendment and invented poll taxes, literacy tests and other devious means to subvert change. It took the passage of the Voting Rights Act of 1965 to insure that the majority of African Americans in the South were registered to vote. Even during the election of 2004 I heard disturbing stories about blacks in Florida and Texas who were denied the ability to vote in their districts through some unconscionable modern maneuvers.

But here I was, in 2009, watching Barack Hussein Obama as he was about to become the forty-fourth president of the United States. One simply had to suspend all disbelief, because it was true.

Only minutes were left before the inauguration ceremony would begin. The anticipation was now palpable, rising and expanding outwards like a billowing canopy above our heads. I suddenly asked myself: What could I, as a Jewish woman in the midst of mostly a black, Christian audience, relate to from my own background that could help me grasp what this moment meant to the black Americans around me?

In my mind I flashed on the documentary footage I had seen many times when I was growing up. I vividly recalled the scratched archival footage showing images of Jewish families in Palestine huddled tightly around huge bulky radios in their living rooms, waiting to see how their political fate would be determined. It was November 29, 1947. In every household at least one person served as the official "counter" with pencil and paper, recording the votes as they came in, one by one, from the delegates of the United Nation General Assembly in New York City.

The moment Russia cast the deciding vote, creating the needed majority to approve Israel's bid for statehood, people in Israel spontaneously spilled into the streets. They formed hundreds of circles to dance and celebrate. Their faces glowed with both joy and wonder. At last the Jewish people had an internationally, politically sanctified homeland, after thousands of years of persecution and statelessness. The exultation of the dancers literally leapt from the badly scratched film into my heart.

That was my personal frame of reference as I stood among my African-American brothers and sisters that day, but I realized there was something else my heart needed to acknowledge. Because of my interfaith activism, and my personal ongoing concern about the Israeli-Palestinian conflict, at that moment I also found myself wishing that the Palestinians would have an opportunity to celebrate their own independent homeland in my lifetime.

I was pulled away from my private reverie by the arrival of Barack Hussein Obama at the podium. He placed his hand on the Bible. Everywhere I turned people were crying. A wild and thunderous cry of jubilation rose up when he finished taking his oath. In an eloquent speech that will be quoted for many decades and centuries to come, President Obama then gave what would probably become the first "interfaith" address made by any American president. He praised our multicultural nation and made clear references to our interreligious composition. These were not veiled references or intimations. This was a head-on, direct comment that he had obviously crafted with great care.

> *For we know that our patchwork heritage is a strength, not a weakness. We are a nation of Christians and Muslims, Jews and Hindus—and non-believers. We are shaped by every language and culture, drawn from every end of this Earth; and because we have tasted the bitter swill of civil war and segregation, and emerged from that dark chapter stronger and more united, we cannot help but believe that the old hatreds shall someday pass; that the lines of tribe shall soon dissolve; that as the world grows smaller, our common humanity shall reveal itself; and that America must play its role in ushering in a new era of peace.*

"Christians and Muslims, Jews and Hindus," was the way President Obama had phrased it—in a clear break with tradition, later noted by all of the media pundits and social commentators. He didn't say "Christians and Jews," or refer to us as a "Judeo-Christian country," which was

A New Interfaith Era in Washington

the customary way our elected officials have referred to our pluralistic society.

President Obama was marking a new interfaith era in American life, and I gloried in it, but there was one additional epiphany for me in that vast expense of Mall. It happened during Pastor Rick Warren's invocation.

Many people had expressed doubts and dismay about Obama's choice of an evangelical preacher to give the invocation, but for me those doubts were dispelled when Pastor Warren began to speak.

"Let us pray," he said.

Immediately all of the heads around me bowed in prayer.

"Almighty God, our Father, everything we see and everything we can't see exists because of you alone. It all comes from you. It all belongs to you. It all exists for your glory."

He then borrowed from both Jewish and Muslim liturgy. He first quoted the most sacred of all prayers said by Jews around the world, known as the *Shema*.

"The Scripture tells us, "Hear O Israel, the Lord is our God. The Lord is One.""

Immediately afterwards he used the opening lines of the Muslim call to prayer.

"And you are the compassionate and merciful one."

This is a translation from the first chapter of the Kor'an, which in Arabic reads *Bismillah ir-Rahman ir-Rahim* (in the name of God, the Compassionate, the Merciful).

For those of us familiar with both Jewish and Muslim prayer, his intention was not lost on us. This was a new era, where Christian prayer was joined by Jewish and now Muslim liturgy.

"Now, today, we rejoice not only in America's peaceful transfer of power for the forty-fourth time…We celebrate a hingepoint of history with the inauguration of our first African-American president of the United States. We are so grateful to live in this land, a land of unequaled possibility, where the son of an African immigrant can rise to the highest level of our leadership. And we know today that Dr. King and a great cloud of witnesses are shouting in heaven…"

All around me, in a series of echoes, I heard the clear refrain "Thank you, Jesus. Thank you, Jesus."

Pastor Warren then alluded to our ideals of pluralism.

"Help us, O God, to remember that we are Americans, united not by race, or religion, or blood, but to our commitment to freedom and justice for all."

Again the refrain reverberated in front of me, behind me, to my right and my left, "Thank you, Jesus. Thank you, Jesus."

Pastor Warren then concluded with the Lord's Prayer. By this time, everyone was either reciting the prayer out loud with him or mouthing the familiar words.

Our Father, who art in heaven, hallowed be Thy name. Thy kingdom come, Thy will be done on earth as it is in heaven. Give us this day our daily bread and forgive us our trespasses as we forgive those who trespass against us. And lead us not into temptation, but deliver us from evil. For Thine is the kingdom and the power and the glory forever. Amen.

Once again a heartfelt response undulated in a wave across the Mall of 1.5 million people. "Thank you, Jesus. Thank you, Jesus."

I heard myself thanking God in Hebrew, the language of my people, and at the same feeling completely and intimately connected to the people around me as they were calling to Jesus.

How often during their times of greatest woe and suffering had black men and women in my country prayed to Jesus to keep them safe, to give them courage, and to lead them out of exile. I was a descendent of a people who had been rescued from Pharaoh and a life of slavery, and I could imagine the Israelites tasting freedom for the first time on the far side of the Sea of Reeds. And I could comprehend why, at that moment, they wanted to thank God. Our scripture tells us that after crossing the Sea of Reeds, the Israelite women began to rejoice in song and dance, with tambourine and drum.

It dawned on me then that I was participating in a gargantuan interreligious "Passover" ceremony: the Washington Mall had been transformed into a giant cathedral under the January winter sky; the congregants were assembled in the open-air cathedral thanking God for the privilege of seeing the day when a people once enslaved could now experience freedom; and the summation of that realization was embodied in the tall, elegant figure of Barack Hussein Obama.

All of us present and witness to that moment had crossed the Sea of Reeds together.

A New Interfaith Era in Washington

Washington, DC—January 20, 2009—Barack Obama takes the oath as the 44th U.S. President with his wife, Michelle, by his side at the U.S. Capitol in Washington, DC. Daughters Malia, center right, and Sasha look on. (Credit: Chuck Kennedy – Pool via CNP)

Minefields & Miracles

Washington, DC—January 20, 2009—Wide shot looking towards the National Mall where some 1.5 million people witnessed the swearing-in ceremony for Barack Obama.
(Credit: Mark Wilson – Pool via CNP)

A New Interfaith Era in Washington

Washington, DC—January 20, 2009—U.S. President Barack Obama takes the oath of office.
(Credit: Matthew Barrick – CNP)

Washington, DC—January 20, 2009—Pastor Rick Warren (center) gives the invocation as President-elect Barack Obama and President George W. Bush bow their heads during the 2009 Presidential Inauguration ceremony.

(Credit: Pat Benic – Pool via CNP)

"But peace, too, is a living thing and like all life it must wax and wane, accommodate, withstand trials, and undergo changes."

~Herman Hesse

CHAPTER 24

Lessons from the Rain Forest

Once you manage to get there, Monteverde, true to its name (Green Mountain), with its immediate access to the rain forest, is understandably one of the most popular tourist sites in Costa Rica. Tourists from around the world will simply not be dissuaded by the bumpy, winding dirt roads one needs to navigate no matter whether you come from north, south, east, or west. Some locals in Monteverde claim that even though the city has received government funds to modernize the roads, the big hotels refuse any opportunity to make the city more accessible because they want tourists to stay as long as possible, and not have an easy way to escape to the beaches on the coasts.

I arrived for a four-day stay in Monteverde, promising myself a half-day foray into the rain forest, in spite of the fact that I had committed to writing at least ten chapters of this book. It had been two years since I first began writing in Rome and I was determined to complete the book by the end of the year.

I had booked a room in advance, at a bargain rate of $30 a night. When I arrived at the hotel I understood why it was such a bargain. The room had one bed and one nightstand. No writing table or chair was available, and even if they had been available, there was not enough room to accommodate either of them. It was basically wall-to-wall bed. Agitated by my discovery, I told the hotel owner the room was not suitable, and that I would have to find other accommodations.

"I need a writing table and a chair, and that's not negotiable," I explained. I was about to leave and look for another hotel when he made a new offer.

"We're just finishing an apartment in a house next door," he said. "It has never been rented, but you can have it for $40 a night instead of $60. There are some problems that we haven't quite resolved yet, but they are not serious. And it does have a table and a chair."

What did I have to lose? I asked myself. I decided to check it out. I climbed the stairs to the second floor of a large house adjacent to the hotel and found an airy apartment with a private kitchen, private bath, and a combination bedroom-living room dominated by an enormous picture window twenty feet in length, facing the rainforest. Opposite the window I spied a small square dining table that could be used as a desk, and four dining room chairs. I visited the upstairs loft, which housed a queen size bed and another large picture window of the rain forest.

"I'll take it," I said immediately. They brought my luggage upstairs while I was marveling at my stroke of good luck. A few hours later I knew why I had been offered the bargain price. The main door wouldn't close--it banged back and forth with every blast of the wind. Also the kitchen sink dripped continuously, which meant I would have to open and close the valve under the sink after each use. But the most annoying discovery for me was that the wind howled day and night. I could enjoy watching the majestic green velvet mountains of the rain forest through the window, but the windowpanes rattled each time the wind blew, and because both sides of the house were unprotected, the noise of the wind was constant and unrelenting.

I sat down for a moment to review my situation. I felt the howling wind penetrating my thoughts. There was no way to think in silence. The wind never abated, not even for five minutes, and with each gust, the house would tremble anew. I found myself wondering how it had been constructed. How deep and sturdy were the pylons of the foundations? Had the walls been properly tested for wind stress? Could the windows withstand the constant pummeling by the wind, or would they just shatter into a million pieces?

After fretting about my situation for several hours, and unable to do any writing, I made myself a salad in the kitchen, opening and closing the valve under the sink, on and off, over and over again, as I cleaned each vegetable, then the bowl, then the plate, and the silverware. I found myself exhausted just from the energy I expended in preparing the meal and managing the dripping faucet so as not to waste water. I said a blessing, but then I ate the salad without paying attention to how it tasted. I was too busy contemplating my dilemma.

I went down to the hotel lobby to complain about my main door not closing. They apologized sincerely and said the apartment wasn't quite ready yet for someone to live there, but they reminded me that I had agreed to take it. I went back up to the apartment. I still couldn't get the door to close.

Lessons from the Rain Forest

A young man with a hammer and a screwdriver came to fix the door twenty minutes later. He managed to adjust it so it would close, but because there was a huge gap between the bottom of the door and the stoop, the wind still rushed in, in a noisy whoosh. It was too late to go to another hotel so I decided to sleep upstairs in the loft to keep warm and to continue worrying about my situation the next day. The howling of the wind seemed to be less invasive in the loft, but the moment I climbed into the bed, I had a new worry. The bed shook every time the wind pounded against the house, and when I looked up I saw the chandelier above the bed swinging back and forth like a pendulum. I crawled under the covers, wondering how I could survive the night without the chandelier falling on my head. I conjectured how my obituary might read, only half in jest.

"She was found dead in her bed, near the Costa Rican Rain Forest, decapitated by a chandelier." No wonder it was only $40 a night.

I hardly slept my first night there and, in the morning, bleary eyed from lack of sleep, and grumpy from a rocky bed and a howling wind, I went downstairs to greet the day. I was stopped in my tracks by the view. Through the picture window I witnessed a breathtaking panoply of lush green, undulating mountains, expansive blue sky, and early rays of sun creating rainbow prisms through the morning rain. Then I noticed that it was raining only in one part of the sky, on the left, but not on the right. How was that possible, I longed to know? (No one had yet explained to me about the Continental Divide.) I felt awe and gratitude as I slid open the door to the balcony and stepped outside to survey my private view of heaven and earth. I smelled the freshness of the morning, saw the sparkling dew on nearby leaves, heard the warbling of the birds, and I simply fell in love.

I stayed outside for a few more moments and then went inside to have a talk with myself. I found a pillow to put on one of the hard wooden dining chairs. I sat down, opened my laptop, clicked on Word, and up popped a blank page. The wind howled and pounded the glass window while I contemplated my situation.

I could look for another place to write and sleep. That was one possibility, I told myself, but that would take time, valuable time, and how did I know I wouldn't have to confront similar problems in the next place as well? Good point, I told myself.

There still was one other possibility. I could change my point of view. I could engineer a paradigm shift in my head.

'What if … the wind was not my enemy but my ally?'

I felt that I was poised on the edge of an "aha" moment.

'What if … instead of being bothered and distracted by the howling of the wind I could use the sound to inspire me?'

'What if … while I was writing I could create mental alchemy by transforming the raw energy of the wind into words and ideas in my book?'

'Wind is wind, and sound is sound,' I reasoned. 'Wind doesn't intrinsically have either a negative or a positive quality, so the sound of the wind doesn't have to be disruptive unless I choose to interpret it as disruptive. If I can change my attitude, I can make my stay here enjoyable, and I can continue writing my book.'

I sat in silence for a moment and then asked myself 'What if I could do that right now? I know there is such a thing as mind over matter.'

So I decided, there and then, that the wind would be my friend, and help me write ten chapters of my book.

Everything changed for me in Monteverde from that moment. When I went to sleep that night, I imagined I was out on the ocean sleeping in a canoe, and so the rocking of the bed actually became the rocking of my sea cradle. The overhead chandelier, which used to shake above the bed, now became the Big Dipper, my guide among the constellations, and it no longer terrified me. I slept peacefully that night and for the next three nights, and every time I heard the wind howl, I felt protected and safe. The wind was my protector at night, and my inspiration by day.

I did indeed write the ten chapters I'd promised myself to complete in Monteverde, but more important were the two lessons I learned.

The first lesson took place in my hotel room when I discovered that I could actually engineer my own paradigm shift just by consciously choosing a new interpretation of my surroundings. That process, if mastered, could actually become an extremely valuable tool for participants engaged in interfaith dialogue. What if people were encouraged to give up their current critical attitudes towards other religions by reframing their thoughts? Could we begin to develop a genuine appreciation and respect for one another by a simple paradigm shift?

The second lesson came on Saturday, my Sabbath, when I went to visit the rain forest nearby. I arrived there early with a group of tourists who wanted to enjoy the canopy ride above and across the rainforest, strapped into a harness, and hooked onto giant cables. I heard them screaming with delight as they careened down from the treetops to the sweet-smelling earth. I decided not to go on the cables, but instead to walk, and to savor my journey slowly.

I was putting off my entry into the rain forest itself, hoping to miss the crowds. To stall a bit longer, I decided I would take a tour of the butterfly exhibit, along with a tourist from Germany. Our guide was twenty-four year-old Sergio, a native Costa Rican, who knew every detail and nuance about the lives of the butterflies. He knew how long they spent in their cocoons, what plant was most hospitable to them, what they liked to eat, how you could tell when their metamorphosis from cocoon to butterfly would occur, and how long they could live. As we moved around the butterfly habitat, he gently lifted up various butterflies by their wings, pointing out their main characteristics, and then let them fly off again. We continued along the path and next he pointed out some mangos that had been cut open and spread out on a plate, as an offering for the "owl butterflies," named for the speckled brown patterns on their wings that actually looked like owls' eyes.

I was surprised to see the butterflies lying motionless on the plate, interspersed with the mango slices. "Are they dead?" I asked with concern.

"No, they're just drunk," our young guide explained with a wide grin and a wink. "They eat too much and then they fall asleep, drunk from the mango nectar."

Later in the morning, I experienced being drunk myself, not on mangos but on nature. I finally entered the rainforest and, except for a young couple and their children who passed by briefly, I was able to explore the rainforest on my own.

For twenty years I had been connected to the Costa Rican rain forest through the lush oil paintings of my artist friend, Rosita Gottlieb. Now I was here in person. I found myself praying to God, using the words of the Sabbath prayers I knew by heart, *Mi Kamocha, Adonai*? Who is like onto you, O God? *No-rah t'hilah, oseh feleh*. Grand and awesome are you, creator of miracles.

I walked very slowly, marveling at the diverse formations of the plants and trees. They seemed connected by their proximity and intimacy, one to another, even though they were not of the same genus. I noticed the thick overcoat of moss on many tree trunks and the great varieties of vegetation populating the forest, even in the smallest areas. My senses feasted on the colors of the forest, especially the greens: pale green, blue-green, lime green, pea-green, gray green, Kelly green, sage green, and deep forest green—and there were shades of green I could not even name. I also observed how the shape of each leaf and plant was unique; some had short spiky leaves, others were wide and textured, or thick and velvety, some tall and graceful. The variety was endless.

At one point, I found myself swaying and holding on to one of the many rope bridges that had been erected for tourists, high above the ground. I looked down and caught my breath in wonder at the vast green carpet below me, spread out like a giant Oriental rug, woven from green strands of chlorophyll. I was so far above the plants it became hard to distinguish one from another as I had done when I was inches away.

Somehow a divine arrangement had been arrived upon by an agreement between God and nature. The trees, the plants, the blossoms, the leaves, the thorns, the fruit, the insects. They existed in perfect cohabitation in a forest that allowed them to flourish as a community. No one plant seemed to be more important than the next. All were an integral and essential part of the eco-system.

The comparison between plants and humans was inescapable.

Even the parasite flowers seemed to have made an agreement with the host trees that allowed them a place to live and flourish, at the host tree's expense. Symbiosis and cooperation ruled the forest wherever I looked.

Suddenly I understood. We, the people of the world and the religions of the world, can also reach a mutual arrangement among ourselves, in order to cohabit the earth peacefully. We don't need to look farther than the rain forest to understand how that could be achieved. Here it was before me, a verdant affirmation of agreement and collaboration, of diversity and unity, of growth and support.

'How can we humans integrate this lesson from nature and manifest it in the way we live?' I asked in my heart. In the cycle of life, every aspect of creation, every creature is important.

I returned to my temporary abode, now a beloved place where the door was too small for the frame, the faucet dripped, the bed shook, the house trembled, the chandelier swayed, and the wind howled.

The rain forest filled my window and my heart. The sky was rainy to the left and sunny to the right, and I was grateful to be alive.

Lessons from the Rain Forest

Sergio, my guide at the butterfly exhibit.

Owl butterflies get drunk from eating too much mango.

A rope bridge leading into the heart of the Monteverde Rain Forest.

The beauty of diversity in the rain forest.

The much sought-after table and chair I used while writing 10 chapters of this book.

"Without being peace, we cannot do anything for peace. If we cannot smile, we cannot help other people to smile. If we are not peaceful, then we cannot contribute to the peace movement."

~*Thich Nhat Hahn*

CHAPTER 25

Is There Peace Among the Peacemakers?

Eliyahu McLean and I were given a blessing and a challenge by our mentor, Reb Zalman Schachter-Shalomi, to found a school to teach peacebuilding for lay people and clergy, with emphasis on grass roots engagement. Eliyahu and I were speaking on the phone one day (he lives in Jerusalem and I in Los Angeles), envisioning the theoretical and practical curriculum we would offer our students. We decided to call Reb Zalman in Boulder, Colorado, to ask for his advice.

The three of us were discussing the nature of the experiential skills we wanted to teach and mentioning names of potential guest lecturers when Reb Zalman suddenly inquired: "Tell me, my friends, is there peace among the peacemakers?"

I remember that moment distinctly because it is one of the most direct and unsettling questions that those of us who are engaged in interreligious activity can ask. Can we, the peacemakers, get along? Can we put aside our egos and our personal agendas as we work towards a common goal of harmony and cooperation? Can we be role models for the world we ourselves want to create?

As I write these words, several anecdotes come to mind that are not related directly to interfaith engagement, but I believe they reveal an important aspect of human nature and can help us understand how every human endeavor, however noble and inspired, can be derailed by our own egos.

The first experiment in communal living that was attempted in the United States took place in 1831. Sophia Willard Dana Ripley and her husband, the Unitarian minister George

Ripley, founded Brook Farm in rural West Roxbury, Massachusetts, on a 175-acre dairy farm. The Ripley's were deeply engaged in the Transcendentalist movement—inspired mainly by Ralph Waldo Emerson's writings—and their dream was that Brook Farm would become a utopian community.

In the 1830s dozens of communes began to sprout up across the U.S., parallel with the rise of important social movements that championed the causes of abolition, temperance, peace, and women's sufferage. Social historians compare that decade to the 1790s and the 1960s because those individuals, committed to the notion of a utopian society, were utterly convinced that they could actually change the fundamental structure of society, and create a new and positive way of living together.

Unfortunately, Brook Farm's experiment in communal living and in favoring the community above the individual did not ultimately suit the passionate individualists and intellectuals who spearheaded the movement. Their biggest challenge became how to find a way to harmonize their idealism with every day reality, and they failed. The Brook Farm utopian experience lasted only six years.

One historian I read put another spin on the failure of Brook Farm, citing that the practical reason it didn't work was that the women could not get along in the communal kitchen. Each woman had her own way of doing things, he said. Even if it were only a partial truth, it nevertheless does point to the difficulty of transcending our personal preferences and habits for the common good.

What do transcendentalist idealism and interfaith idealism have in common? Well, for one, the belief that the world can become a better place if we work together and, secondly, the belief that those who share the birth pangs together will be better parents for the future. Those may both be true, but there are some issues that need to be considered on the way to utopia.

A psychologist friend of mine likes to cite a major fallacy in the way we think about the psychological development of children. We mistakenly believe, she maintains, that only children of divorced families have deep-seated psychological problems. The egalitarian way she phrased it still makes me smile: "Children of divorced families grow up to have psychological problems, and children of happily married parents grow up to have psychological problems."

The common denominator is our humanity, she summarized, and no one can escape the challenges of coping, sharing, interacting, giving and receiving love, no matter how happy our home, or how elevated our ideals.

And so it goes even among my colleagues. Even in the best of scenarios, when people are assembled for peacemaking and for the highest causes, problems will arise, and so will our "shadow," (Karl Jung's term for the dark side of the psyche), especially when we are in close proximity. The more intimately we work together, the more opportunities there are for our shadow side to intervene and subvert our goals.

A good friend of mine once accompanied me to a meeting of an interfaith group dedicated to social and economic justice. After the meeting she remarked to me with genuine surprise in her voice, "Did you see how they were all at odds with one another, arguing and bickering, grandstanding and debating? They can't even get along with one another, so how are they going to influence the world to be kind and loving and just?"

This subject of how peacemakers resolve conflict among themselves continued to intrigue me. I had a chance to further explore the matter In November 2010 when Steve Olwean, a dedicated Muslim peacemaker who heads the Common Bond Institute, invited me to lead an interfaith panel on the Ground Zero Mosque Controversy at a conference held at Sonoma State University in California. A featured seminar leader, Dr. Maureen O'Hara, psychotherapist, organizational consultant and futurist, spoke in depth about the shadow side of "virtuous organizations." She emphasized how high the stakes can become in an organization based on values.

"We invest ourselves, including our soul in a way that we wouldn't do in a corporate situation," she began. It is dangerous work when we ask people to "bring your heart and soul" into an organization, she cautioned, because when things go awry, the concept of "betrayal" is not just an idea, but it is an "attack to the core," she emphasized.

Lack of faith can plunge people into the "dark night of the soul," she continued, "and people who are betrayed, exiled, or banished from a virtuous organization, are then cast into a world where they become the other. You can be left with no compass and disintegrating pain," Dr. O'Hara warned, recounting the story of a woman who, when banished from her volunteer group, later committed suicide.

"This is the inevitable risk we must take when we get involved in transformational work," said Dr. O'Hara. "Meltdowns are guaranteed." She concluded her comments with these poignant words, "We need to be chaplains for the dying and midwives for those about to give birth."

Learning about the shadow side of virtuous organizations from Dr. O'Hara gave me pause. How does this "life and death" dynamic actually play out in the world of peacemaking? I have witnessed stiff competition and unfair practices between rival peacemaking groups, on the one hand, and I have also noticed even within an individual organization people jockeying for power and dominance, in total contradiction to their stated mission and principles of collaboration. Groups and organizations, like people, also have their egos. An organization dedicated to peace may be just as easily sabotaged as any other variety of organization. An ego is an ego is an ego.

When our own peacemaking group encounters this particular challenge, efforts to find resolution should be doubled, because the world is watching us, to see if we will reach what we preach. But if we discover that we cannot continue to function harmoniously, regardless of our efforts to reconcile, we should "go away sad, not mad," organizational consultant Bob Petersen advises.

One thing has become crystal clear to me after more than twenty years of working in the interfaith community. In a peaceful world, as I envision it, there will still be conflict, but we will have achieved non-violent ways to resolve the conflict. We will have perfected techniques to diffuse anger, resentment, and fear, and we will have developed expertise in achieving forgiveness and reconciliation among enemies and aggrieved parties. We will also be increasingly devoted to the well-being of each member of our society.

This brings me to a highly personal example in my own life which I am willing to share because I believe it can be helpful as we continue to investigate how best to expand our interfaith community around the world, and also how to determine what skills we most need to hone. Hopefully, by sharing this example, I will encourage deep self-searching for all of us engaged in interfaith dialogue, a self-exploration we must be willing to undertake if we, the peacemakers, want to serve as examples for the world we say we wish to create.

In my local interfaith community, about two years ago, I found myself in a painful and frustrating relationship with a Muslim woman colleague, Noor Malika, who has given me permission to use her name and to publish this account.

A series of small misunderstandings between us led to larger discord, and suddenly we found ourselves locked in a major confrontation. It was clear that we needed some serious healing between us.

There were several signposts on the way to our falling out, as I recall, all of which began as minor issues. Individually, we were each convinced about our own moral high ground as every new point of contention arose, and it was easy to make the other one "wrong." An exchange of petulant emails inspired exaggerated interpretations of each other's behavior, adding fuel to the fire. We had reached a dangerous place of both mistrust and suspicion, a highly combustible situation that not only threatened our long-term personal relationship, but also compromised the integrity of our group. It was a reality check for both of us because we were self-defined as peacemakers.

Is There Peace Among the Peacemakers?

Where did it all begin? I don't remember the genesis of our discord, but from my recollection there seemed to be one particular event that brought the matter to a head. I had suggested that our local women's interfaith dialogue group attend an event honoring the Somali author and activist, Ayaan Hirsi Ali, a champion for women's rights in the Muslim countries, and also a serious critic of Islam.

In her best-selling book, *Infidel*, Hirsi Ali singled out Somalia's brutal treatment of women and lambasted Islam for causing it. She became a hero and champion to many women in the Western world because of her outspoken activism, and in 2005 she was named by *Time* magazine as one of the one hundred most influential people in the world. She also received several awards for her work, including Norway's Human Rights Service's Bellwether of the Year Award, the Danish Freedom Prize, the Swedish Democracy Prize, and the Moral Courage Award for commitment to conflict resolution, ethics, and world citizenship.

But, at the same time—and this is the key issue in this matter—Hirsi Ali was considered a *persona non grata* by the mainstream Muslim community for having "thrown out the baby with the bathwater." Many Muslims felt and probably still feel that she has caused great damage by publicly maligning Islam. They may have been sympathetic to her campaign to help women but, as a result of her public proclamations and writings criticizing Islam, she had distanced herself from Islam and from many people who loved Islam.

Her defamation of Islam was especially hurtful to Noor Malika and other Muslim women in our local dialogue group of Muslim and Jewish women that had been meeting once a month for more than six years. The Muslim women in our group were already experiencing, on a daily basis after 9/11, the world's collective displeasure with Islam, through news and TV reports, portrayals of Muslims in feature films as terrorists, and most personally through racial profiling that was an ongoing occurrence in America, especially in airports and public places.

Noor Malika had sent me an email a year earlier pointing out Hirsi Ali's questionable status after I had asked what she thought about the writer/activist. At the time Noor Malika had referred me to several websites which detailed why Hirsi Ali was not well liked by the mainstream Muslim community. Because I literally receive hundreds of emails daily, I honestly had no recollection of my asking her about Hirsi Ali. As a result, my suggestion to attend a ceremony honoring the outspoken Somali crusader became a lightning rod that provoked a full-fledged storm in my women's group. When I asked about Hirsi Ali the second time, Noor Malika became very annoyed at my oversight. She located in her files and sent to me the same letter opposing Hirsi Ali she had emailed me a year before.

The Muslim members in the group refused to attend the award ceremony, but I actually went to the Hirsi Ali event myself. After she accepted her award and spoke about her crusade to protect Muslim women, she agreed to take questions from the audience. I approached the microphone, took a deep breath, and said with great sincerity, "I greatly admire the work you have done to protect women, but I am in trouble for being here tonight to honor you."

The audience perked up and Hirsi Ali looked at me with greater interest.

"Many of my Muslim girlfriends would be angry to know that I am here. These are women that I dearly care about," I told her, "women with whom I have been meeting once a month for six years in a Muslim/Jewish interfaith dialogue group. They are outraged and deeply wounded by your flagrant criticism of all of Islam," I explained.

"Why are you so willing to condemn the entire religion instead of just regional and cultural practices that you abhor?" I asked her. "We know that Muslim women have different experiences in different countries, and that many of the practices you decry are not supported by scriptural text in the Kor'an, so why do you have to criticize the entirety of Islam when so many millions of people around the world honor and find meaning in that religion? What should I tell my Muslim girlfriends when I meet them next time about why you publicly malign Islam?"

She was obviously taken aback by my comments. She paused and then she replied, in a gentle voice. "I wish I could talk with your girlfriends and explain my views to them, based upon my life experience," she explained. "I wish they were here tonight, or that I could come to your group so that we could discuss it together."

In retrospect, I don't think she really answered my question, but I felt better for airing my concerns and I was glad to have had the opportunity to say it publicly. Several people who were in the audience approached me later to thank me for my honesty. But that was not the terrain where I truly needed resolution. I still had a thorny problem in my own backyard, a problem that could not have been resolved by Hirsi Ali's response, no matter what she might have said.

Time to mend fences, my own fences, I told myself.

I apologized for my *faux pas* to my Muslim sisters in the group, by email, and by phone. I explained that I did not fully realize how offensive Hirsi Ali's position was to them, and that I had not meant to offend them by my invitation. I told them I was just beginning to understand how sensitive the issue of public criticism had become for the Muslim community, especially in America, where they were constantly under the microscope. They accepted my apology and they were very gracious. But my relationship with Noor Malika was not so easily healed. It had spiraled downward and I observed that it was at its lowest point since we had first met, more than nine years earlier. Also, there was continuous talk about our unresolved conflict swirling among the members of our group, making communication between the two of us even more difficult.

It was a very unhappy situation, so what were we going to do about it?

It was at that very moment that our good friend, Thomas, a Christian chaplain, a psychotherapist, and a member of our local interfaith community, stepped up to the plate. Thomas was someone who knew and appreciated both of us. He offered to mediate. "Give me the honor of creating a safe space where you can work out your differences," he suggested generously.

I immediately thought of a wonderful book that had been given to me by a minister from Evanston, Illinois, entitled *The Third Side: Why We Fight and How We Can Stop*, by William L. Ury. In reading the book I learned that anthropologists who devoted themselves to studying the earliest cooperative societies noted that the most effective way those societies were able to solve a conflict between two parties had been to find a third, neutral party who would be willing to sit and hold sacred space for those having the conflict. Furthermore, the third side would not let anyone go home until such time both sides had been fully heard, a solution had been reached, and then each side had expressed his satisfaction with the outcome.

Our third side was to be Thomas.

Thomas invited us to his home to do the important work of reconciliation. Noor Malika and I both eagerly accepted his offer, though we later confessed that we were apprehensive and had no idea what would materialize.

So there we were: a Christian, a Muslim, and a Jew. We recognized that we were not only creating a space for peace in our own lives, but we were enacting the rituals and teachings that were offered to us by our own religions. We were being asked to follow a path of reconciliation and forgiveness. Were we up to the challenge?

Thomas began by reciting a quote from Psalms: "Be still and know that I am God." Then he asked us to sit together in silence for a few minutes. When he next spoke he humbly acknowledged that he considered himself no better than either of us. "We are all faced with daily challenges to be true to our Creator and to the path laid out to us." He said that he, too, found himself recognizing his own imperfections as he sat with us, and he expressed a fervent desire to be of service to us, not as a clergyman, but as a fellow traveler.

He then began by asking me to tell Noor Malika what I liked most about her. I did not have to hesitate. I immediately spoke about her leadership skills, her courage and her dedication, her amazing ability to organize events, her wisdom, and her quest for spiritual growth.

When he asked Noor Malika to say what she appreciated about me, she replied: "I could say the very same things Ruth said about me." We both laughed for a moment, realizing that in many ways we were a mirror image of one another.

Then Thomas entered the "minefield" zone, but with extreme caution. I could tell he was aware of it by the way he framed each and every one of his words. I also realized that he was feeling the whole endeavor could blow up in his face—that is always the risk one takes when entering the minefield.

He asked us to share specifically what were our difficulties with one another, what we viewed as the other person's limitations or stumbling blocks. Our responses tumbled out, first in spurts and then like gushers, and with that the accompanying tears of feeling misunderstood, offended, and alienated. The session continued on that note for quite a while until we both had unloaded our burdens into the center of the room, where they were fully visible to all three of us.

The next part was, of course, the hardest. We each had to accept responsibility for our role in creating the conflict, feeding it, and perpetuating it through our thoughts as well as our deeds. We would have to stop blaming one another and admit how we were clinging to our "stories" so that we could feel justified and safe. Before our meeting, our survival had required layers of protective covering. Now our survival required that we be naked.

And then something miraculous happened. I have a vivid memory of light and clarity that literally came showering down on our heads. We opened our hearts to one another, and we were flooded with love. Noor Malika and I experienced it as a spiritual awakening and with it came a genuine appreciation for one another which had been obfuscated by our layers of hurt. As the layers were peeled away, one by one, the air in the room became light and buoyant. I experienced the sensation of floating; maybe it was the experience of the "unbearable lightness of being." Whatever it was, something had shifted in our relationship and in the configuration of energies in the room, with Thomas no longer a witness or a mediator but a full partner. Our collaboration together as a trio took us higher than Noor Malika and I could have achieved on our own. It was deeply moving for all three of us when we realized that the three representatives of the Abrahamic faiths were doing God's work together.

Afterwards, when embraces and blessings had been distributed all around, we ended the session, but the session never truly ended. The next day Noor Malika and I called each other four to five times, to reaffirm our friendship and the feeling of love that had been evoked by our healing. We were filled with affection and compassion for one another, for Thomas, and for the world. We were reborn through the process of reconciliation. And, by asking for forgiveness from one another, the heavens responded by opening up and filling us with gratitude and joy. And the most beautiful part of all is that it has never ceased. Even now, when we see one another or speak on the phone, Noor Malika and I continue to express our gratitude for one another and for the part we have played in each other's lives.

The incident didn't end there, because people in our interfaith community were also profoundly affected by our peacemaking, like concentric rings of water expanding outward. Since then we have continued to share our experience with other people. No one fails to be moved by our story, because each person can immediately conjure the image of the individual with whom he or she is longing for reconciliation, and a chance for true healing. We all have people like that in our lives.

So, in answer to Reb Zalman's provocative question, "Is there peace among the peacemakers?" I would say, "Not always. But we, the peacemakers, must exercise our greatest efforts to heal our own internal rifts, because then we will actually be able to live in a world we so passionately yearn to create."

Thus we can become not only interfaith activists, but also interfaith alchemists, transforming our own minefields into miracles.

Members of "The Cousins," our LA Muslim/Jewish women's dialogue group, eight years strong.

Keeping peace among the peacemakers (l. to r.) Noor Malika Chishti, Thomas Hedberg and Ruth.

Is There Peace Among the Peacemakers?

Interfaith panel members discussing the Ground Zero Controversy at the Common Bond Institute Conference, 2010. Seated (l. to r.) Rev. Guo Cheen, Ruth, Aisha Morgan; standing (l. to r.) BK Sister Elizabeth Padilla, Harold Joseph, Anya Cordell.

With Eliyahu McLean (seated center) and our students in a class to teach Peacebuilding Skills, sponsored by the Aleph Jewish Renewal movement.

"When you're finally up on the moon, looking back at the earth, all these differences and nationalistic traits are pretty well going to blend and you're going to get a concept that maybe this is really one world and why the hell can't we learn to live together like decent people?"
~Astronaut Frank Borman

CHAPTER 26
Weaving the Global Interfaith Web

The once fragile threads of interfaith engagement are now luminous unbreakable strands on the interfaith web, growing exponentially, spreading outwards daily and linking hundreds of thousands of kindred spirits across the globe. As Marilyn Ferguson described some 30 years ago in her prophetic novel, *The Aquarian Conspiracy*, there are people scattered around the world all engaged in parallel activity, but they don't know one another. Though they feel compelled to do the work, they often feel alone. Ferguson insists they are actually part of a global "conspiracy," but they are not aware of it yet. There will come a moment, she postulates, when all these individuals quietly doing their work will realize that their efforts are being mirrored throughout the world and, at that moment as they experience the connection, the world will shift, and a new era will begin.

Malcolm Gladwell calls it "the tipping point," the point at which critical mass is established, when profound changes occur. Even though they appear to have occurred miraculously overnight, changes and trends in the interfaith arena have been in the making for years. Much credit goes to the internet for weaving the global web that we now all take for granted, but I believe real credit should go to the desire of people all over the world to create that connection. In this case, function followed collective longing.

The tipping point is now.

In the old days (35 years ago) an interfaith event in a major city might be held once every six to nine months. However, if you could position yourself to see an astronaut's view of the contemporary interfaith scenes in LA, NYC, Washington, DC, London, New Delhi, Istanbul or Jerusalem, you would be amazed to observe that perhaps as many as six interfaith events are taking place simultaneously in each city on the same day.

Interfaith is on the move. Sometimes the competition is fierce. People are being invited to participate in multiple activities by multiple organizations. A Los Angeles friend of mine, Anthony Manousos, a Quaker, is on the board of four separate local interfaith organizations. Each one, he emphasizes, serves a different constituency and none is redundant.

Today thousands of interfaith organizations, foundations and grass roots groups abound. Interfaith dialogue and engagement are indeed alive and well-- and needed more than ever— as we painfully discovered in September of 2010 during the Ground Zero Mosque debate, a debate that has persisted to this day.

The debate erupted when the Muslim community in New York expressed a desire to build a mosque and an interfaith community center for all religions not far from Ground Zero. Hateful invective—not civil discourse—spewed forth from those opposed to the idea of the mosque. Angry demonstrations were quickly and effectively organized against American Muslims, including threats to burn the Kor'an. For those of us following the sequence of events, it was clear that irresponsible "media superstars" had succeeded in fanning the flames of hatred, encouraging interfaith suspicion and dissention across the country.

Many people around the world were also caught off guard because of the vitriol and extreme reactions that the Ground Zero debate provoked in the United States. Social scientists and observers of American pluralism had maintained that Muslims who lived in America had achieved the highest level of integration and acceptability of any Muslim minority in the world—certainly more than in Western Europe. Was that no longer true?

Although the constitutionality of building a mosque near Ground Zero at first seemed to be the main issue, what the controversy unearthed was a realization that many Americans, a decade past 9/11, were still not ready to accept American Muslims as they had accepted other minorities. The wound caused by the 9/11 Islamic terrorists was still open and weeping, and reason and good will did not seem to stand a chance at healing that wound. The religion of Islam, rather than the individuals who caused the events, was being held responsible for the suffering. The motives of the mosque project organizers were interpreted as triumphalism rather than an honest attempt at reconciliation. The rawness of the emotions that erupted through this controversy startled many of us in the interfaith movement. It made many of us question what would happen to the interfaith movement. Could this controversy potentially imperil ties with Muslim communities around the country?

In retrospect, the answer to that question was a grateful "no." The controversy actually served to demonstrate the power and reach of the interfaith movement in America. Interfaith groups in major cities around the country quickly organized to counter the rhetoric of hate and suspicion by staging mega interfaith protests, unity walks, and email chains to protest bigotry and Islamophobia. The Interfaith Witnesses, a newly formed group in Orange County, California, spontaneously organized itself to show up and hold vigil at anti-Muslim rallies. The members are determined to provide a non-violent but solid support for Muslims who are the object of hate rallies and public demonstrations. I also remember receiving an email not long ago encouraging women of all faiths to fight the bigotry by donning the "hijab" (Muslim women's head covering) in solidarity with Muslim women.

On September 12, 2010 I participated in a multi-generational, multi-religious Unity Walk in Pomona and Claremont in California, moving as a group from synagogue to church to mosque. The walk drew almost 600 people including the mayors of Pomona and Claremont. Similar walks were staged around the country, such as in Washington, DC, where they have been organizing Unity Walks for 10 years, each year attracting more and more participants. Yesterday I received an email which reported that Unity Walks were being held in 17 countries around the world.

The tipping point is now.

These recent events lead me to conclude that, indeed, "in numbers there is strength." Clearly the most effective way to curb bigotry on a global scale is to support local interfaith communities while simultaneously enlarging the global interfaith networks. We can now maintain contact with thousands of local interfaith organizations that have emerged and continue to sprout up in cities large and small.

There are too many to mention them all, but I would like to highlight several of the groups and individuals I know about personally, to offer a taste of what is happening simultaneously in many parts of the globe.

The North American Interfaith Network (NAIN), a volunteer-led organization, gathers interfaith activists from the U.S. and Canada once a year to share their experiences, best practices, and develop new friendships. The idea for NAIN emerged out of what was affectionately termed a "North American Assisi," hosted by the Interfaith Ministries of Wichita, Kansas—one of the oldest interfaith councils in the US. The first NAIN conference was held in Wichita in 1988.

In New York City, Samir Selmanovic, a Muslim from Croatia who converted to

Christianity and then became a minister, was the driving force for the establishment of Faith House Manhattan in 2007. Their inter-religious community, with paid staff, meets twice monthly for wide-ranging and innovative events. Their mission is "to deepen their personal and communal journeys, share ritual life and devotional space, and foster a commitment to social justice." Their motto is: experience your neighbor's faith. They started out catering primarily to the Abrahamic religions, but very soon expanded their wings to include all religions.

Also in New York is a new organization called Groundswell, led by Valarie Kaur, an award-winning filmmaker, Harvard-educated theologian, and social justice advocate who produced the documentary *Divided We Fall*. Groundswell is a multifaith social action network that generates moral force around social justice causes. In their own words: "We **convene** and connect faith and moral communities in new partnerships that amplify their collective impact. We call this multifaith network to action, creating a groundswell around urgent social causes. And we **proclaim** and amplify these voices as part of a visible multifaith movement for justice."

In Chicago, the Interfaith Youth Core (IFYC) was the brainchild of visionary Eboo Patel, an Ismaili Muslim. In 1998 when he was attending an interfaith conference at Stanford University, he and his peers realized they were the only young people there. "Why isn't there a huge movement of young people from different faiths working together to apply the core value of all faiths--service to others?" they asked themselves. They answered their own question by creating the Interfaith Youth Core in 2002, using service as the bridge, a model that has been emulated by many other interfaith organizations around the world. The best news is that it works for all generations, not just for youth.

In Omaha, Nebraska, the heartland of America's bread basket, Project Interfaith, launched by Executive Director Beth Katz in 2005, offers a great diversity of face-to-face and online programs including interfaith arts programs, study circles, and an annual speaker series. Their religious and cultural diversity trainings have been cited by Harvard University's Pluralism Project as "among the most innovative interfaith work in the country."

In Detroit, Brenda Naomi Rosenberg, a Jewish activist, has collaborated with other interfaith activists to create award-winning interfaith projects including "Reuniting the Children of Abraham, a multi media tool kit 4 peace." Recently Brenda joined forces with Samia Bahsoun from New Jersey, an American Arab of Lebanese Muslim descent, to establish the Tectonic Leadership Center, for conflict transformation and cross-cultural communication. By providing workshops, seminars, retreats, and coaching, their mission is to bring together pairs of leaders from opposite sides of the Israeli/Palestinian conflict to take joint ownership in transforming conflict.

S.A.R.A.H. (Spiritual and Religious Alliance for Hope), based in Orange County, California, is an interfaith organization to empower girls and women of all religious backgrounds. SARAH "sisters," as they like to call themselves, led by the energetic Sande Hart, actively engage in and facilitate dialogue, and shine in their devoted service to their community--for which they have received multiple awards. Each year they galvanize more than 1,000 people from a variety of religious communities to serve as volunteers for an annual day of service.

Len and Libby Traubman, a couple living in San Mateo, California, established the Jewish-Palestinian Living Room Dialogues over 19 years ago. December 2011 marked their 236th meeting and, yes, they are counting! Aside from establishing a user-friendly and easily replicable model for living room dialogue, which primarily emphasizes the art of listening-to-learn, they are responsible for creating and maintaining a web site which lists hundreds of inspirational examples of collaboration among Muslims, Jews, and Christians in multiple arenas: music, art, film, sports (skiing, mountain-climbing, surfing), storytelling, and even kite-flying. They always accentuate the positive in their persistent, day-after-day presentation of victories on the ground. As a result, where the media have failed, they have succeeded in publicizing many of the instructive, heartwarming interactions and ongoing interfaith programs that are taking place around the world.

The Interfaith Center at the Presidio in San Francisco, founded in 1995, is dedicated to developing local and global connections and creating innovative interfaith learning environments and resources. Rev. Paul Chaffee and his wife Jan, after serving on the Center's staff for its first 15 years, have just launched an online interfaith publication called The Interfaith Observer (TIO).

The Arizona Interfaith Movement, guided by the enterprising Dr. Paul Eppinger, made interfaith history when it convinced senators and representatives of the Arizona state government to permit the interfaith alliance to sell license plates to residents with the designation "Golden Rule State," thereby earning money to run their vibrant interfaith organization and expand their activities.

In Guadalajara, Mexico, Gaby Franco, Carlos Rodriguez and Father Jorge Manzano founded Fundacion Carpe Diem Interfaith Foundation, a house of interfaith gathering and learning, which as a bonus includes Carlos' course in quantum physics for spiritual seekers and Father Manzano's courses in philosophy. The three friends and colleagues are the turbo-chargers of the organization, joined by many dedicated individuals in Guadalajara who represent the full spectrum of religious, spiritual, and civic leadership.

In Toronto, Canada, the Scarboro Missions has branched out from its original Catholic outreach program (established in 1918) to develop a strong interfaith arm. They developed a poster (the brainchild of my good friend Paul McKenna), which highlights the Golden Rule in the sacred writings of 13 religious traditions. The poster comes accompanied by lesson plans for elementary and high school as well as a study guide for adults. *Animating the Golden Rule*, Tina Petrova's documentary about the poster, has been aired on national TV and the poster is now in the permanent collection at the UN in New York.

In England, Spirit of Peace, headed by the dedicated Jane Ozanne, was set up in 2008 to foster greater peace and equality globally. They work closely with renowned international peace partners, primarily in the UK, with a special focus on the Middle East. Also based in England, the Coexist Foundation promotes education, research, and dialogue to advance understanding between the three major Abrahamic Faiths. Their US affiliate, based in New York, is led by Rev. Bud Heckman.

In perpetual motion, the Interfaith Encounter Association in Israel, headed by Dr. Yehudah Stolov, is dedicated to promoting peace in the Middle East through interfaith dialogue and cross-cultural study. Their multiple, ongoing programs are tailored individually to youth, men and women, but they also encourage intergenerational initiatives. Their topics range from the parallel study of similar passages in the Kor'an, Torah, and the Bible to wedding and birth rituals, dietary laws and dating rituals.

And the list goes on: Jerusalem Peacemakers, The Open House of Ramle, Bethlehem Encounter, The Compassionate Listening Project, Abraham's Vision, Seeds of Peace, 20,000 Dialogues, Children of Abraham, Common Bond Institute, Rumi Forum, Guibord Center—Religion Inside Out, Just Vision, Interfaith Communities United for Justice and Peace, NewGround, Fellowship of Reconciliation, Interfaith Alliance of Washington, DC, Pacifica Institute, St. Ethelburga's Centre for Reconciliation and Peace, Orange County Interfaith Coalition for the Environment, Raoul Wallenberg Institute of Ethics, The Elijah Interfaith Institute, Dalai Lama Centre, California Interfaith Power and Light, Thanksgiving Square Foundation, Peace X Peace, Unity-and-Diversity World Council, Inc., Be the Cause, Odyssey Networks, Tony Blair Faith Foundation, Clergy Beyond Borders, The Global Peace Initiative of Women, Raindrop Turkish House, The Progressive Foundation, Interfaith Conference of Metropolitan Washington, Women of Spirit and Faith, World Pilgrims of Atlanta, Interfaith Center of New York, Monks Without Borders, Bridge Builders of Alaska, Canadians for Compassion, Wisdom, the Levantine Cultural Center, Rasur Foundation.

These are but a few of the independently run (non-governmental) organizations I have personally encountered that dedicate themselves to interfaith goals and grass roots outreach. Their website information, along with an extended list of similar organizations across America and in other parts of the world can be accessed at www.minefieldsandmiracles.com. I am also hoping that my readers will send me more listings as we update the link regularly.

Like many of my colleagues, I have come to the conclusion that there is a "Combined Law of Physics and Spirit," demonstrating that the two phenomena are irrevocably interconnected. When we are willing to get involved and make a commitment to positive change, we become co-creators, and we can actually re-weave the cosmic fabric of our world.

What is occurring is happily both a bottom-up and top-down phenomenon. While local interfaith groups are sprouting up around the globe, there are also many global organizations that are conscientiously working to broaden the scope of the interfaith landscape. The three that lead the way are:

- A Council for the Parliament of the World's Religions (CPWR), which convenes the largest interfaith gatherings in the world once every five years. First launched in 1893 and activated again in 1993, CPWR is described at length in Chapter 16.

- Religions for Peace is the world's most representative multi-religious coalition advancing common action for peace. While the origins date to 1961, the first World Assembly of Religions for Peace was held in Kyoto, Japan in 1970. The Religions for Peace global network consists of a World Council of senior religious leaders from all regions of the world, six regional inter-religious councils (IRC's) and more than eighty national ones, a Global Women of Faith Network, and a Global Interreligious Youth Network. *Religions for Peace* works to build peace by focusing on addressing conflict, ending poverty, and protecting the earth.

- United Religions Initiative (URI), formed in 1995, is a global network of over 500 grassroots organizations, called Cooperation Circles, dedicated to peace and justice through interfaith and cross-cultural cooperation. Its nearly half a million members are overcoming distrust and hostility every day for the good of their communities—mediating religiously motivated conflict; building schools, orphanages and health clinics; campaigning for citizenship rights and more in 78 countries. They touch the lives of an estimated 2.5 million people.

The UN is also part of the global interfaith picture. The Committee of Religious

NGO's at the United Nations collaborates with many religious communities around the world, seeking to draw attention to the importance of interfaith engagement as an extension of the UN's global concerns. In fact, a pioneer of the interfaith movement, the Temple of Understanding (TOU), founded in 1960 by Juliet Hollister, was encouraged by Eleanor Roosevelt to become an NGO. The Temple of Understanding immediately embraced Article 18 of the *Universal Declaration of Human Rights*, protecting freedom of thought, conscience and religion. In 2000 the Millennium Declaration, signed by 189 Member States, identified eight *Millennium Development Goals* (MDG) to be achieved by the year 2015. TOU's representative to the United Nations interweaves these goals throughout the organization's programs at the UN, in addition to sponsoring conferences and workshops on religious freedom.

The growing interfaith movement has also affected academia. The New Seminary in New York opened its doors in 1979, specifically for interfaith education, but the real news is how traditional theological seminaries, once supported and directed by a single religious denomination, are now expanding their curricula significantly.

A fine example is Claremont School of Theology in California, under the bold leadership of Jerry Campbell, which recently received a grant of $50 million to establish a ground-breaking interfaith institution called Claremont Lincoln University. Though it was always conceived of as a multi-faith seminary, says Campbell, they began with the Abrahamic group because, as he explains, "The Academy for Jewish Religion/California (AJR/CA) was already trans-denominational, the Claremont School of Theology was ecumenical, and the Islamic Center of Southern California was pan-Islamic." They planned to gradually add other religions to the consortium but their initiative became an instant juggernaut. Religious communities all over the city began to call, wanting to be part of the new interfaith hub. The Jains are now included—just a few months after they began—and the organizers are currently in dialogue with members of the Buddhist, Bah'ai, Sikh and Indigenous communities.

At the historic inauguration ceremony of Claremont Lincoln University on September 6, 2011, the Ambassador of South Africa to the US, Ebraim Rassoul, delivered the keynote address and eloquently summed up the new role of the university in propagating the values of the interfaith movement, for which he received two standing ovations:

> *This is what the Claremont Lincoln University offers: an opportunity to share fragments of truth and pieces of the puzzle, firstly to overcome our own demons represented by the extremism, exclusivity and intolerance we spawned, and the way we have allowed some,*

in our name, not to follow God, but to appropriate God, and so contribute to the misery of society.

Simultaneously, we must allow the graduates of this institution to revel in the multiplicity of worship, ritual, pageantry and tradition, of the many faiths that must come to the Claremont Lincoln University, but they must also seek to enjoy the wonderment that comes from recognizing the Divine in each other, and acting on this insight in ways which cultivate a better world through compassionate relationships, collaborative efforts, and peaceful acceptance.

In Los Angeles the Center for Muslim-Jewish Engagement (CMJE) was established in 2010 to "promote dialogue, understanding and grassroots, and congregational and academic partnerships among the oldest and the newest of the Abrahamic faiths." CMJE represents a collaboration of three distinct entities, the Omar Ibn Al Khattab Foundation, Hebrew Union College-Jewish Institute of Religion, and the USC Center for Religion and Civic Culture. Rabbi Reuven Firestone, Professor of Medieval Judaism and Islam, and Dafer M. Dakhil, the Director of the Omar Ibn Al Khattab Foundation, were the key players in this significant interfaith undertaking.

At Harvard University in Boston, the Pluralism Project, founded in 1991 and expertly guided by Diana Eck, documents the changing religious landscape of the United States of America, including the interfaith infrastructure, and convenes interfaith grass roots organizations from across the country in order to share best practices and interfaith resources.

Auburn's Center for Multifaith Education, part of the historical Auburn Theological Seminary in New York City (founded in 1818), "equips people of all faiths, from senior religious leaders to teens in conflict-torn countries, to reach across lines of religious difference and build a more just and peaceful world." Their emphasis on interfaith education began some 20 years ago. Rabbi Justus Baird, director of the Multifaith Education Center, underscores the importance of the interfaith component in contemporary religious education because, as he writes, "a great lack of education about other faiths, stereotypes and misunderstanding continue to proliferate, which fuels conflicts around the world and at home."

Also on the East Coast, Hartford Seminary in Connecticut, a traditional seminary with a history going back 100 years, has now introduced a new interfaith program for religious leaders of all faiths, facilitated by Yeheskel Landau and Lucinda Mosher. Collaboration, in all cases, is the operative word.

And, finally, one of the most exciting new models of interfaith collaboration—which will surely transform the religious landscape of America—can be found in Omaha, Nebraska. There the Tri-Faith Initiative and three faith partners, Temple Israel, the Episcopal Diocese of Nebraska, and the American Institute of Islamic Studies and Culture have purchased four adjacent parcels of land to accommodate separate prayer sites for the three faith groups and a communal space for an interfaith center to serve the wider community. This project, expected to be completed by 2015, will occupy a 35-acre campus and represents the first initiative of its kind in the nation to purposefully build houses of worship of the three Abrahamic faiths next to each other.

In my capacity as a Partner Cities Associate for the Parliament of the World's Religions during 2008 and 2009, I had an opportunity to travel extensively and stretch the strands of the global web to communities in North Carolina, Washington, DC, Texas, Mexico, Costa Rica, Colombia, Argentina and Morocco.

It was during my trip to Morocco that I learned that the very first university of the Middle East, Al-Karaouine, was founded in Fez in 859 by a woman, Fatima al-Fihri, the daughter of a wealthy merchant. At that institution, professors of the three Abrahamic religions taught side by side, on an equal status. In fact, in medieval times, Al-Karaouine played a leading role in the cultural exchange and transfer of knowledge between Muslims and Europeans. Historical precedent informs the modern-day movement.

But modern day phenomena also color the interfaith world. In 2007, at an interfaith conference in Monterrey, Mexico, I screened *God & Allah Need to Talk* with Spanish subtitles to a crowd of 600. I addressed the audience in Spanish and they went wild, treating me like a rock star. They stayed afterwards in droves, pressing forward for souvenir photos and for my autograph. My colleague, Joseph Prabhu, present at the event, said half-seriously, "Ruth, you could have been elected Mayor of Monterrey today!" It was unexpected and unsettling, but later I began to see it as an indication that people around the world are preparing for a new form of social interaction in which interfaith activity will be one of the most popular themes of their lives. And not a minute too soon.

Wherever I went I found *co-conspirators*, people like myself who were preparing themselves for a "new world order," not a geopolitical monopoly of resources and assets—as some people are predicting—but a new world community that offers inclusivity.

The tipping point is now.

On my travels in Mexico, I met Gaby, Carlos, Jorge, Rosalia, Gerardo, Roberto, Consuelo, Elmer, Jose, Fernando, Joshua, and others. In Buenos Aires their names were Gabriel, Bernardo, Sergio, Maria Elisa, Moira, and many more. In Bogota, they were Fabian,

Virginia, Blanca, Leonel, Jorge, Ana, and Jose. In London they were Jane, Steve, Esther, Rita and Reyaaz. In Toronto they were Leslie, Paul, Samira, Terry, and Lucy. In Alaska it was Christina, Patrick, Skookums, Paola, Karma, Carole, and Esther. In India it was Parvinder, Balwant, Vinay, Jay-esh, Nimo, Niraly, Edward, Mohamed, and Rajshree. And last year I met Mirna from Singapore. They were men and women of diverse ages and appearances, representing diverse religious communities and ethnic backgrounds, but somehow I felt I was meeting the same person again and again.

I entered into a reverie one day and was suddenly overcome with an image so realistic that I could not put it out of my mind. It moved me to tears because it gave form and reason to my feelings of familiarity with all of the unique individuals I had encountered around the world. During my reverie I sensed that I was present at a gathering of souls. All of us were assembled in the presence of the Divine, to receive instructions, at a time before we incarnated into our present selves.

For those who do not accept reincarnation, you may have another explanation. But for me, in that moment of lucidity, I understood why, as I traveled the globe, I was able to experience an immediate, deep connection to individuals I barely knew.

"Look around very carefully," we were told at the gathering of souls during my reverie. "Be aware that you are all brothers and sisters and know that you will meet again and you will perceive, in short order, that your mission is identical. Even though you will be born in different countries, speak different languages, and follow different religious or spiritual paths, you are family. Take a good look around now and remember who you are because soon you will be scattered around the globe. Do not worry. When you meet, you will immediately resonate with one another, because you will be of one unifying purpose: to help birth the era of world peace."

And so it has been. There is an immediate and undeniable spark of recognition that I have experienced with colleagues who are involved in this noble and challenging work all around the world—and they have reported similar occurrences to me.

When we say, "Don't I know you from somewhere?" we are echoing our common experience of remembering one another from another time, another place, another dimension, a sensation of being part of one entity, one enormous Soul.

Goethe called it *"eine schoene Seele."* And William Penn described it thus: "The humble, merciful, just and divine souls are everywhere of one religion; and when death has taken off the mask, they will know one another, though the liveries they wear here make them strangers."

At the most recent global gathering of the Parliament of the World Religions held in Melbourne, Australia in December 2009, I confirmed that understanding for myself, again and again, when I encountered 6,500 members of my interfaith "family," representing 200 religions. I met many followers of the Abrahamic Religions, as well as devotees of the Hindu, Buddhist, Baha'i, Sikh, Brahma Kumaris, Jain, Zoroastrian, Pagan, and Wiccan communities. A first-time delegation of some 200 people came to represent the Global New Thought movement, and there were many opportunities to interface with representatives of the Indigenous communities from around the world whose wise counsel was sought and appreciated.

In May 2011 my understanding of Indigenous teachings deepened when I was graciously invited by the Easter Island healer/ambassador Mahina Raputuki to attend the *Ninth International Council of Thirteen Indigenous Grandmothers*, held in Anchorage, Alaska. The grandmothers hailed from Nepal, Africa, Brazil, Mexico, and many parts of North America. They spoke different languages and were often aided by interpreters, but they were clearly united by their cosmology and the urgency of their mission. They held fire ceremonies daily, for healing and for blessing, and to call attention to our sacred responsibility to care for our planet and for one another. They all emphasized the interconnectedness of humanity with nature, and the importance of respecting what we received "on loan," from the Source of all life, or as they call it "Father Heaven, Mother Earth." They reiterated the same message Indigenous leaders have been communicating for thousands of years. Perhaps now we are truly beginning to hear them.

My global experiences with people of such different philosophies and traditions have caused me to embrace a new understanding about my work and my mission, which I now see as a way to bring individuals from the full spectrum of spiritual, religious, and Indigenous communities together with agnostics and atheists. I sense that I have been asked to assist in weaving an even wider web than I originally imagined. No one can be left out of the essential conversation, a life-and-death dialogue affecting each and every one of us, and our entire planet.

Karen Armstrong, the master chronicler of and commentator on religious history, brought that message home to us in a concrete and innovative way when she was awarded the TED (Technology, Entertainment, Design) Prize, granted $100,000, and a "wish to change the world." Karen envisioned a universal Charter for Compassion for all peoples, because no one, she maintained, should be left out of the conversation. In fulfillment of her wish, a group of spiritual leaders representing all the major religious faiths joined with her in Vevey, Switzerland and crafted the charter, incorporating contributions from diverse individuals in countries around the world. Though many prominent religious leaders were involved, there was no hierarchy established and the language that emerged was not a religious language, but the language of our common humanity, as illustrated in the following excerpt from the document they created.

> *…We urgently need to make compassion a clear, luminous and dynamic force in our polarized world. Rooted in a principled determination to transcend selfishness, compassion can break down political, dogmatic, ideological and religious boundaries. Born of our deep interdependence, compassion is essential to human relationships and to a fulfilled humanity. It is the path to enlightenment, and indispensible to the creation of a just economy and a peaceful global community.*

I met Karen Armstrong in October 2010 when she was the guest speaker at a Parliament event in Palo Alto, California. She told the audience that when she spoke publicly in Holland about the Charter of Compassion, the word compassion was mistakenly translated as "pity." She underscored that compassion does not mean either pity or "sloppy benevolence," as she put it, but the ability to feel empathy for another human being.

That ability is now being exemplified before our eyes around the world. Thousands—no hundreds of thousands—of organizations, based on the premise of compassion and personal responsibility and care for the planet, are leading the way.

In an awe-inspiring internet presentation, Paul Hawken, from the Bioneer Organization, says the number of all of these new organizations could soon reach 500,000. He points out that even if we were to watch the screen night and day for four days, listing all of the organizations that are currently engaged in making the world a better place, we would still not be able to mention all of them. The media may not publish that information, but it is a fact, and it should give the world pause and cause for celebration.

The tipping point is now.

People are also beginning to realize that beyond the organizations we form, we must teach our children "the culture of peace." An organization called re:Generation, the inspiration of Shepha Vainstain from California, trains Palestinians and Israelis to effectively teach peace to students on both sides of the border. and to support Ein Bustan, a joint Jewish-Arab Waldorf School in Israel. Shepha and her colleagues are convinced that even when peace treaties are signed between nations, the most effective method for sustaining peace will be found in the children's textbooks and through teachers who love and promote peace.

More than any other factor, I believe this new era of interfaith fellowship is driven by an innate desire for collaboration, and for forming alliances. Following the revolution in Egypt in February 2011, I enlisted a close friend of mine, singer/songwriter Dalit Argil, to help me organize a Universal Freedom Seder in Los Angeles. Our goal was to recognize and honor the bravery of the long-silent people of Egypt, Libya, Tunisia, Algeria, Bahrain, Yemen, Syria and elsewhere, who were gathering in public squares across the Middle East. Those courageous individuals were willing to jeopardize their lives in order to have a voice in their future, something that may be hard for westerners to appreciate.

I know from personal experience that citizens in those countries could be jailed just for being interfaith activists. In one case I was even asked to delete from my manuscript specific details about an individual's past detainment and imprisonment because of the potential repercussions to him and his family if I had used his name. The stakes were clearly very high! The "Arab Spring" was a stirring moment in world history, an open declaration against tyranny, and Dalit and I wanted to mark it with an interfaith, multicultural Seder, modeled on the annual Passover Festival of Freedom.

We invited officials from the Egyptian and Israeli consulates, and from all the consulates located in Los Angeles, as well as the U.S. State Department, La County Sheriff Lee Baca, and representatives from more than 12 religious communities. The non-traditional Seder, held on April 14, 2011, was co-led by four religious leaders: Rabbi Mordecai Finley of Ohr HaTorah Congregation, Imam Jihad Turk and Dr. Mahmoud Abdel-Baset from the Islamic Center of Southern California, and Rev. Dr. Gwynne Guibord, an Episcopalian priest and founder of the Guibord Center—Religion Inside Out.

The Seder leaders reaffirmed the high value their religions place on human rights, and they also underlined the importance of recognizing our collective responsibility for caring for the earth and one another.

(For seder highlights: http://www.youtube.com/watch?v=Lba3AZOjttY)

The final benediction featured an interreligious group reading from the Universal Declaration of Human Rights, which was adopted by the General Assembly of the United Nations in December 1948. We read in unison:

NOW, THEREFORE THE GENERAL ASSEMBLY

proclaims

THIS UNIVERSAL DECLARATION OF HUMAN RIGHTS

as a common standard of achievement for all people and all nations, to the end that every individual and every organ of society, keeping this Declaration constantly in mind, shall strive by teaching and education to promote respect for these rights and freedoms and by progressive measures, national and international, to secure their universal and effective recognition and observance.

About 250 people were in the audience that night, among them musicians, artists, photographers, and others who had generously volunteered their time and talent because they understood the universal significance of the event. Conception to delivery for the entire event was approximately six weeks—which in itself seemed miraculous. Dalit and I marveled at the generous contributions of all the people involved; we saw it as an example and proof of "holy collaboration." We believe it is the only way to go forward and, in our opening words to the audience, we intoned together, "Collaboration, collaboration, collaboration."

At the conclusion of the evening, Jilla, an Iranian-American woman, came up to me, took my hands in hers and said, with tears glistening on her face, "I never had a vision of what the world could look like until tonight. Tonight I saw what was possible."

By next year we would like to see 100 Universal Freedom Seders taking place around the country and around the globe, 500 the year after, 2,000 the year after that.

Yes, I come from a long line of dreamers, but this is the age of miracles and of miracle-workers. We have been empowered to make the connections that will develop into a new era of peace and harmony. Everywhere around me, as I turn, I see people involved in miracle-making. It brings to mind a Kabbalistic belief which says that alongside every blade of grass in the universe at least two angels are hovering, offering their encouragement. "Grow. Grow," they whisper.

I blink and then, as clearly as Jacob must have envisioned the angels ascending and descending the ladder to heaven, I see a panorama laid out before me in great detail. But this is no dream. The tipping point is now and I can make out the contours of two angels surrounding every person in the world, and I hear them saying:

"Be the miracle. Be the miracle."

Unity Walk in Pomona, 2010.

(Right) With Gaby Franco (l.) and Carlos Rodriguez, leaders of the Carpe Diem interfaith organization in Guadalajara, Mexico.

Parliament of the World's Religions Staff Members, 2010.

Weaving the Global Interfaith Web

Staff and volunteers of Carpe Diem in Guadalajara, Mexico.

Interfaith leaders in Mexico City.

Participants in the Bogota, Colombia Pre-Paliament Event.

Sufi group in London.

Weaving the Global Interfaith Web

Working together with interfaith leaders in Buenos Aires, Argentina.

With interfaith leaders in San Jose, Costa Rica.

Interfaith friends: L to R: Virginia Pardo from Bogota, Colombia, Rosalia Lozano from Monterrey, Mexico, and Ruth.

In Mt. Abu, India with Dadi Janki, the administrative head of the worldwide Brahma Kumaris World Spiritual University and community.

With Parvinder Khalsa, my Sikh guide for the Golden Temple in Amritsar, India.

In Oxford with Mary and Rev. Dr. Marcus Braybrooke, author of more than 40 books on interfaith engagement.

Memorable Scenes from the 2009 Melbourne Parliament

Australian Aborigine at opening ceremony.

Buddhist Presentation.

Youth participants in the Melbourne Parliament.

King Robert Hounon, supreme leader of Vodun Hwendo tradition from Benin.

His Holiness the Dalai Lama encourages social action as well as dialogue.

More than 6,500 people representing 200 religions from 90 countries crossed this bridge daily. (Credit: Leah Abrahams)

Memorable Scenes from the 2009 Melbourne Parliament

Parliament participants gather on bridge at the conclusion of the conference. (Credit: Leah Abrahams)

Andras Corbin representing the Pagan Community.

Confucian dance.

Weaving the Global Interfaith Web

Our interfaith group from Los Angeles at the Parliament. (Credit: Leah Abrahams)

With my interfaith colleagues Noor Malika Chishti (r), and Anthony Manousos (l) after our presentation "Listening With a Heart of Mercy." (Credit: Leah Abrahams)

With Rabbi David Rosen (l.) and H H Pujya Swami Chidanand Saraswati.

With Sister Joan Chittister, champion of religious equality for women.

Holy Land interfaith activists are interviewed by Jordanian journalist.

Serving as a translator for my Israeli Arab friend, Ibtisam Mahameed, during her presentation on Muslim women's rights.

Participants in the Spanish Salon from Europe, the U.S. and Latin America.

Highlights from the LA Universal Freedom Seder, April 2011

With my Seder Co-Chair, singer/songwriter Dalit Argil. (Credit: Yael Swerdlow)

Idan Reichel, Israeli musician. (Credit: Myra Vides)

With Dr. Mahmoud Abdel Baset (l.) and Imam Jihad Turk (r.), the Muslim co-leaders of the Universal Freedom Seder. (Credit: Myra Vides)

Highlights from the LA Universal Freedom Seder, April 2011

Musician and producer Larry Klein.
(Credit: Myra Vides)

Dancer Maya Gabay. (Credit: Myra Vides)

(L. to r.) Rabbi Mordecai Finley. Sister Mary and Sister Gita from the Brahma Kumaris community, and Rev. Dr. Gwynne Guibord. (Credit: Yael Swerdlow)

Seder participants Nirinjan Khalsa (l.) and Andre Van Zyl (r.). (Credit: Yael Swerdlow)

Representatives from the Egyptian Consulate.
(Credit: Yael Swerdlow)

A full house with representatives from 13 religious communities. (Credit: Yael Swerdlow)

Karen Armstrong, creator of the Charter for Compassion.

(Credit: Nadine Priestly)

The Thirteen Indigenous Grandmothers with H.H. the Dalai Lama.

Bibliography

Abu-Nimer, Mohammed, Welty, Emily and Khoury, Amkal I. *Unity in Diversity: Interfaith Dialogue in the Middle East.* U.S. Institute of Peace Press, 2007.

Afridi, Mehnaz M. *Shoah Through Muslim Eyes, (The Holocaust: History & Literature, Ethics & Philosophy).* Academic Studies Press, 2017.

Albanese, Catherine L. *America: Religions & Religion.* 4th ed. Thomson Wadsworth, 2007.

Alpert, Steven. *Interfaith Manual,* www.allfaithcenter.org, 2008.

Appiah, Kwame Anthony. *Cosmopolitanism: Ethics in a World of Strangers.* W. W. Norton, 2006.

Ariarajah, S. Wesley. *Not Without My Neighbor: Issues in Interfaith Relations.* WCC Publications, 2003.

Aslan, Reza and Aaron J. Hahn Tapper. *Muslims and Jews in America: Commonalities, Contentions, and Complexities.* Palgrave, 2011.

Ayoub, Mahmoud and Irfan Omar, ed. *A Muslim View of Christianity: Essays on Interfaith Dialogue.* Orbis Books, 2007.

Banchoff, Thomas, ed. *Democracy and the New Religious Pluralism.* Oxford, 2007.

Bender, Courtney and Pamela E. Klassen, eds. *After Pluralism: Reimagining Religious Engagement.* Columbia University Press, 2010.

Berling, Judith. *Understanding Other Religious Worlds: A Guide for Interreligious Education.* Orbis, 2004.

Berthrong, John H. *The Divine Deli: Religious Identity in the North American Cultural Mosaic.* Orbis, 1999.

Braybrooke, Marcus. *Peace in Our Heart, Peace in Our World,* lulu.com, 2017.

Braybrooke, Marcus. *Christians and Jews Building Bridges,* lulu.com, 2015.

Braybrooke, Marcus. *1000 World Prayers.* John Hunt Publishing Ltd., 2003.

Braybrooke, Marcus. *A Pilgrimage of Hope.* SCM Press, 1993

Braybrooke, Marcus. *A Heart for the World: The Interfaith Alternative.* O-Books, 2006.

Brockman, David R. *The Gospel Among Religions: Christian Ministry, Theology, and Spirituality in a Multifaith World,* Orbis, 2010.

Buttry, Daniel L. *Interfaith Heroes,* Front Edge Publishing, 2007.

Chittister, Joan, Murshid Saadi Shakur Chishti, and Rabbi Arthur Waskow. *The Tent of Abraham: Stories of Hope and Peace for Jews, Christians, and Muslims.* Beacon Press, 2006.

Cobb, John B. Jr. *Beyond Dialogue: Toward a Mutual Transformation of Christianity and Buddhism.* Wif and Stock Pub, 2014.

Cohn-Sherbock, Dan. *Interfaith Theology: A Reader.* Oneworld, 2001.

Coppola, David L, ed. *What Do We Want the Other to Teach About Us? Jewish, Christian, and Muslim Dialogues.* Sacred Heart University Press, 2006

Cornille, Catherine. *Many Mansions.* Orbis Books, 2002.

CrossCurrents, Vol. 51: 1 (Spring 2001)—entire issue, entitled "Godscape, Cityscape."

Dalai Lama. *The Mystic Heart: Discovering a Universal Spirituality in the World's Religions.* New World Library, 2003.

Eck, Diana L. *A New Religious America: How a "Christian Country" Has Become the World's Most Religiously Diverse Nation.* HarperCollins, 2001.

Eck, Diane L. *Encountering God: A Spiritual Journey from Boseman to Banaras.* Beacon Press, 2003.

Eppinger, Dr. Paul, Ed. *Voices of Faith.* Arizona Interfaith Movement, 2008.

Eppinger, Dr. Paul, Ed. *Interfaith Inspirations for Our Globalized World.* Arizona Interfaith Movement, 2010.

Falcon, Ted and Rahman, Jamal and Mackenzie, Don. *Getting to the Heart of Interfaith: The Eye-Opening, Hope-Filled Friendship of a Rabbi, a Pastor and a Sheikh.* Quality Paperback Edition, 2009.

Firestone, Reuven. *An Introduction to Islam for Jews.* The Jewish Publication Society, 2008.

Firestone, Reuven. *Children of Abraham: An Introduction to Judaism for Muslims.* American Jewish Committee/Ktav Publishing House, 2001.

Forward, Martin. *Inter-religious Dialogue: A Short Introduction.* Oneworld, 2001.

Gabbay, Alyssa. *Islamic Tolerance: Amir Khurraw and Pluralism.* Routledge 2010.

Goldberg, Philip. *American Veda.* Doubleday, 2011.

Goldberg, Philip. *Roadsigns on the Spiritual Path, Living at the Heart of Paradox.* Rodale Press, 2003.

Gopin, Marc. *Holy War, Holy Peace: How Religions Can Bring Peace to the Middle East*, Oxford University Press, USA, 2005.

Gopin, Marc. *Between Eden & Armageddon, The Future of World Religions, Violence & Peacemaking.* Oxford University Press, 2002.

Gopin, Marc. *To Make the Earth Whole: The Art of Citizen Diplomacy in an Age of Religious Militancy.* Rowman & Littlefield Publishers, Inc. June 15, 2009.

Greenbaum, Steven. *Practical Interfaith: How to Find Our Common Humanity as We Celebrate Diversity*, Skylights Paths, 2014.

Greenberg, Irving (Yitz). *For the Sake of Heaven and Earth, Judaism and Christianity: A New Encounter*, The Jewish Publication Society, 2004.

Hawken, Paul. (Bioneer Organization) youtube speech, http://tinyurl.com/4xmysfl

Haddad, Yvonne Yazbeck and Esposito, John L. *Daughters of Abraham: Feminist Thought in Judaism, Christianity, and Islam.* University Press of Florida, 2001.

Heckman, Bud and Neiss, Rori Picker. *Interactive Faith, The Essential Interreligious Community-Building Handbook.* SkyLight Paths Publishing, 2008.

Heim, Mark. *Salvations.* Orbis Books, 1995.

Heschel, Abraham Joshua. *No Religion Is An Island.* Wif and Stock Pub, 2009

Hicks, Douglas A. *With God On All Sides: Leadership in a Devout and Diverse America.* Oxford University Press, 2009.

Hill, Fletcher. *Motherhood as Metaphor: Engendering Interreligious Dialogue*, Fordham University, 2013.

Hinze, Bradford E. and Irfan A. Omar, eds. *Heirs of Abraham: The Future of Muslim, Jewish, and Christian Relations.* Orbis, 2005.

Hirschfield, Brad. *You Don't Have to Be Wrong for Me to Be Right: Finding Faith Without Fanaticism.* Random House, 2009.

Hussain, Amir. *Muslims and the Making of America.* Baylor Press, 2016.

Hussain, Amir. *Oil and Water, Two Faiths: One God.* CopperHouse, 2006.

Hutchinson, William R. *Religious Pluralism in America: The Contentious History of a Founding Ideal.* Yale University Press, 2003.

Idilby, Ranya, and Oliver, Suzanne and Warner, Priscilla. *The Faith Club, a Muslim, a Christian, a Jew: Three Women Search for Understanding.* Free Press, 2007.

Inayat-Khan, Pir Zia. *Mingled Waters:Sufism and the Mystical Unity of Religions.* Omega, 2017.

Kamenetz, Roger. *The Jew in the Lotus: A Poet's Rediscovery of Jewish Identity in Buddhist India.* HarperCollins, 2007.

King, Roberta R. and Tan, Sooi Ling. *(Un)Common Sounds: Songs of Peace and Reconciliation Among Muslims and Christians.* Cascade, 2014.

Klass, Morton. *Ordered Universes: Approaches to the Anthropology of Religion.* Westview Press, 1995.

Knitter, Paul. *Introducing Theologies of Religion.* Orbis Books, 2002.

Kraybill, Ron & Evelyn Wright. *The Little Book of Cool Tools for Hot Topics: Group Tools to Facilitate Meetings When Things Are Hot*. Good Books, 2007.

Kurs, Katherine. *Searching for Your Soul: Writers of Many Faiths Share Their Personal Stories of Spiritual Discovery*. Schocken, 1999.

Küng, Hans. *Yes to a Global Ethic*; SMC Press, London, 1996.

Kuwaja-Holbrook, Sheryl A. *God Beyond Borders*. Horizons in Religious Education, 2014.

Lerner, Michael. *Embracing Israel/Palestine: A Strategy to Heal and Transform the Middle East*. Tikkun Books, 2011.

Magonet, Jonathan. *Talking to the Other: Jewish Interfaith Dialogue with Christians and Muslims*. I.B. Tauris, 2003.

Manousos, Anthony, Ed. *Quakers & the Interfaith Movement*. Quaker University Fellowship, 2011.

Marshall, Kathryn. *Interfaith Journeys: An Exploration of History, Ideas, and Future Directions*. Ebook, 2017.

Marty, Martin E. *When Faiths Collide*. Blackwell, 2005.

Massa, Mark, S.J. *Anti-Catholicism in America: The Last Acceptable Prejudice*. Oxford University Press US, 2003. The Crossroad Publishing Company; First Edition (September 1, 2003); 2nd edition (October 1, 2005).

Matlins, Stuart M. and Arthur J. Magida, eds. *How to Be a Perfect Stranger: The Essential Religious Etiquette Handbook*. 5th edition. SkyLight Paths Publishing, 2010.

Matlins, Stuart M., ed. *The Perfect Stranger's Guide to Funerals and Grieving Practices: A Guide to Etiquette in Other People's Religious Ceremonies*. SkyLight Paths Publishing, 2000.

Matlins, Stuart M, ed. *The Perfect Stranger's Guide to Weddings: A Guide to Etiquette in Other People's Religious Ceremonies*. SkyLight Paths Publishing, 2000.

Mays, Rebecca Kratz, ed. *Interfaith Dialogue at the Grass Roots*. Ecumenical Press, 2008.

McCarthy, Kate. *Interfaith Encounters in America*. Rutgers University Press, 2007.

McGraw, Barbara A. and Jo Renee Formicola, eds. *Taking Religious Pluralism Seriously: Spiritual Politics on America's Sacred Ground*. Baylor University Press, 2005.

Meet Your Neighbors: Interfaith Facts. Faith Communities Today/Hartford Institute for Religion Research, 2003.

Merton, Thomas. *Zen and the Bird of Appetite*. The Abbey of Gethsamani, Inc., 1968.

Montaldo, Jonathan; Rohr, Richard; Beaugeaut, Cynthia; Moore, Thomas; Thurman, Robert; Smith, Huston; Ware, Kallistos; Chittister, Joan; Forest, James; Fox, Matthew; Lipsey, Roger; Simmer-Brown, Judith, Hossein Nasr, Seyyed. *We Are Already One: Thomas Merton's Message of*

Mosher, Lucinda. *Faith in the Neighborhood: Belonging*. Seabury, 2005.

Mosher, Lucinda. *Faith in the Neighborhood: Loss*. Seabury, 2007.

Mosher, Lucinda. *Faith in the Neighborhood: Praying: Rituals of Faith*. Seabury, 2006.

Niebuhr, Gustav. *Beyond Tolerance: Searching for Interfaith Understanding in America*. Viking, 2008.

Numrich, Paul D. *The Faith Next Door: American Christians and Their New Religious Neighbors*. Oxford University Press, 2009.

Orsi, Robert. *Gods of the City: Religion and the American Urban Landscape*. Indiana University Press, 1999.

Panikkar, Raimon. *The Intra-Religious Dialogue*, revised edition. Paulist Press, 1999.

Patel, Eboo. *Interfaith Leadership: A Primer*. Beacon Press, 2016.

Patel, Eboo. *Acts of Faith: The Story of an American Muslim, the Struggle for the Soul of a Generation*. Beacon Press, 2010

Patel, Eboo and Patrice Brodeur, eds. *Building the Interfaith Youth Movement: Beyond Dialogue to Action*. Rowan & Littlefield, 2006.

Prabhu, Joseph, editor. *The Intercultural Challenge of Raimon Panikkar*. Orbis Books, 1996.

Prabhu, Joseph. *Raimon Panikkar as Modern Spiritual Master*. Orbis Books, 2011.

Pranis, Kay. *The Little Book of Circle Processes*. Good Books, 1969.

Pratt, Douglas. *Being Open Being Faithful: The Journey of Interreligious Dialogue*. World Council of Churches, 2014.

Putnam, Robert D. and David E. Campbell. *American Grace: How Religion Divides and Unites Us*. Simon & Schuster, 2010.

Sacks, Jonathan. *Not in God's Name*. Schocken Books, 2017.

Sacks, Jonathan. *The Dignity of Difference: How to Avoid the Clash of Civilizations*. Continuum, 2002.

Sacks, Jonathan. *The Home We Build Together: Recreating Society*. Continuum, 2007.

Salmonic, Samir. *It's Really All About God: Reflections of a Muslim Atheist Jewish Christian*. Jossey-Bass, 2009.

Schirch, Lisa. *The Little Book of Dialogue for Difficult Subjects*. Good Books, 2007.

Seager, Richard. *The Dawn of Religious Pluralism, Voices from the Parliament of Religions 1893*. Open Court, 1993.

Seager, Richard. *The World's Parliament of Religions.* Indiana University Press, 1995.

Shafiq, Muhammad and Muhammed Abu-Nimer. *Interfaith Dialogue: A Guide for Muslims.* International Institute for Islamic Thought, 2007.

Shapiro, Rami. *World Wisdom Bible: A New Testament for Global Spirituality.* Skylight Paths, 2017

Smart, Ninian. *Worldviews: Crosscultural Explorations of Human Beliefs*, third edition. Prentice-Hall, 2000.

Smith, Jane. *Muslims, Christians and the Challenge of Interfaith Dialogue.* Oxford University Press, 2007.

Smock, David R., ed. *Interfaith Dialogue and Peacebuilding.* U.S. Institute of Peace, 2002.

Swidler, Leonard, Khalid Duran, and Reuven Firestone. *Trialogue: Jews, Christians, and Muslims in Dialogue.* Twenty-Third Publications, 2007.

The Student Journal of Scriptural Reasoning (Vol. 1, No. 1, October 2006). 35 pages at http://etext.lib.virginia.edu/journals/abraham/sjsr/issues/volume1/number1//.

Tapper, Aaron J. Hahn and Azlan Reza, Co-Editors. *Muslims and Jews in America: Commonalities, Contentions and Complexities.* Palgrave MacaMillan, 2011.

Teasdale, Wayne, ed. *Awakening the Spirit, Inspiring the Soul: 30 Stories of Interspiritual Discovery in the Community of Faiths.* Skylight Paths, 2004.

Tippet, Krista. *Speaking of Faith.* Viking, 2007.

Trible, Phyllis and Letty M. Russell, eds. *Hagar, Sarah, and Their Children: Jewish, Christian, and Muslim Perspectives.* Westminster John Knox, 2006.

Volf, Miroslav. *Exclusion & Embrace: A Theological Exploration of Identity, Otherness, and Reconciliation.* Abingdon Press, 1996.

Wuthnow, Robert. *America and the Challenges of Religious Diversity.* Princeton University Press, 2005, 2007.

Yankelovich, Daniel. *The Magic of Dialogue: Transforming Conflict into Cooperation.* Touchstone, 1999.

Women of Wisdom, Friendship & Faith: The Wisdom of Women Creating Alliances for Peace. Read the Spirit Books, 2010.

Wuthnow, Robert. *America and the Challenges of Religious Diversity.* Princeton University Press, 2005.

Zaslow, David. *Roots and Branches: A Sourcebook for Understanding the Jewish Roots of Christianity.* The Wisdom Exchange, 2011.

Minefields & Miracles Acknowledgements

It seems fitting and totally apropos that this book about my interfaith journey was literally produced *en route*. The first words of this book were written at 4:00 o'clock one sleepless morning in 2007, when I was visiting New York City.

I worked on the first ten chapters a few months later in an apartment in Trastevere, Rome, shared for three weeks with my dear friend, Marion Weil. She wanted to spend time in Italy because she was on a mission to learn Italian, so she invited me to join her. The deal we struck (mostly in my favor) was that we would sightsee and visit museums during the day, she would shop and cook for both of us and, in the evenings and late into the night, I would write my book on my laptop. Mornings Marion would listen attentively as I read the chapters composed the night before. I would eagerly wait to hear her cogent and always on-point comments that would send me back to the keyboard to edit and refine. *Mille grazie*, Marion, for that gift.

It took two more years until I returned to my manuscript, not for lack of interest but for lack of time. I promised myself I would complete 10 more chapters and so I did, during a three-day writing marathon in March 2009, while intermittently gazing through a picture window at the lush Costa Rican rain forest.

Five more chapters emerged after a self-imposed weeklong confinement in the downstairs recreation room of my sister's home in Green Bay, Wisconsin, in August 2009. Chapter 26, the last chapter, was written in my Los Angeles home. These final words of acknowledgement were penned in June 2011 in Hartford, Connecticut, where I was invited to attend an interfaith course offered by Hartford Seminary, "Religious Leadership in an Interfaith World."

From New York to Rome, Green Bay to Los Angeles to Hartford. *En route*.

Home, I have discovered, is not a physical place but an emotional realm in which I feel and experience love daily from my family and friends, my teachers and mentors. I am also indebted to my critics who, in the end, have brought the important issues of my life into clear focus and have helped me define my role and purpose. I am acutely aware of the contributions these individuals have made in my life, and I am grateful to each of them.

Thank you, Ellie Katz, for your incandescent friendship and your loyal support of my work in all of its forms. Thank you, Peter Lotterhos, for your inspired coaching and helping me reach new understandings about unlimited potential.

Special mention goes to my sister and publisher, Leah Abrahams, CEO of Mixed

Media Memoirs LLC, a brilliant editor, and a superb photographer in her own right. She is a woman of many talents, and of enormous generosity of spirit. Wherever I found myself in the world, Leah remained a constant friend and faithful big sister. Moreover, in the midst of my fanciful and often impractical projects, she has been a clear and intelligent voice of reason. Every one should have the good fortune to have a "Leah" as a sister!

My heartfelt thanks for their mentoring and friendship to two individuals who figure prominently in my interfaith memoir: Rabbi Zalman Schachter-Shalomi and Rabbi David Rosen. I would also like to pay tribute to Michael Bernard Beckwith, founder of the Agape International Spiritual Center in Los Angeles, for his encouragement and powerful support when I first launched the Festival of Freedom Movement in 1993, and to Rabbi Mordecai Finley, my rabbi and teacher, who accepted my invitation to co-lead a citywide Universal Freedom Seder with a priest and an imam in the spring of 2011. Rabbi Finley subsequently dubbed me a "spiritual entrepreneur," a name I will always cherish.

I also wish to acknowledge H.H. the Dalai Lama, another one of my great spiritual teachers, whom I was privileged to meet in Jerusalem in 1994. The Dalai Lama has continued to deliver the same steady, direct, and unwavering message in all of his public and private pronouncements: Love, compassion, forgiveness; love, compassion, forgiveness. His mantra has informed my life on a daily basis, but I am also indebted to him for his response when he was once challenged with the question: "What is the best religion?"

> *The best religion is the one that gets you closest to God. It is the one that makes you a better person. Whatever makes you more compassionate, more sensible, more detached, more loving, more humanitarian, more responsible, more ethical. The religion that will do that for you is the best religion.*

It takes a village to raise a child and to publish a book. Many friends agreed to read individual chapters and also the final manuscript. Their feedback was invaluable. Thank you, Marcus Eliason, Marty Zucker, Gene Rothman, Doris Davis, Miri Koral, Julie Whitten, Valerie Hasely, Joseph Prabhu, Zmira Birnbaum, Dinah Berland, Paul Chaffee, Sheri Manning, Swami Shiva Atmatattwananda, Fernanda Rossi, Jaelle Dragomir, Shimon Katz, and Stanley Kaplan.

I am very grateful to: Laura Treichel, the graphic artist who designed the book and the cover; artist Sebastian Schimpf for his powerful mandala that appears on the cover; Cesiah Carrera Torres for the group photograph on the back cover; the Council for a Parliament of the World's Religions for allowing me to use their historical photos; Gulcin Anil for her kinetic image of Dervish Art; Sohrab Akhavan for his photographs of our interfaith journey to Turkey; Ron Sachs for helping me obtain photos of President Obama's inauguration; the Pluralism Project for their list of interfaith organizations; and Yvonne Teofan for assembling the resource section. A special note of gratitude goes to Zia Iampietro who created a magnificent web site for the book, and whose eagle eye as a proof reader was key in the final hours before publication.

To my myriad interfaith friends and colleagues around the world: You are my sisters and brothers in spirit and faith, and I am privileged to know you, to work with you, and serve alongside you.

My penultimate acknowledgement goes to my children, Alexander and Leora. Their comments and suggestions were brilliant, and the book has benefitted enormously from their contributions. I also am deeply indebted to them for being my teachers in ways that they will never fully comprehend, perhaps until they have children of their own.

My final thanks and praise go to G-d, our Creator, who has sustained me, guided me and brought me to this day, a day of wonder and gratitude for all that I have been privileged to experience and to learn about Creation and the reason why we are here.

Baruch Atah Adonai Eloheinu Melech Ha'olam,
S'hechiyanu, V'kiyamanu, V'higiyanu Lazman Hazeh.

This is the *S'hechiyanu* prayer we say in Hebrew to mark special, sacred moments in our lives and to acknowledge how we rely upon the love and grace of the Divine in everything we do.

Discussion Questions for Interfaith Groups and Book Clubs

1) Chapter 1

Have you ever been discriminated against … because of your religion … your political beliefs, economic status, color, ethnic background, gender, religion, gender, size, weight? What did it feel like? How did that experience influence your life?

2) Chapters 2 & 3

Have you ever had an identity crisis? What brought it about? How did you feel when it happened? What makes up your identity? Who are you if you can't refer to your name, heritage, religion, family role, profession, age, physical characteristics, likes and dislikes? Would you still be you? What makes you you?

3) Chapter 6

Have you ever had a very close friendship or fallen in love with someone of a different religious background or culture that resulted in censure from your family or friends? What was that like? How was it resolved? Is there anything you might have done differently knowing what you know now?

4) Chapter 7

What does Rumi's poem mean: "Out beyond ideas of wrongdoing and rightdoing, there is a field. I'll meet you there"? Can there be peace without justice?

5) Chapter 10

Should some sacred religious rites and rituals remain private? Is it advisable to celebrate someone else's religious practices? When should you take part and when should you decline? What is forbidden in your religion concerning other religions? What do you think about that restriction? Do you follow two distinct religious/spiritual practices? Is that comfortable for you?

6) Chapter 13

Where were you when 9/11 occurred? At the time, what did you think happened? Have your ideas about 9/11 changed since that time? Have your ideas about Muslims changed from 9/11 until today? Have you met any Muslims, spent time with them, visited a mosque since 9/11? How has your life changed personally since 9/11?

7) Chapter 15

Have you ever had a friendship with someone whose social or political convictions differed significantly from yours? How did you handle conflicts when they arose? Were you able to maintain a friendship in spite of those fundamental differences?

8) Chapter 19

Did you ever feel that you have a divine mission? Could you describe what that was like?

9) Chapter 20

Have you ever been a "citizen diplomat"? If so, under what circumstances? Can you picture yourself in that role?

10) Chapter 22

If you were in Ruth's shoes, how would you have resolved this conflict?

11) Chapter 23

Can you describe an experience in nature that deeply affected or even transformed your life? Have you ever made a conscious decision to look at a situation in a totally new way in order to experience it differently?

12) Chapter 25

Have you ever observed or experienced conflict among people who are dedicated to peace? What conclusions did you draw?

13) Chapter 26:

What would a peaceful world be like? Look like? Taste like? Feel like? How can we make the ideal real? Take a few minutes to think about it, with your eyes closed, and then share one or two things about your image of a peaceful world. Economically? Politically? Religiously? Educationally? Scientifically? Artistically? Spiritually?

Suggestions for capturing the answers to Q. 13: Write the ideas as they are expressed either on a blackboard or on an easel pad. Or write them on small index cards/post-its and stick them up on a board or wall where everyone can move around to read them. What palpable, visceral world emerges from all of the ideas? Is that world possible? Probable? Achievable? Inevitable? (If you would like to share your group's vision of a peaceful world with others, please email me. rabsharone@gmail.com)

Interfaithfully yours,
Ruth Broyde Sharone

Coming soon: **INTERFAITH: The Musical**, created by Ruth Broyde Sharone
To order a CD, go to: www.InterfaithTheMusical.com
To learn how you can bring the musical to your community, write to:
interfaiththemusical@gmail.com

Stay in touch with the author and receive updates about her forthcoming publications including *SOME OF MY BEST FRIENDS:*
Muslim Women Who Are Changing the World

Visit **www.MinefieldsAndMiracles.com**
or contact her directly:
(310)733-8313, rabsharone@gmail.com

www.ingramcontent.com/pod-product-compliance
Lightning Source LLC
Chambersburg PA
CBHW060418010526
44118CB00017B/2259